— A —

# BRIT'S GUIDE

— TO —

# ORLANDO

— AND —

# WALT DISNEY WORLD®
## RESORT FLORIDA
# 1999

— SIMON VENESS —

## foulsham

LONDON • NEW YORK • TORONTO • SYDNEY

# foulsham

The Publishing House, Bennetts Close, Cippenham, Berkshire, SL1 5AP, England

ISBN 0-572-02469-X

## DEDICATION

To my wife, Karen, without whose non-stop support and assistance the Brit's Guide would never have become a reality.

## SPECIAL THANKS

Special thanks for this edition go to: First Choice Holidays, Virgin Holidays, The Walt Disney Company, The Peabody Orlando, The Delta Orlando Resort, Dollar Rent A Car and All Cellular Phone Rental.

My sincere thanks also go to all the hard-working people at Foulsham who help to bring my work to life every year.

Printed in Malaysia.

# Contents

# 8. Off The Beaten Track

(or, When You're All Theme Parked Out). **A taste of real Florida** – Winter Park, Aquatic Wonders Boat Tours, Boggy Creek Airboats, Island Tours, Orange Blossom Balloons, Warbird Air Museum, Green Meadows Petting Farm, Florida Fun-Train, Disney and Cruising, Seminole County, Beach Escapes, Sports, including Disney's Wide World of Sports; **Orlando by Night** – Church Street Station, Downtown Disney, Universal's CityWalk, The Pointe*Orlando, Disney Shows, Arabian Nights, Pirate's Dinner Adventure, Capone's, Mark II Dinner Theater, Medieval Times, King Henry's Feast, Sleuth's, Wild Bill's, Night Clubs, Live Music, Discos, Bars.

# 9. Eating Out

(or, Watching the Americans at Their National Sport). Full guide to local-style eating and drinking, run down of the fast-food outlets, best Family restaurants, American diners and Speciality restaurants.

# 10. Shopping

(or, How to Send Your Credit Card into Meltdown). Your duty free allowances, full guide to the main tourist shopping complexes, discount outlets, malls and speciality shops.

# 11. Safety First

(or, Don't Forget to Pack Your Common Sense!). General tourist hints, the Dos and Don'ts, how to look after your money and be safe behind the wheel.

# 12. Going Home

(or, Where Did the Last Two Weeks Go?). Avoiding last-minute snags, full guide to Orlando International and Orlando/Sanford Airports and their facilities for the journey home.

# 13. Your Holiday Planner

Examples of how to plan for a two-week holiday, with a Four-Day Walt Disney World pass, with a Five-Day pass, and blank forms for *your* holiday!

# Foreword

When I started writing the first edition of this book, back in 1993, I was blissfully unaware of all the huge changes and new projects in store for the Orlando area. It seemed a relatively straightforward project to visit central Florida annually and up-date all the various elements that make up this tourist wonderland. Wrong! Nowadays, the three counties that make up this vast holiday resort (Orange, Osceola and Seminole) are all vigorously engaged in making things newer, bigger and better almost by the day, and keeping up with their developments is a positively mind-boggling experience (not to mention exhausting. All together now – aaaahhh!). And, when I look at all the new attractions being unveiled by the likes of Disney and Universal, it is enough to make even this Orlando veteran blink in sheer amazement. However, despite all these attempts to keep us dazed and dazzled, the **Brit's Guide** remains dedicated to the simple principle of providing the most informed and user-friendly travel service you can find, especially for first-time visitors to the area. I like to think it is written with a real tourist's eye for detail and value for money, and it includes all the information you *really* need to know, not just what the glossy brochures want you to know. It aims to give you a good idea of what to expect and (most importantly) how to plan for it, how to budget for things like hotels, meals and days out at the theme parks, as well as being a useful companion while you are there. Prepare to be amazed by what's in store, but don't say I didn't tell you so. Now excuse me while I put my feet up for a while … have a nice day now!

Simon Veness

**Orlando is a roller-coaster holiday all the way!**

# 1 Introduction
## (or, Welcome to the Holiday of a Lifetime)

It's the biggest, brashest theme park on the planet – and we're not talking just about Walt Disney World® Resort Florida.

For Orlando itself is now the nearest thing there is to an Amusement City, an almost non-stop land of adventure rides, thrills, fun and fantasy. It is so bewilderingly vast that any holiday to Florida's Funland now needs to be organised with the precision of a military operation.

In the course of a week or two, your senses will be bombarded by an absolutely dazzling array of attractions, from the corny to the highly sophisticated, all vying for your attention and exacting a high physical toll. There is something to suit all tastes and ages, and it is guaranteed to bring out the kid in everyone. You'll walk a lot, queue a lot and probably eat a lot. You'll have a good time, but you'll end up exhausted as well.

## Seven theme parks

In simple terms, there are seven (eight later in 1999) big theme parks which are now generally reckoned to be essential holiday fare, and at least one of those will require two days to make you feel it has been well and truly done. Add on a day at one of the water fun parks, a trip to see some of the wildlife or other more 'natural' attractions, or the lure of the nearby Kennedy Space Center, and you're talking at least 10 days of pure adventure-mania. Then add in the night-time attractions of Church Street Station, Downtown Disney and Universal's new CityWalk and the various and numerous dinner shows, and you start to get an idea of the awesome scale of the entertainment on offer. Even given two weeks, something has to give – just make sure it isn't your patience/pocket/sanity!

So, how do we Brits, many of us making our first visit to the good ol' US of A, make the most of what is still without doubt the most magical of holidays?

There is no set answer of course, but there are a number of pretty solid guidelines to steer you in the right direction and help you avoid some of the more obvious pitfalls. Central to most of them is **planning**. Towards the back of this guide there is a useful 'calendar' to fill in and use as a ready reference guide. Don't be inflexible, but be aware of the time requirements of each of the main parks, and (importantly) allow yourself a few quiet days either by the pool or at one of the smaller attractions to recover your strength!

Also, be aware of the vast scale and complexity of this theme park wonderland, and try to take in as much of the clever detail and great breadth of imagination on offer, especially in Walt Disney World.

# Orlando

Orlando itself is a relatively small but bright young city which has been taken over to the immediate south-west by the Walt Disney World® Resort Florida, to give it its full title, which opened with the Magic Kingdom® Park in 1971 and has encouraged a massive tourist expansion ever since. New attractions are being added all the time and the city of Orlando is in danger of being swamped by this vast out-pouring of rampant commercialism and aggressive tourist marketing. However, there is still a genuine concern for the environment and the dangers of over-commercialisation, and the development should not get out of hand, at least in the near future (although it is easy to imagine it already has in some parts).

The tourist area generally known as Orlando actually consists of three counties. Orange County is the home of the city of Orlando, but much of Walt Disney World is in Osceola County, with Kissimmee its main town. Seminole County, home of Sanford Airport, is immediately to the north of Orange County.

The local population numbers less than 1.5 million, of which some 150,000 are actively employed in the tourist business, but in 1998 more than 37 million people were forecast to decide on Orlando as the place for their holiday, spending in excess of $7 billion in central Florida! Britain accounts for more than a third of all foreign visitors to Orlando, and in 1998 that was likely to be around 1.2 million. Those figures represent a near 100 per cent increase in the last 10 years, with the international airport seeing its traffic boom from eight million passengers in 1983 to a massive 28 million just 15 years later. In addition, the full Orlando area boasts some 90,000 hotel rooms and 3,500 places to eat.

# Walt Disney World® Resort Florida

Walt Disney World now consists of four distinct, separate theme parks, 24 speciality hotel resorts, a camping ground, a nature reserve, three water fun parks, a new resort centre of arts and recreation called the Disney Institute, a state-of-the-art spectator sports complex, five 18-hole golf courses, two mini-golf courses and a huge Downtown Disney shopping and entertainment complex. It covers 40 square miles (almost 30,000 acres): Alton Towers and Thorpe Park would comfortably fit into one of its car parks. Indeed, Alton Towers, Britain's biggest theme park, is 60 times smaller than Walt Disney World. Disney's most-frequented park, the Magic Kingdom®, has a single-day record attendance in the region of 92,000 – Thorpe Park in Surrey (size 500 acres) peaks at around 20,000. The Disney organisation still does things with the most style, but the others have caught on fast and they are all creating new amenities almost as fast as they can think of them.

Intriguingly, only half of Walt Disney World's massive site is currently developed, leaving plenty of room for accommodation and attractions. They think and plan on a massive scale (up to 20 years ahead), and have just completed the biggest expansion programme in their history with the opening of Disney's Animal Kingdom™ Theme Park, a huge redevelopment of the Downtown Disney area of shops, restaurants and nightclubs, and the launch of their own cruise line. The world's largest entertainment company just does not stand still, and there are sure to be other new elements announced after our deadline.

Here's a quick run-down of what's on offer. **The Magic Kingdom®**

# FLORIDA

How far from Orlando to . . .

| | | | |
|---|---|---|---|
| Bradenton | . . . . 130 miles | Key West | . . . . . 375 miles |
| Clearwater | . . . . 110 miles | Miami | . . . . . . . . 220 miles |
| Cocoa Beach | . . . 40 miles | Sarasota | . . . . . 140 miles |
| Daytona | . . . . . . . 60 miles | St Petersburg | . . 105 miles |
| Fort Myers | . . . . 190 miles | Tampa | . . . . . . . . 75 miles |
| Jacksonville | . . . 155 miles | Venice | . . . . . . . 160 miles |

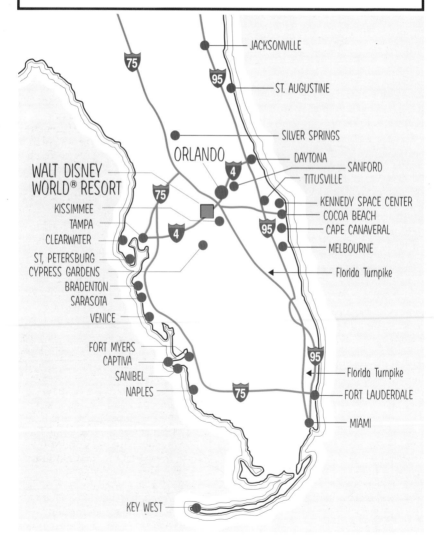

**Park**: this is the essential Disney, including the fantasy of all its wonderful animated films, the adventure of the Wild West and African Jungles, and the excitement of some classy thrill rides like

**Lake Eola, downtown Orlando**

Space Mountain, a huge indoor roller-coaster, and The ExtraTERRORestrial Alien Encounter. **Epcot®**: This is Walt Disney World's look at the world of tomorrow through the gates of Future World, plus a potted journey around our planet in World Showcase. It's more educational than adventurous, but still possesses some memorable rides and some great places to eat. **Disney-MGM Studios**: here you can ride the movies in style, meeting up with Star Wars, the Muppets and Indiana Jones, drop into the fearsome Tower of Terror and learn how films are *really* made. **Disney's Animal Kingdom™ Theme Park** is billed as 'a new species of theme park' and delivers another contrasting and hugely entertaining scenario. With cleverly realistic animal habitats, including a 100-acre safari savannah, captivating shows and a stunning thrill ride, it offers a chance to change pace from the other parks, especially with the new Asia area opening in '99. **Disney's Typhoon Lagoon Water Park**: bring your swimming costume and spend a lazy afternoon splashing down water slides and learning to surf in the

world's biggest man-made lagoon. **Disney's River Country Water Park**: more water fun 'n' games, with some great slides and the accent on nature. **Disney's Blizzard Beach Water Park**: this is the big brother of all the water parks, with a massive spread of rides 'n' slides all in a 'snowy' environment. **Discovery Island Park**: a man-made 12-acre zoological garden attraction of peaceful walks and local wildlife habitats. **Disney's Wide World of Sports** offers the chance to watch world-class events like tennis, baseball, basketball, athletics, volleyball and many others. **Downtown Disney** incorporates **Pleasure Island, Marketplace** and the new **West Side** of themed restaurants, cinema complex, the unique DisneyQuest arcade of interactive games, Virgin Megastore and world-famous Cirque du Soleil theatre/circus company. New Year's Eve is the Pleasure Island theme, with a choice of seven nightclubs. For Walt Disney World hotels, see Chapter 4, while Walt Disney World's **Wedding Pavilion** now features in many brochures for the chance to get married in true fairytale style.

Most people buy one of the multi-day passes which allow you to move between the various parks on the same day, while all grant unlimited

**An animation programme at the Disney Institute**

access to Walt Disney World's transport system of monorails, buses and ferries (always get your hand stamped if you leave one park but intend to return later on). Make no mistake, you can't walk between the parks, and trying to do more than one in a day in any depth is a recipe for disaster. The choice of tickets for Disney in particular is becoming bewildering, and the addition of seven- and nine-day passes hasn't helped. Here are the main ones you should consider: **5-Day Park Hopper** gives you unlimited access for five days to the four main theme parks, so you can visit more than one on any of the five days, and it is best suited to families who have been here before but still want to visit all the parks; **5-Day All-in-One Hopper** adds free admission to the water parks, Pleasure Island and Disney's Wide World of Sports for your five days, but it can be tough trying to fit everything in; a better bet, especially for first-timers, is the **7-Day All-in-One Hopper Pass** which gives you just about enough time to enjoy all the attractions on the ticket; there is also a **9-Day All-in-One Hopper Pass** which is even better value if your visit is long enough (and if you want to spend nine full days on Disney, although you don't have to use them consecutively any more and unused days stay valid indefinitely. It is also worth shopping around for your All-in-One Hopper tickets before you leave. TicketShop USA (tel. 0181 600 7000), Keith Prowse (tel. 01232 232425) and Seligo (tel. 0121 693 4321) offer the 5-, 7- and 9-Day All-in-Ones for around £150 (for adults; £120 for 3–9s), £180 (£145) and £205 (£160), subject to the exchange rates, as do all the UK's Disney Stores, while the tour operators also pre-sell tickets, but I have noticed a £20 difference in some prices for the same ticket. **You should also be wary of buying too many**

**attraction tickets in advance.** The **Orlando FlexTicket** is a good buy as the 3-Park ticket gives seven days unlimited access to Universal Studios Florida®, SeaWorld and Wet 'n' Wild, while the 4-Park Ticket gives 10 days' access to those three plus Busch Gardens. However, you should check you have enough time to use a Disney pass as well as a FlexTicket. Obviously, if you are going for only a week you would be wasting your money on both. Pre-buying your Disney tickets (and even the FlexTicket for an Orlando visit of at least two weeks) gives you the benefit of being able to budget on one of your main expenditures, but **beware** the temptation (and any travel agent pressure) to buy ALL your tickets in advance. It is easy to buy too many and find you don't have enough time to fit everything in, while, for many of the attractions, you can buy CHEAPER in Orlando.

A first word of warning: you don't want to try to do Walt Disney World in one big chunk. Apart from ending up with serious theme park indigestion, you'll probably also hit one of the parks on a busy day (check the Theme Park Planner on page 242). The Magic Kingdom® Park and Epcot® can be particularly exhausting (especially with children), and you'll need a quiet day afterwards.

## The others

If Walt Disney World is what you think Orlando is all about, then you'll be in for a pleasant surprise when you encounter the likes of Universal Studios Escape, SeaWorld Adventure Park, Busch Gardens, Cypress Gardens, the Kennedy Space Center and Silver Springs. They may be built along smaller lines (although Universal have their big expansion, the Islands of Adventure, opening in 1999), but they deal successfully in the same

# GETTING AROUND ORLANDO

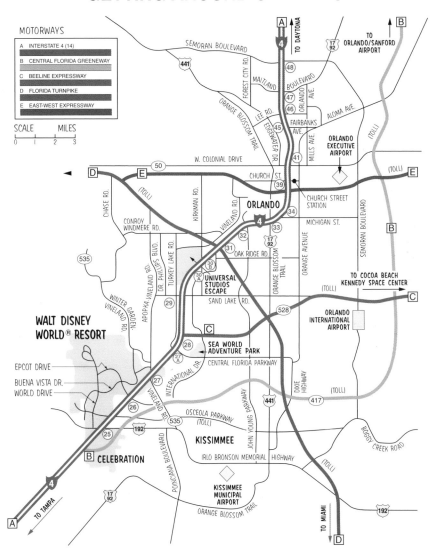

MOTORWAYS

| | |
|---|---|
| A | INTERSTATE 4 (14) |
| B | CENTRAL FLORIDA GREENEWAY |
| C | BEELINE EXPRESSWAY |
| D | FLORIDA TURNPIKE |
| E | EAST-WEST EXPRESSWAY |

SCALE MILES
0 1 2 3

areas of excitement and sophistication. **Universal Studios Florida®**: this features the state-of-the-art simulator ride Back to the Future, the mind-boggling Terminator 2 attraction, Jaws, King Kong, the new Twister experience, Earthquake, the Blues Brothers and ET. **SeaWorld**: don't be put off thinking it's just another dolphin show, this is *the* place for the creatures of the deep, with killer whales being the main attraction, a bright, refreshing atmosphere and a pleasingly serious ecological approach, plus their serious thrill ride, Journey to Atlantis. **Busch Gardens**: the sister park to SeaWorld, here it's creatures of the land, with the highlight being the Myombe Reserve, a close-up look at the endangered Central African

**Cypress Gardens**

highland gorillas and the Edge of Africa safari experience. A real treat, plus a number of brain-numbing roller-coasters and other rides. **Cypress Gardens**: a chance to slow down and take in the more scenic attraction of beautiful gardens, water-skiing shows and circus acts. **Kennedy Space Center**: the dramatically upgraded home of space exploration, a must for anyone even vaguely interested in One Giant Leap for Mankind. Many free attractions, plus coach tours, giant-screen film shows and the unmissable new Apollo/ Saturn V centre. **Silver Springs**: a close look at Florida nature via jeep and boat safaris through real swampland, with

**Kennedy Space Center**

the addition of several alligator displays. **Splendid China**: a magnificent recent attraction, a 5,000-mile journey through the country of China with elaborate miniaturised reproductions of features like the Great Wall and the Terracotta Warriors, plus films, live shows, including the White Tiger spectacular, and great shopping and food. **Fantasy of Flight**: this aviation museum experience features the world's largest private collection of vintage aircraft plus fighter-plane

BRIT TIP: The humidity levels – up to 100 per cent – and fierce daily rainstorms in summer take a lot of visitors by surprise, so take a lightweight, rainproof jacket with you if possible or buy one of the cheap plastic ponchos available in local supermarkets and other shops.

simulators and a balloon ride.
So that's what's on offer, the next question is when to go? Florida's weather does vary a fair bit, from bright but cool winter days in November, December and January, with the odd drizzly spell, to furiously hot and humid summers punctuated by tropical downpours.
The most pleasant option is to go

# KEY TO ORLANDO – MAIN ATTRACTIONS

A1 = DISNEY'S ANIMAL KINGDOM™ THEME PARK
A = MAGIC KINGDOM® PARK
B = EPCOT®
C = DISNEY-MGM STUDIOS
D = UNIVERSAL STUDIOS ESCAPE
E = SEAWORLD ADVENTURE PARK
F = BUSCH GARDENS
G = KENNEDY SPACE CENTER
H = US ASTRONAUT HALL OF FAME
I = SPLENDID CHINA
J = CYPRESS GARDENS
K = SILVER SPRINGS
L = GATORLAND
M = DISNEY'S TYPHOON LAGOON WATER PARK

N = DISNEY'S BLIZZARD BEACH WATER PARK
O = DISNEY'S RIVER COUNTRY WATER PARK
P = WATER MANIA
Q = WET 'N' WILD
R = DISNEY'S DISCOVERY ISLAND PARK
S = MYSTERY FUN HOUSE
T = RIPLEY'S BELIEVE IT OR NOT
U = TERROR ON CHURCH STREET
V = CHURCH STREET STATION
W = DOWNTOWN DISNEY
X = GREEN MEADOWS PETTING FARM
Y = FANTASY OF FLIGHT
Z = DISNEY INSTITUTE

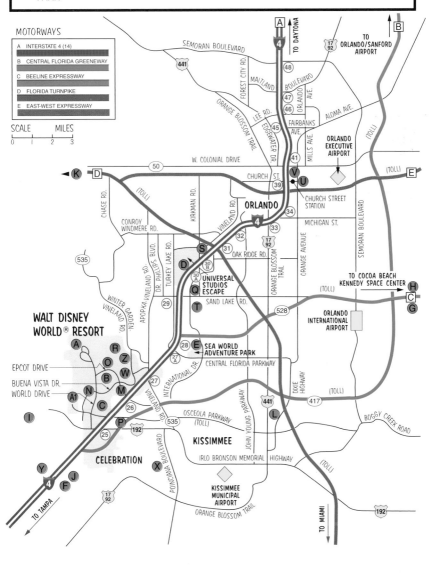

in between the two extremes, i.e., in spring and autumn. You will also avoid the worst of the crowds. However, as the majority of families are governed by school holidays, July to September remain the most popular months for Brit visitors, and so there will also be some pertinent advice on how to get one jump ahead of the high-season crush.

And now to business. Hopefully, we've whetted your appetite for the excitement in store. It's big, brash and fun, but above all it's American, and that means everything is exceedingly well organised, with a tendency towards the raucous rather than the reserved. It's clean, well-maintained and very anxious to please: Floridians generally are an affable bunch, but they take affability to new heights in the main theme parks, where staff are almost painfully keen to make sure you Have A Nice Day. Also close to every American's heart is the custom of TIPPING. With the exception of

> BRIT TIP: Sterling travellers' cheques will cause only confusion. Americans are notoriously bad at dealing with 'foreign' money.

petrol pump attendants and fast-food restaurant servers, just about everyone who offers you any sort of service in hotels, bars, restaurants, buses, taxis, airports and other public amenities will expect a tip. In bars, restaurants and taxis, 15 per cent of the bill is the usual going rate while porters will expect $1 per bag. Brits are notoriously forgetful of this little habit but, as all service industry workers are automatically taxed on the assumption of receiving 15 per cent in tips, you will be doing a major service to the local economy if

you remember those few extra dollars each time. It is also useful to know that dollar travellers' cheques can be used as cash, so it is not necessary (as well as not being advisable) to carry large amounts of cash around. **Take note also that all Orlando prices, both where indicated in this book and on every price-tag you see over there, do not include the 6–7 per cent Florida Sales Tax. There is also a 4 per cent Resort Tax on hotel rooms.**

The use of credit cards is very nearly essential as they are accepted everywhere, are easy to carry and use and provide an extra degree of buying security. In some cases, notably car hire, you can't operate without your flexible friend, so don't leave your Visa or Mastercard at home!

Holiday visitors to America do not need a visa providing they hold a valid British passport showing they are a British Citizen (and which does not expire before the end of your holiday). Instead, all you do is fill in a green visa waiver form (from your travel agent or airline) and hand it in with your passport to the US immigration official who checks you through first thing after landing. However, British Subjects do need a visa (costing £30), and you should apply at least a month in advance to the US Embassy.

In England, Scotland and Wales write to the Visa Office, US Embassy, 5 Upper Grosvenor Street, London W1A 2JB (tel 0891 200 290)

In Northern Ireland write to US Consulate General, 3 Queens House, Belfast BT1 6EQ.

Alternatively, call 0991 500 590 (£1.50/minute) for more detailed visa advice, or log on to their internet site at www.usembassy.org.uk.

## Plan your visit

The next few chapters will help you *plan* your Walt Disney World days and lazy ways, as well as including a guide to American-speak so you know what they mean when they ask if you have any change in your fanny-pack(!); get to grips with the perils and pleasure of *driving* on the wrong side of the road; understand American *accommodation* styles; unravel the secrets of the main *theme parks*; get to know the best of the rest of the *other attractions*; enjoy *eating out*, US-style; become world-class in the *shopping* stakes; stay safe in this tourist wonderland (not as big an issue as the media would have you believe, but learn to be *safety-conscious* anyway); and take the sting out of *going home*. Read on and enjoy . . .

# WHAT'S NEW IN 1999

**Universal Studios Escape** will be making the biggest noise this year with the opening of their second theme park, the **Islands of Adventure**, continuing growth of their **CityWalk** entertainment district and the creation of their first hotel resort, **Portofino Bay** that effectively turns the old single park of Universal Studios Florida® into a whole, self-contained resort complex. The six Islands of Adventure are scheduled to open in 'summer 1999' but my guess is by June at the latest.

Disney, of course, will not stand still and plan to complete the final part of **Disney's Animal Kingdom™ Theme Park**, the land of Asia, with two outstanding new attractions, the Tiger Rapids raft ride and the Maharajah Jungle Trek. There is also talk of a new roller-coaster ride in Dinoland USA. **Disney-MGM Studios** is due to debut its new ride, the Rock 'n' Roller-Coaster, hot on the heels of the dynamic Fantasmic! show that now concludes the day's entertainment. **The Magic Kingdom™ Theme Park** should have Buzz Lightyear's Space Rangers in Tomorrowland as its latest offering. At **Epcot®**, the long-awaited debut of the Test Track adventure should finally take place after a long wait. A new film-themed **All Star Resorts** hotel complex with 1,920 rooms is also due to open in '99. Outside the theme parks, **Orlando City Center** is a new development in the downtown heart of the urban district, part of the drive to regenerate this area, with a mixed spread of offices, shops and restaurants. Burdines opens its newest department store at the **Florida Mall**, while 1999 should also see the completion of the fourth terminal at **Orlando International Airport**.

# WHAT'S HOT

Inevitably in a resort area as big and complex as this, there are always attractions and features which are the current 'in-thing'. And here is the Brit's Guide list of the 'must-see' things for your schedule:

**Theme Parks:** Disney-MGM Studios for Fantasmic! and the Rock 'n' Roller-Coaster; Disney's Animal Kingdom™ Theme Park for Asia; Universal Studios Escape for ALL their new developments; Busch Gardens for a chance to escape the crowds. **Other attractions:** Gatorland/Boggy Creek Airboat Rides, for the best combo ticket of the lot; Skull Kingdom, for the scariest experience in town; Richard Petty Driving Experience, for genuine high-speed thrills; Green Meadows Petting Farm, a surprise hit with young kids. **Nights Out:** Sleuth's, for the most amusing dinner-show; House of Blues at Downtown Disney, for top-name acts and a cool Sunday Gospel Brunch; 08 Seconds in downtown Orlando, the top locals' Country & Western hot-spot; The Groove at Universal's CityWalk for the best disco around; Jimmy Buffett's Margaritaville at CityWalk for a truly original bar-restaurant-venue. **Eating Out:** anywhere at Downtown Disney and Universal's CityWalk; The Players Grill at The Pointe*Orlando; Bahama Breeze, a regular International Drive favourite; California Grill on top of Disney's Contemporary Resort, for great food and fabulous views; Peter Scott's, for an up-market dinner-dance evening.

The Touchdown Hotel at Disney's All Star Sports Resort

The baseball stadium at Disney's Wide World of Sports

# Planning and Practicalities

*(or, How to Do It All and Live to Tell the Tale)*

There is one simple rule involved once you have decided Orlando is the place for you.

Sit down (preferably with this book) and **PLAN** what you want to do very carefully. This is **NOT** the type of holiday you can take in a freewheeling, carefree 'make it up as you go along' manner. Frustration and exhaustion lie in wait for all those who do not have at least a basic plan of how to fill in their seven to 14 days in the fun capital of the world.

So this is what you do. First of all work out WHEN you want to go, then decide WHERE in the vast resort is the best place for you. Then consider WHAT sort of holiday you are looking for, WHO you want to entrust your holiday with and finally HOW much you want to try to do.

## When to go

If you are looking to avoid the worst of the crowds, the best periods to choose are October to early February (but not the week of the Thanksgiving holiday in November or the Christmas to New Year period), mid-February (after George Washington's birthday holiday) to the week before Easter, and April (after Easter) to the end of May. Orlando gets down to some serious tourist business from Memorial Day (the last Monday in May, the official start of the summer season) to Labor Day (the first Monday in September and the last holiday of summer),

peaking on the 4th of July, a huge national holiday. The Easter holidays are similarly uncomfortable (although the weather is better), but easily the busiest is the Christmas period, starting the week before December 25th and lasting until January 2nd. It is not unknown for some of the theme parks to close their gates to new arrivals as their massive car parks become full by mid-morning.

The months offering the best combination of comfortable weather and smaller crowds are March (pre-Easter) and October, but never let wet weather put you off. Few of the main theme park attractions are affected by rain, and you will be one jump ahead if you have remembered to bring a waterproof jacket as the crowds noticeably thin out when it

> BRIT TIP: Thanksgiving is always the fourth Thursday in November, while George Washington's birthday, or President's Day, is the third Monday in February. The weeks including those dates are to be avoided!

gets wet. Don't worry if you haven't brought rain-gear – all the parks do a major trade in cheap, plastic ponchos to keep you dry while you carry on queuing. In the colder

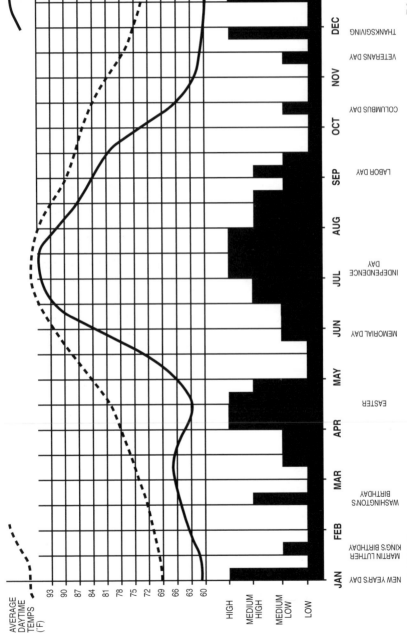

DIAGRAM 1

months, take a heavy sweater or coat for early-morning queues, then, when it warms up later in the day, leave it in the handy lockers that are provided in all of the parks. And, when it's too hot, take advantage of the air-conditioned facilities (of which there are many) during the warmest parts of the day, although you may also find the indoor facilities can be a bit chilly.

## Where to stay

The choice of where to stay is equally important, especially if you have a family who will demand the extra amenities of swimming pools and games rooms. Having the use of a swimming pool is also a major plus for relaxing at the end of a busy day. Inevitably, there is a huge choice of hotels, motels, apartments and private houses, and there are pros and cons to each of the main tourist areas, as well as a slight difference in price. As a guideline, there are four main areas that make up the greater Orlando tourist conglomeration.

**Walt Disney World® Resort Florida**: some of the most sophisticated, convenient and fun places to stay are to be found in Walt Disney World's 'resort' hotels sprinkled around its main attractions. The same imagination that has gone into the creation of the theme parks has been at work on the likes of Disney's Wilderness Lodge and Disney's Contemporary Resort. They all feature free, regular transport to all of the attractions and guests also get extra perks like special baby- and child-care services, early admission to theme parks on selected days, free parking and being able to book in advance for restaurants and shows in the parks, while Disney characters pop up for meals at some of them. The drawbacks here are that, with the exception of the new Disney's All Star Resort, the Walt Disney World resorts are among the most expensive in Orlando, especially to eat in, and you still have a fair drive to get to the other attractions like Universal Studios Escape and the Kennedy Space Center. For a one-week holiday it takes some beating, though.

**Lake Buena Vista**: this is a loosely-defined area around some very pretty lakes to the eastern fringes of Walt Disney World and along Interstate 4 that again features some of the more up-market hotels. It also has the convenience of being handy for all the Walt Disney World parks, with most hotels offering free transport, and excellent leisure and shopping facilities. Once again, it tends to be a bit pricey, but its proximity to the main highway, Interstate 4, makes it convenient for the whole of Orlando.

**International Drive**: this ribbon development lies midway between Walt Disney World and downtown Orlando and is therefore an excellent central location. Running parallel to Interstate 4, you are not much more than 15–20 minutes away from the main theme parks, while it is also a well-developed tourist area in its own right, with some great shopping, restaurants and minor attractions like Wet 'n' Wild, Ripley's Believe It Or Not, WonderWorks, Skull Kingdom, mini-golf and go-karting. The down side is it can get extremely congested and occasionally hazardous with tourist traffic in peak periods and you have to make a slightly earlier start in the morning for Walt Disney World. But it does represent good value for money and it also possesses a rarity in Orlando in that you can go for a long stroll along real, well laid-out pavement.

**Kissimmee**: budget holiday-makers can be found in their greatest numbers along the tourist sprawl of Highway 192, an almost unbroken 12-mile strip of hotels, motels, restaurants and shops. It offers some of the best economy accommodation in the whole area and is handy for Walt Disney World's attractions, although it gives you the longest journey to Universal Studios and downtown Orlando. A car is just about essential here, though, as you are not intended to walk anywhere, and the area generally lacks that sophistication to be found elsewhere (although a general beautification project is underway, notably along the western stretch of 192).

## Split holidays

The type of holiday you fancy also comes into the equation at this point, although it is fair to say you can't really go far wrong no matter what you're seeking. The Atlantic coast and some great beaches are only an hour's drive away to the east, the magnificent Florida Everglades are little more than two hours to the south, and there are more wonderful beaches and pleasant coast roads to the west. There are great shopping opportunities almost everywhere you turn, while Orlando is also home to some of the best golf courses in the world, and there are plenty of opportunities to either play or watch tennis, baseball and basketball as well. There really is something for everyone, and it just serves to emphasise once again the need to plan what you want to do. An increasingly popular choice these days is to split the holiday by having a week or two in Orlando as well as a week on the Florida coast or somewhere more exotic like the Caribbean. The main tour companies have caught on to this trend quickly and now offer a huge variety of different packages, with cruise and stay options increasingly popular.

If you can afford the time (and the expense), the best combination is to have two weeks in Orlando itself

Florida's east coast beaches are just an hour's drive from Orlando; west coast beaches are 90 minutes away

and then a week relaxing and recuperating on one of Florida's many fabulous white-sand beaches. A two-week half-and-half split is a popular choice, but can tend to make your week in Orlando especially hectic fitting everything in, unless you pick your additional week on the Atlantic coast at somewhere like Cocoa Beach. This resort, near to Cape Canaveral and the Kennedy Space Center, is only an hour from Orlando and offers the choice of being able to return to Walt Disney World for the day. A few companies offer a 10-day Orlando and four-day coast split, and this is worth seeking out if you are limited to two weeks. Fly-drives obviously offer the greatest flexibility of doing Orlando and seeing something else of Florida, but again there is a lot to tempt you in just two weeks and you may find it is better to book a one-centre package that includes a car as well as your accommodation so you can still travel around a bit and avoid too much packing and unpacking in different hotels and motels.

## Travel companies

The briefest of glances into the nearest travel agent will reveal there is some serious competition for your hard-earned money before you have even left these shores. In the last couple of years the travel companies have worked hard to keep the cost of an Orlando holiday down, making it excellent value for money, whether you fly-drive, book your own flights or take a straightforward package. As with anything these days, it is important to shop around to get the best value for your holiday £, but I always recommend making sure your package is booked with an ABTA agent for holiday security should anything go wrong. At the last count, there were some 60 tour operators offering package holidays or fly-drives to Orlando, and here is a run-down of the biggest and best.

**Virgin holidays**: The biggest operator to MCO (that's Orlando Airport in travel-agent speak), Virgin also have the biggest and most exhausting brochure. They offer the largest variety of combinations, including Miami, New York, the Bahamas, Mexico, seven Caribbean islands and some tempting cruises, as well as the Florida coasts. A strong selling point is Virgin's non-stop scheduled service to Orlando (now from Manchester as well as Gatwick) with award-winning in-flight entertainment, free drinks and special kids' meals and games. They have a veritable army of well-briefed reps in Orlando and a good, all-round choice of accommodation in the different areas, and are popular for fly-drives, flying into Orlando and out from Miami. They average out slightly on the expensive side, but there are some special deals to be had every year, including 'kids eat free' and single parent offers, and you are assured of good quality service. Orlando is also an increasingly popular choice as a wedding venue, and Virgin have their own wedding co-ordinators, featuring even balloon weddings! For golf, tennis and scuba-diving enthusiasts there are also activity packages. Other bonuses include single parent discounts, non-driver packages, 'kids-eat-free' deals at

selected hotels and help and advice for disabled passengers. Virgin also have a unique return flight check-in service at Downtown Disney, open at 9am on your final day so you can get rid of your suitcases and make good use of the time. You can also check out their internet site on www.virginholidays.co.uk.

**Thomson**: Another of the largest, mass-market operators, Thomson

**Downtown Orlando**

have an excellent reputation in Orlando, where they have a large team of reps and Service Centres on International Drive and at Fort Liberty in Kissimmee, and offer the widest choice of departure airports (13 of them, including Newcastle, Cardiff and Belfast) to the new Orlando/Sanford Airport, flying with Britannia Airways and the majority non-stop. You can now pre-book your flight seats in advance for a small charge, and they also feature great in-flight entertainment, with Britannia's 360 USA programme in partnership with Universal Studios. Thomson price their packages very competitively for the family market, with special children's fares and bonuses like 'kids eat free' and 'extra value' hotels, while they offer a wide selection of coastal resorts for two-centre holidays and an increasing number of private villas. Walt Disney World passes can also be pre-booked to help with your holiday budgeting and they organise wedding packages, at either Walt

Disney World, the Gulf Coast or the landscaped surroundings of beautiful Cypress Gardens. From summer '99, Britannia flights will also offer upgrade options at £60 and £120 extra for more leg-room and other services.

**Airtours**: They complete the Big Three group who each take in the region of 100,000 British tourists to Orlando every year. They fly mainly non-stop from nine UK airports, with a comprehensive in-flight entertainment programme and fun-pack for kids. Families can also pre-book (for a small fee) their seats in the designated family areas, a valuable in-flight service. Like Thomson, they now use Orlando/Sanford Airport for its quicker ease of transit (see also Chapter 3) and also offer an additional comfort up-grade at £99 per person. They work hard to be one of the most price-friendly outfits and also offer some imaginative two- and three-centre combinations, including the Cayman Islands, Mexico and New Orleans. Airtours also make a feature of their fly-drive packages, with a range of 'Drive and Stay' holidays which offer a wide choice to the Florida sun-seeker, especially return visitors, with a good value hotel pass as well. They now feature an upgraded villas selection, car rental with pre-bookable insurance (praise be!) and operate a KinderCare baby-minding service in Orlando itself.

**Unijet**: Their takeover in 1998 by First Choice raised some doubts about their future as a brand name, but FC insist Unijet will continue to operate from seven UK airports with direct flights to Orlando/Sanford Airport with Air 2000 and Monarch and British Airways flights (for an average £150 supplement) to Orlando International. On Air 2000 seats can be pre-booked for a small charge to ensure families get to sit together. Unijet pride themselves on their value-for-money family

packages (including 'kids-eat-free' hotel deals) and offer an increasing number of holiday homes as well as hotels, which are great value for larger families or groups. They also feature nine of Walt Disney World's big resort hotels, from the budget options to the top of the range, and an expanded range of two-centre holidays (including some popular Caribbean cruises).

**British Airways Holidays**: Another company to benefit from their direct, scheduled air service, BAH also offer a great variety of combinations, including some first-class cruises, and have a very experienced staff in Orlando. They present a good range of Walt Disney World properties and provide a 'Without cash' holiday deal that enables you to pay a one-off price that includes tickets for Walt Disney World, Universal, SeaWorld and Busch Gardens, as well as a buffet breakfast daily at your hotel, but this is not a cheap option.

**Jetsave**: A revamped brochure, 30 new properties, two new resorts (Antigua and Cancún) for their excellent range of twin-centre options, an extended range of UK departures (with Britannia to Orlando/Sanford Airport and several scheduled airlines to Orlando International), Disney cruise options and an enlarged range of wedding packages highlight Jetsave in 1999. They cater well for repeat visitors with a large selection of up-market holiday homes, which work out good value for family groups. Jetsave's proud boast as the first major operator in this field also gives them an edge in experience.

**Cosmos**: Another familiar name in the travel world, although they tend to concentrate more on the European market. Their Orlando operation is nonetheless very well organised with one of the most readable brochures, catering as it does mainly for the family market and offering a good variety of middle-range accommodation. Flights, operated mainly on chartered airlines, are not always non-stop (and some also use Orlando/Sanford Airport), but they do offer a large variety of departure points, including Newcastle, Cardiff and Birmingham, and they are one of the most competitively priced operators. Their 'Dream Weddings' feature includes balloons, Cypress Gardens and Walt Disney World's wedding specialities.

**First Choice**: Flights with Monarch (from Gatwick, Birmingham, Glasgow and Manchester) and Air 2000 (from Manchester, Birmingham, Newcastle and Glasgow) offer pre-bookable seats (£10) and a new Classic Premium upgrade for £99. All flights use Orlando/Sanford Airport. Other new features include an extended choice of Disney hotels, coastal resorts and twin-centre holidays, including the Bahamas and cruises. First Choice also have an imaginative teenagers' programme, free tickets for under-12s to a number of attractions and a useful optional coach transfer (£18) for drivers who want to get a good night's sleep before picking up their car. They aim firmly at the family market and offer some of the best deals, with price reductions, low-start prices and 'kids eat free' options, plus they now feature Walt Disney World hotels and a range of private villas and apartments. Their Florida Weddings programme presents a choice of four venues, from Walt Disney World to Cypress Gardens. The expanding First Choice plc have two other brands selling Florida holidays, **Sovereign,** which offers a more up-market product (notably for villas), and **Eclipse**, a direct-sell operation. Their new web site is definitely worth checking out at www.first-choice.com.

**Sunworld**: Another firm which concentrates on family appeal, Sunworld also offer competitive rates for kids and some of the best middle-range prices in the market (plus a growing reputation for providing one of the most quality-conscious mass-market products). Free kids' passes to some attractions, free kids' meals (under 12s), more villa accommodation and a 'Florida Gold' hotel selection are all recent additions to their programme. They use Leisure Air, Caledonian and Monarch flights to Orlando/Sanford from five UK gateways. In keeping with the majority, they also offer Dollar hire cars with free rental, plus a new range of two-centre options, including the Florida Keys, Jamaica and a Bahamas cruise.

**Jetlife**: Another company who specialise in a tailor-made service, Jetlife are especially popular with second-time visitors as they offer an increasing number of what they call 'easy-living' homes – private villas and apartments that represent great value for larger family groups, and three- and four-bedroom houses with a private or communal swimming pool – plus the full range of Walt Disney World accommodation. Jetlife use scheduled airlines, with a large number of non-stop flights, have an excellent variety of two-centre holidays, including Jamaica, Mexico, Hawaii and various American cities, and their packages are competitively priced with some clever extras.

**Kuoni**: As in all their holidays, Kuoni offer the up-market version of Orlando, with some of the best hotels, what they call their Florida Classics, and a strong tie-up with Walt Disney World. Recent additions are the exclusive and picturesque Gulf Coast resorts of Sanibel and Captiva plus a range of executive holiday homes in keeping with Kuoni's high-class profile. The average price reflects the more exclusive nature of the packages, but there are some big child reductions (and some free kids' holidays) and Kuoni use only scheduled air services, which means non-stop flights (except for United Airlines, who go via Washington) to Orlando International Airport.

**TransAtlantic Vacations**: You won't find this firm in the big league of any operation world-wide other than Florida and, more particularly, Orlando. That means they offer a specialist American service with almost 10 years' experience of the Sunshine State and a good family-orientated product. In keeping with the bigger players in this market, TransAtlantic offer an increasing range of holiday homes and apartments, as well as hotels, which are more popular with return visitors and larger family groups. Their two-centre options are the fairly routine Gulf and Gold Coasts, the Bahamas and Jamaica, plus three-, four- or seven-day cruises. Flights feature a choice of charters to Orlando/Sanford or scheduled airlines into Orlando International for greater flexibility.

**Funway Holidays:** This UK offshoot of a large American company specialises in US destinations, hence they offer a tailor-made service to match Orlando with *any* other choice. Like many of the specialists, their private homes are a big feature of the Florida programme, but they also serve up some terrific-value deals, especially with low children's prices, if you get in quickly enough. They use only scheduled airlines, so offer non-stop flights to Orlando International Airport. Jamaica and the Bahamas can also be joined in the two-centre options, which also feature the Gulf Coast. Other extras include 'kids eat free' hotels, free kids' clubs and free shuttle bus services at selected hotels for non-drivers.

**Bridge Travel:** In many ways, Bridge are *the* specialists to Orlando, although they are now diversifying to cover more of Florida and the US. Their Orlando bias means they

**Busch Gardens, Tampa**

often get in first with new deals (notably with Disney Cruise Line) and their brochure is easily one of the most descriptive, not to mention comprehensive and accurate for all aspects of Walt Disney World. A five-day All-in-One Hopper Pass is included in the basic price, while they offer a first-day transfer option for drivers allowing them to pick their car up on day two when they might be in better shape. They also fly from seven UK airports, using BA and Virgin from Gatwick and Manchester (to Orlando International) and Airtours and Air 2000 charters (to Orlando/Sanford) from Glasgow, Newcastle, Birmingham, Cardiff and Belfast.

There are, of course, plenty of other options apart from the main tour companies, and scanning the holiday pages of the national press or Teletext will often reveal many special deals on full packages or flights alone.

The best idea is to establish some sort of plan of what you want to do and then get a selection of brochures and compare the various prices and attractions of each one.

## What to see when

Once you arrive, the temptation is to head immediately for the nearest theme park, then the next, and so on. Hold on! If there is such a thing as theme park indigestion, that's the best recipe for it, so once again try to establish a basic plan of campaign. Some days at Walt Disney World, Universal Studios, etc, are busier than others, while it is simply not possible to cover fully more than one a day, and is sometimes inadvisable to attempt two of the main parks on successive days. So here's what you do.

With the aid of the Holiday Planner at the back of this book, make a note of all the attractions you want to try to see and then pencil them in over the full duration of your holiday.

The most sensible strategy is to plan around the seven (or eight!) 'must see' parks of The Magic Kingdom® Park, Epcot®, Disney-MGM Studios, Disney's Animal Kingdom™ Theme Park, Universal Studios Florida® (and the new Islands of Adventure theme park), SeaWorld and Busch Gardens. If you have only a week to try to pack everything in, consider dropping Busch Gardens from your itinerary (it's furthest away from Orlando and doesn't have quite the same magical appeal as the others) and concentrate on the Disney parks and Universal Studios, with SeaWorld as an 'extra' if it fits into your plan. Science fiction addicts like myself and others fascinated by the realities of space travel will be hard-pressed not to include the Kennedy Space Center in their 'must see' list, but it will probably bore small children.

As a basic rule, the Magic Kingdom® is the biggest hit with children, and families often find it requires two days to feel they have seen and done everything on offer. The same can be said of Epcot®, but there are fewer rides to keep small

children happy, and as much of the emphasis is on education as on entertainment, although it all has Walt Disney World's slick, easily-digestible coating. Only the most fleet of foot, coupled with the benefit of a relatively crowd-free period, will be able to negotiate Epcot® successfully in a day. Disney's Animal Kingdom™ Theme Park is also a little short on attractions for the youngest kids, but it still requires nearly all of its 7am–8pm opening hours. Disney-MGM Studios is a 9–5 park (where you can comfortably fit in all the attractions in the daylight hours), while SeaWorld needs rather longer and Universal Studios Florida® can be a two-day park when Orlando is at its busiest. Busch Gardens is another full day affair, especially as it is 75–90 minutes drive away to Tampa in the south-west, but an early start to the Kennedy Space Center (an hour's drive to the east coast) will mean you can be back in your hotel swimming pool by tea-time, confident you have fully en-joyed One Small Step For Man. All the main attractions, plus the smaller ones, are detailed in Chapters 5–8, so try to get an idea of the essential time requirements of them all before you pick up your pencil!

## Smaller attractions

Of the other, smaller-scale attractions, the nature park of Silver Springs is a full day out as it also involves a near two-hour drive to get there, but everything else can be fitted around your Big Seven Itinerary. The waterparks of Disney's Typhoon Lagoon, River Country and Blizzard Beach, Wet 'n' Wild and Water Mania are all a good way to spend a relaxing afternoon, while Cypress Gardens is another quieter place to while away four to five hours. There are also a number of smaller-scale attractions in Orlando which will probably keep the children amused for several hours. Gatorland is a unique look at some of Florida's oldest inhabitants, with three different shows to display the various reptilian creatures. The Mystery Fun House is a good bet for two to three hours, as are Ripley's Believe It Or Not, an American version of the Guinness World of Records and the new Wonderworks interactive museum. The new Haunted Mansion, Skull Kingdom and Terror on Church Street (not for the faint-hearted – see Chapter 6) guarantee a 20- to 30-minute journey through various indoor horrors, while Discovery Island Park at Walt Disney World is quite the opposite, two or three hours of gentle Florida nature, with a walk-through aviary and animal shows. DisneyQuest, another new venture in Downtown Disney, is a hugely imaginative interactive 'arcade' that guarantees 1–2 hours of fun. Each main tourist area is also well served with imaginative mini-golf and go-kart tracks that will happily absorb any excess energy for an hour or two from those who haven't, by now, been exhausted!

## Evenings

Then, of course, there is the evening entertainment, with a similarly wide choice of extravagant fun-seeking. By far the best, and a must for at least one evening each, are Downtown Disney Pleasure Island at Walt Disney World, Universal's new CityWalk and Church Street Station in downtown Orlando. Both will keep you fully entertained from 5pm until the early hours if you so wish – and you don't want to have an early start planned for the next morning! An increasingly popular and rapidly proliferating source of fun are the various dinner shows Orlando has to offer: a two- to three-hour cabaret based on themes

like the Wild West (predictably), Medieval England (not so predictably) and murder mysteries (the unpredictably fun Sleuth's) that all include a hearty meal.

## What to do when

Getting down to the fine detail: there are a couple of handy general guidelines for avoiding the worst of the tourist hordes, even in high season. It may well be stating the obvious, but the vast majority of fun-seekers in town are American, and they tend to arrive at the weekends, get settled in their hotels, and then head for the main theme parks, i.e., Walt Disney World, first. That means that Mondays and Tuesdays are generally bad times to join the queues for the Magic Kingdom® and Epcot®. In addition, Thursdays and Saturdays are almost as congested at the Magic Kingdom®, while Fridays and Saturdays are above average for crowds at Epcot®. Disney-MGM Studios is slightly different in that their busiest days tend to be Wednesdays and Sundays, while Walt Disney World's most popular water parks, Blizzard Beach and Typhoon Lagoon, hit high tide at the weekend and Thursday and Friday during the summer. The advent of Disney's Animal Kingdom™ Theme Park has meant peak crowds there in mid-week, with Sunday distinctly quieter. Like Disney-MGM Studios, the best days to visit Universal Studios are Friday and Saturday, with Mondays also a little quieter. By the same logic, if Walt Disney World is humming in the early part of the week, that makes it a good time to visit SeaWorld, Busch Gardens, Cypress Gardens, Silver Springs or the Kennedy Space Center. Wet 'n' Wild and Water Mania are best avoided at the weekends when the locals come out to play.

Making sure you get the most out of your days at the main theme parks is another art form, and there are a number of practical policies to pursue. The official opening times of the theme parks are all well-publicised in and around Orlando and don't vary much between 8.30 and 9am. However, apart from the obvious advantage of arriving early to try to get at the head of the queues (and you will encounter some VERY formidable queues – or lines, as the Americans call them – at regular intervals), all the parks will often open earlier than scheduled if the crowds build up quickly before the official hour. So, you can get a step ahead of the masses by arriving at least 30 minutes before the expected opening time, or an hour early during the main holiday periods. Apart from anything else, you will be better placed to park in the vast, wide open spaces of the public car parks and catch the tram service to the main gates (which can be anything up to half a mile away!).

Once you've put yourself in pole position for that eagerly-anticipated opening, don't waste time on the shops, scenery and other frippery which will lure the unprepared first-timer through the gates. Instead, head straight for some of the main rides and get a few big-time thrills under your belt before the main hordes arrive. You will quickly work out where the most popular attractions are as the majority of the other early birds will be similarly prepared and will flock in the appropriate direction. Go with the flow for the first hour or so and you'll enjoy the general tourist buzz as well as some of the best rides in relative comfort. Chapters 5 and 6 provide a full run-down of exactly what's what, so you can plan your individual park strategies.

As another general rule, you can also benefit from doing the opposite of what the masses do after the initial rush has subsided into a steady stream. But a word of warning first: the Walt Disney World parks, notably the Magic Kingdom®, stay open late in the evening during the main holiday periods, occasionally until midnight, and that can make for a long day for young children.

## Pace yourself

Therefore it is important to pace yourself, especially if you have been one of the first through the gates. There are plenty of opportunities to take time-outs and have a well-earned drink or bite to eat, and you can take advantage of the American propensity to take meal-times very seriously by avoiding lunchtime (around 12.30pm) and dinnertime (around 6pm) for your own breaks. So, after you've had a couple of hours of real adventure-mania, it pays to take an early lunch (i.e., before midday), plunge back into the hectic thrill of it all for another three hours or so, have another snack-sized meal in mid-afternoon and then return to the main rides, especially if your appetite has been only whetted by the early morning fun, as the parks tend to quieten down a little in late afternoon. If your hotel is not far from the park, it is worthwhile even taking a couple of hours out to return for a hotel siesta, providing you have your hand stamped for re-entry when you leave (your car park ticket will also be valid all day so you won't have to pay for re-admission there either), and then enjoying the evening entertainment back at the park, which is often the most spectacular part of the day.

Finally, if all this talk of how to tackle the main attractions isn't enough to wear you out, a word about shopping in Orlando – it's world class. Chapter 10 deals fully with the huge variety of temptations guaranteed to lure even the most miserly shopper, but suffice it to say here that your battle plan should also include at least an afternoon to visit one of the spectacular shopping malls in Orlando, as well as a chance to sample some of the discount outlets and speciality centres like Old Town in Kissimmee, the Church Street Exchange in downtown Orlando, and the stunning new Pointe*Orlando on International Drive.

## Clothing and comfort

The most important part of your whole holiday wardrobe is your footwear. Hopefully, the message will now have sunk home that you are going to spend a lot of time on your feet, even during the off-peak periods. The smallest of the parks covers 'only' 100 acres, but that is irrelevant to the amount of time you will spend queuing. Your feet will

BRIT TIP: Avoid the temptation to pack a lot of smart or semi-formal clothing – you really won't need it in hot, informal Florida.

definitely not thank you, therefore, if you decide this is the trip to break in those new sandals or trainers. Comfortable, well-worn shoes or trainers are ESSENTIAL. Otherwise, you need dress only as the climate dictates. T-shirts and shorts are quite acceptable in all of the parks (but not bare torsos, even for men!) and most restaurants and other eating establishments will happily accept informal dress.

If, after a long day, you feel the need for a change of clothes or a sweater for the evening, use the handy lockers which all the theme parks provide to leave personal belongings. For parents with small children and babies, Walt Disney World in particular is well equipped to ease your stay. Push-chairs (or strollers in American-speak) are available for a small charge at all parks, while baby services – for nursing mothers and nappy-changing – are freely located at regular intervals.

It is often necessary to point out the absolutely vital need to carry and use high-factor sun creams at all times, even during the winter months when the sun may not feel that strong but can still burn all the same. Nothing, but nothing is guaranteed to make you feel uncomfortable for several weeks like severe sunburn. Orlando has a sub-tropical climate and requires higher-factor sun creams than our summers

BRIT TIP: The summer is also the time when the local mosquito population starts to get busy. Make sure you take a spray-on insect repellent, especially for evening use. Alternatively, try to get hold of the Avon skincare product Skin So Soft which works wonders at keeping the bugs at bay.

or even a holiday in the Mediterranean. Use sun blocks on sensitive areas like your nose and ears, and splash on the after-sun cream liberally once you are back in your hotel room. Local skincare products are widely available in Orlando and usually inexpensive (especially at Wal-Mart or K-Mart stores), while many tour operators now have a skincare specialist available for advice at their welcome meetings.

Be aware, however, that if you are

2

in and out of the pool, or spending a day sliding down all the fun rides and slides of one of the water fun parks, you will need a waterproof sun cream to avoid becoming lobsterised! Wear a hat if you are out theme park-ing in the hottest parts of the day, and try to avoid alcoholic drinks until the evening as there is nothing like alcohol for making you dehydrated (except, perhaps, strong coffee and caffeine-based soft drinks) and susceptible to heatstroke, a more advanced stage of sunburn. You will need to increase your fluid intake significantly during the summer months in Orlando, but stick to still soft drinks or water!

Should you require medical treatment, whether it be for sunburn or other first aid, consult your tour company's information about local hospitals and surgeries. In the event of a medical, or other, emergency dial 911 as you would 999 in Britain.

It cannot be over-stressed you should have comprehensive travel and health insurance for any trip to America as there is NO National Health Service and ANY form of medical treatment will need to be paid for – and is usually expensive.

Emergency out-patients departments can be found at Florida Hospital Medical Center (in four locations: 12125 South Apopka-Vineland Road, near the Crossroads at Lake Buena Vista, 7848 West Irlo Bronson Memorial Highway, near Splendid China; 6001 Vineland Road, near Universal Studios; and 1462 West Oakridge Road, near Florida Mall) and Sand Lake Hospital on 9400 Turkey Lake Road, while the East Coast Medical Network (407 648 5252) and House Med Inc (407 239 1195) both make hotel 'house calls' 24 hours a day. House Med also operates MediClinic, another walk-in facility on 2901 Parkway Boulevard, Kissimmee, which is open daily from 9am to 9pm, and Orlando Regional

Healthcare System (operators of Sand Lake Hospital) have Walk-In Medical Care centres on International Drive (phone 407 351 3035 and 239 6679) open from 8am to 8pm. If you visit a doctor during your stay, make sure you let your tour rep know afterwards. For a chemist (the Americans call them drug stores), the two biggest chain stores are Eckerd Drugs and Walgreens. Eckerd Drugs on 8330 International Drive is an easy-to-find chemist that is open until midnight, while their branch at 908 Lee Road is open 24 hours a day, as is Walgreens at 6201 International Drive (opposite Wet 'n' Wild).

## Travellers with disabilities

Holiday-makers with disabilities will be pleased to note that the main parks pay close attention to their needs, too. There are few rides and attractions that cannot cater for them, while wheelchair availability and access is almost always good. Walt Disney World publish a *Guidebook for Disabled Guests*, as do Universal, which is available in all three main parks. Life-jackets are on hand at River Country and Typhoon Lagoon, while there are special tape recorders and cassettes for blind visitors, and guide dogs are in no way discouraged.

**Seminole County**

---

## American-speak

Another thing to watch out for are those words or phrases that may have a different meaning across the Atlantic, or which need a complete translation. When I sat down to compile this lis, I surprised even myself at how many words need to be 'translated' back into English. Some of them are obvious, others more obscure. Mind your language …

| American | English |
| --- | --- |
| Check or Tab | Bill |
| Restroom | Public toilet |
| Bathroom | Private toilet |
| Eggs 'over easy' | Eggs fried both sides but soft |
| Eggs 'over hard' | Eggs fried both sides but hard! |
| Eggs 'sunny side up' | Eggs fried on just ONE side (soft) |
| French fries | Chips |
| Chips | Crisps |
| Cookie | Biscuit |
| Grits | Porridge-like breakfast dish made out of ground, boiled corn |
| Biscuit | Savoury scone |
| Hash browns | Grated, fried potato (delicious!) |
| Jelly | Jam |
| Silverware or place-setting | Cutlery |
| Liquor | Spirits |
| Seltzer | Soda water |
| Shot | Measure |
| Liquor store | Off-licence |
| Broiled | Grilled |
| Grilled | Flame-grilled |
| Sub | French bread roll |
| Shrimp | King prawn |
| Sherbet | Sorbet |
| Appetiser | Starter |
| Entree | Main course |
| To go | Take-away (as in food) |
| Candy | Sweets |
| Drug store | Chemist |
| Sidewalk | Pavement |
| Pavement | Roadway |
| Bill | Note (as in $5 note) |
| Crib | Cot |
| Cot or rollaway | Fold-up bed |
| Diaper | Nappy |
| Stroller | Pushchair |

| American | English |
| --- | --- |
| Lines | Queues 'Stand in line' not 'Queue up') |
| Elevator | Lift |
| Underpass | Subway |
| Subway | Underground |
| Mailbox | Postbox |
| Faucet | Tap |
| Collect call | Reverse charge phone call |
| Gas | Petrol |
| Trunk | Car boot |
| Hood | Car bonnet |
| Fender | Car bumper |
| Antennae | Aerial |
| Windshield | Windscreen |
| Stickshift | Manual transmission |
| Trailer | Caravan |
| Freeway | Motorway |
| Divided highway | Dual carriageway |
| Denver boot | Wheel clamp |
| Turn-out | Lay-by |
| No standing | No parking OR stopping |
| Parking lot | Car park |
| Semi | Articulated Truck |
| Ramp | Slip-road |
| Intersection | Junction |
| Yield | Give way |
| Purse | Handbag |
| Fanny pack | Bumbag |
| Pants | Trousers |
| Undershirt | Vest |
| Vest | Waistcoat |
| Pantyhose | Tights |
| Sneakers | Trainers |
| Shorts | Underpants |
| Quarter | 25 cents |
| Dime | 10 cents |
| Nickel | 5 cents |
| Penny | 1 cent |
| Downtown | The city or town centre (not the run-down part!) |
| A/C | Air conditioning |

## Measurements

American clothes sizes are less than we are used to, hence a woman's size 12 dress over there is really a size 14 to us, or an American jacket sized 42 is really a 44. Shoes are the opposite: if an Orlando shoe shop reckons that wicked new pair of trainers are a size 10, they should fit a British size 9 foot! Their measuring system is also still imperial and NOT metric, so we have to get used to everything being in feet and inches, ounces and pounds, pints and quarts and mph (not kph – watch those speeds!).

Finally, be aware when Americans say the first floor, they actually mean the ground floor, the second floor is really the first, and so on.

(Last PS: NEVER ask for a packet of fags! Fag is, ahem, a crude, slang term for homosexual, hence you will get some VERY funny looks. 'A packet?' etc.)

## Wedding Bells

Florida is increasingly sought after by couples looking to tie the knot, and Orlando offers a terrific range of wedding services, from ceremony co-ordinators, photography and flowers to a wonderfully scenic range of venues like Cypress Gardens, Winter Park and Leu Gardens, plus more unusual venues like the pit-lane of the Richard Petty Driving Experience at Walt Disney World or even at 145mph around the speedway itself! **Walt Disney World's Wedding Pavilion** offers true fairytale romance, with the backdrop of Cinderella's Castle and Seven Seas Lagoon. You can opt for traditional elegance in this Victorian setting with up to 260 guests or the full Disney experience, arriving in Cinderella's glass coach and with Mickey and Minnie among the guests! Disney's wedding organisers can tailor-make the occasion for individual requirements (tel. 407 828

3400). All the main **tour operators** feature wedding options and co-ordinated services, and offer ceremonies as varied as aboard a hot air balloon or helicopter (Virgin), Caledesi Island beach (Airtours and Jetsave), Church Street Station (Jetsave) or luxury yacht (Cosmos). **Crownline Wedding Services** (tel. 407 354 0985) are the Orlando specialists for the co-ordinated approach, offering everything from a choice of eight venues to video, flowers and wedding cake. You can also **do it yourself** by calling at the Osceola County Administrative Building, 17 South Vernon Street, Room 231-A, Kissimmee from 8.30am–4.30pm Monday–Friday (tel. 407 847 1424). Both parties must be present to apply for the Marriage Licence, which costs $88.50 (in cash) and is valid for 60 days, while the ceremony (equivalent to a British registry office) can be performed at the same time for an extra $20. Passports and birth certificates are required and, after acquiring a Marriage Licence, a couple can get married anywhere in Florida. The County's Marriage Department can also supply names of public notaries to conduct the ceremony if you want to get married elsewhere, like one of the more picturesque restort hotels, which are usually amenable to providing the venue. For more information, you can call the Orlando/Orange County Convention & Visitors' Bureau for an information pack.

## Budgeting

Of course, all this planning will count for nothing unless you get your sums right, too. So here is a quick guide to what you should reckon on spending on a typical popular package with two of the main tour operators (based on two adults and children aged 8 and 11 travelling at the beginning of April):

© Disney

**The Disney Wedding Pavilion on the Seven Seas Lagoon at Walt Disney World Resort®**

**One week: (with Virgin Holidays)**

| | | |
|---|---|---|
| at Wynfield Inn | = | £1,407 |
| 5-Day Disney Hoppers | = | £630 |
| 1-Day Universal Studios | = | £100 |
| Car hire | = | £189 |
| Meals | = | £236 |
| Souvenirs | = | £60 |
| Miscellaneous | = | £100 |
| **TOTAL** | | **£2,722** |

**Two weeks: (with First Choice)**

| | | |
|---|---|---|
| at Gateway Inn | = | £2,036 |
| 5-Day Disney Hoppers | = | £630 |
| 3-Park Flex Ticket | = | £254 |
| Wild Bill's Dinner Show | = | £72 |
| Other attractions | = | £100 |
| Car hire | = | £357 |
| Meals | = | £470 |
| Souvenirs | = | £120 |
| Miscellaneous | = | £150 |
| **TOTAL** | | **£4,189** |

(Note: Accommodation selected is of budget variety; all passes charged at tour operators' brochure rates; inclusive rates; meals worked out on basis of $54 a day at mixture of hotel and theme parks.)

Obviously, it could well be possible to do things more cheaply, but both examples are intended as a starting point only. However, they should still provide a graphic illustration of the *real* expense involved. Great value it certainly is, but cheap it ain't.

## Know before you go

Finally, while you are still at the planning stage, you might like to make a note of the organisations you can contact in advance for information. Florida Tourism (otherwise known as FLA USA) have an info line on 0891 600555 (calls cost 50p/minute) that lists all Florida destinations and gives other consumer lines in the UK, while they are also on the internet at www.flausa.com. The Orlando Tourism Bureau in London has a 24-hour tourist information line on 0891 600220 (50p/minute) on which you can request a copy of their free area guide and their web site is www.go2Orlando.com. Kissimmee's UK office has a brochure request line on 0171 630 1105 and their web site is www.floridakiss.com and e-mail at kissimmee@compuserve.com. You can also write to the Kissimmee-St Cloud Convention & Visitors' Bureau, Roebuck House, Palace Street, London SW1E 5BA, or fax them on 0171 630 0245.

When you arrive in the area, it is also worth checking out Orlando's ONLY official **Visitor Center** at 8723 International Drive (tel. 407 363 5872) for discounted attraction tickets, free brochures and accommodation advice and free information pamphlets and maps. The Kissimmee **Visitor Center** is at the eastern end of the Highway 192 tourist drag (tel. 407 847 5000) and they have a toll-free accommodation line in the US of 1-800 333 KISS.

Okay, now we've established all that, it's time to get you up and running on the roads of Florida's funland …

# **3** Driving and Car Hire
*(or, The Secret of Getting Around on Interstate 4)*

For the vast majority, introduction to Orlando proper comes immediately after clearing the airport via the potentially bewildering complexity of the local road systems in a newly-acquired hire car. Yet driving here is a lot more simple and, on the whole, enjoyable than driving in the UK. In particular, anyone used to the M25 will certainly find Orlando's motorways more sedate.

Before you get to your hire car, however, a quick note about Orlando International Airport and the new Orlando/Sanford Airport, which is primarily a British charter flight gateway 30 miles to the north of Orlando itself. There is a full breakdown of how both airports work in Chapter 12, but you need to be aware of a couple of little quirks on your arrival.

Orlando International is one of the most modern and enjoyable airports you will encounter, but it does have a double baggage collection system that is a bit bewildering at first. You disembark at one of three Satellite terminals and have to collect your luggage immediately, then put it on another baggage carousel that takes it to the main terminal while you ride the passenger shuttle. Once in the main terminal you will be on Level Three and need to descend to Level Two for baggage reclaim. Package holiday-makers with Dollar Rent A Car will be able to hand their luggage straight over here to the

International Drive at night

porters who will take it down to Level One to await their car pick-up.

The Big Five hire companies who all have check-in desks at the airport are Dollar, Hertz, National, Budget and Avis and all offer the most comprehensive hire services, if rather lacking in the personal touch. However, there is also a telephone desk at Level One that connects you directly to one of another 10 hire companies who often work out

BRIT TIP: Make sure you follow the correct instructions to collect your hire car. There are several different desks for each of the main hire companies and if you do not check in at the right one you will waste a lot of time.

better value if you haven't already booked your car. A quick call brings their bus to pick you up and take you to their nearby depot, which also gives you a look at the surrounding roads before you have to drive on them. Hertz and Avis are the biggest companies in the US, but Dollar and Alamo are the Nos 1 and 2 with the tourist business. Dollar include Thomson, Airtours, Virgin, Cosmos, First Choice and Sunworld in their typical packages, while Alamo are the main clients for Unijet, British Airways Holidays and Thomas Cook Holidays, among others.

Being mobile is very nearly essential in most American cities and Orlando is no exception. Few of the attractions are within walking distance of anywhere and there are few pavements (sidewalks). You can get around to a certain extent by bus, and many hotels are linked to private mini-bus charter firms who charge reasonable rates to the main attractions, while some hotels operate a free shuttle service to Walt Disney World (notably 90% of those in Kissimmee), and some of the other theme parks. Taxis tend to be pretty expensive and usually need to be ordered as they are not plentiful. For example, the journey from the airport to International Drive would cost you the best part of $35, while from International Drive to Universal Studios would be about $15. Three companies who operate a handy fleet of shuttle buses are Mears (tel 407 839 1570), World Transportation (407 826 9999) and Transtar (407 856 7777), with an International Airport transfer to International Drive costing $15 per person and $20 to Kissimmee, and a typical journey from I Drive to Walt Disney World costing $9/10 a head. While buses are not the ideal transport system in somewhere as vast as the metro Orlando area, they do work out extremely cheap at only 85 cents a ride or $7 for a weekly pass. Three routes worth noting are Link 56 from West Highway 192 to the Magic Kingdom®, Link 4 from downtown Kissimmee to downtown Orlando and Link 42 from the International Airport to International Drive. For more information, call 407 841 8240 (Orange County) or 407 348 7518 (Osceola County). Remember to have the right change for an individual journey. All buses should be wheelchair accessible. International Drive also now has its own extensive multi-coloured trolley service, I-Ride, which runs the length of the main tourist area, from SeaWorld in the south right up to the Belz Factory Outlet Malls at the top of the Drive. It is great value at 75 cents each journey (children 12 and under ride free) and buses run daily every 15 minutes from 7am until midnight, with more than 50 stops. There are also 1-, 3-, 5- and 7-day passes for $2–$7, while senior citizens' journeys are only 25 cents each. I-Ride bus-stops are indicated by a circular sign with a large pink paw-print (for the Lynx bus system) and you must have the right money as drivers do not carry change. Your hotel front desk will have all the details, but otherwise Orlando's public transport is pretty sketchy and can involve long waits which are especially inadvisable in the hot summer months.

## The car

Ultimately, having a car is the key to being in charge of your holiday, and on a weekly basis it tends to work out very reasonable price-wise, too.

Weekly rates can be as low as $60 for the smallest size of car

BRIT TIP: The boot size on American cars tends to be much smaller than the British equivalent.

(an **Economy**, usually a Fiesta-sized hatchback; next up is the **Subcompact**, an Escort-sized car; the **Compact**, a small family saloon like an Orion; the **Midsize** is a more spacious four-door, five-seater like a Vectra; and the **Fullsize** would be a large-style executive car like a Granada, and you can get larger still). But beware – these low, low prices are a bit of a catch. There are plenty of insurance and tax extras which soon take the basic price to $220 a week or more. However, all the rental companies are now offering all-inclusive rates which do away with these 'hidden extras'. Special seasonal all-inclusive rates, if booked at home direct with one of the big car hire companies can also be as low as £130 a week.

Once again, the scale of the car hire operation is huge, and, with upwards of 300 tourists arriving at a time, it can be a pretty formidable business getting everyone off and running. The currently widespread practice of British holiday companies offering Free Car Hire with their packages does NOT mean it won't cost you anything. It is only the rental cost which is free and you will still be expected to pay the insurance, taxes and other extras BEFORE you can drive the car away. Having a credit card is essential, and there are two main kinds of insurance, the most important being the Loss Damage Waiver, or LDW. This currently costs around $13.99 a day and covers you for any damage to your hire car. You can manage without it, but the hire company will then insist on a huge deposit in the order of $1,000 on your credit card, and that could wipe out your credit limit in one go (and you are also liable for ANY damage to the car). You will also be offered Supplemental Liability Insurance at around $8–$10 a day. This covers you against being sued for astronomical amounts by any

court-happy American you may happen to bump into. Drivers under 25 have to pay an extra $8–10 per day, while all drivers must be at least 21. Other additional costs (which all mount up over a two-week holiday, so be sure to take out only what you need) include local and Florida state taxes which can add another $4 a day to your final bill, Airport Access Fee at $2 per day and then there's your petrol, although that's only around $1.20 a gallon for unleaded.

Drivers also please note: you may feel the effects of jet-lag for a day or two after arrival, but this can be reduced during the flight by avoiding alcohol and coffee and instead drinking plenty of water.

The thought of tackling American roads and driving on the 'wrong' side can be the main cause of pre-holiday anxiety, but most soon find it is a pleasure rather than a pain, mainly because nearly all hire cars these days are automatics and rarely more than a year old. And, because speed limits are lower than we're used to at home (and rigidly enforced), you won't often be rushed into taking the wrong turn. Keep your foot on the brake when you are stationary as automatics tend to

> BRIT TIP: Be FIRM with the hire company check-in clerk as many are quite pushy and will try to get you to take extras, like car upgrades, you don't need.

creep forward, and always put the automatic gear lever in 'P' (for Park) after turning off the engine.

## Controls

All cars are also fitted with air-conditioning, which is absolutely essential during spring, summer and autumn. The button to turn it on will be marked A/C, Air, or will be indicated by a snowflake symbol. (Handy hint: to make it work, you also have to switch on the car's fan!) Note also that air-conditioning takes power from the engine and, with smaller cars, you may notice a bit of a struggle going uphill. To get full power back, simply turn off the A/C until the road levels off again. Don't

> BRIT TIP: You probably won't be able to take the keys out of the ignition unless you put the car in 'Park' first. This sometimes causes much consternation!

be alarmed by a small pool of liquid forming under your car in summer – it's merely condensation off the A/C unit. Power steering is also a common feature on many hire cars, so if you're not used to it, be gentle around corners until you get the feel of it. Some larger cars also have Cruise Control which lets you set the desired speed and take your foot off the accelerator (or gas pedal in American-speak). There will be two buttons on the steering wheel, one to switch the Cruise Control on, the other which you push to set the desired speed. To take the car off Cruise Control either press the first button again or simply touch the brake. Wait until you have a clear stretch of motorway before you try this, though! The handbrake may also be different to the standard British pull-up variety. Some cars have an extra foot pedal to the left of the brake, and you need to push this to engage the handbrake. There will then be a tab just above it which you pull to release it, or a second push on the pedal if there is no tab. The car probably won't start unless the gear lever is on 'P', which can be

confusing at first. To put the car in 'D' for Drive, you also have to depress the main brake pedal. D1 and D2 are extra gears only for steep hills. N.B. Few cars have central locking so make sure you lock ALL the doors.

## Getting around

Once you are familiar with your car's controls you will want to head straight for your hotel. Your hire car company should provide you with a basic map of Orlando plus directions for getting to the hotel. Insist that these are provided as all the hire companies make a big point of this in their advertising literature. To begin with, familiarise yourself with the main roads of the area and learn to navigate by the road *numbers* (it's much easier than names, and the directional signs will feature the numbers primarily) and the exit numbers of the main roads.

When you drive out of the International Airport (or the hire company's off-airport depot) DON'T look for signs to 'Orlando' – the airport's smart, new signage should be a big help here. The main tourist areas are all south and west of the city proper, so follow the appropriate signs for your hotel. For the International Drive area you want the Beeline Expressway (Route 528) all the way west until it crosses International Drive just north of SeaWorld. The main hotel area of I-Drive (as it is known locally) is to the north, so keep right at the exit. For western Kissimmee and Walt Disney World, go south out of the airport and pick up the new Central Florida Greeneway (Route 417) all the way west until it intersects with State Route 536 at Exit 6. You can then follow 536 straight across into Walt Disney World or take the Interstate 4 motorway west for one junction until it hits the main Kissimmee Routeway, Highway 192

**You'll find modern transport everywhere until you reach places like Cypress Gardens!**

(or the Irlo Bronson Memorial Highway). For eastern Kissimmee, come off Route 417 at its Exit 11 junction with the Orange Blossom Trail (Highway 441), and going south brings you into Highway 192 at the other end of the main tourist drag.

Leaving the new Orlando/Sanford Airport is also a straightforward affair, boosted by the airport's simple design to get incoming British tourists on the road far quicker than Orlando International.

Dollar Rent A Car have made a big impression here with their British-dedicated operation. There is no off-airport shuttle to your car to slow you down, just a quick walk from the airport's baggage reclaim hall to the car hire office and then you're away. But please remember to have your Dollar paperwork and your driving licence with you – now is not the time to realise it's still on the sideboard at home as you WILL find yourself either delayed or refused a car altogether (in the case of forgetting your licence).

It may be much further to the north and involve more driving time, but you should save time overall. You leave the airport on East Lake Mary Boulevard and quickly hit the junction with the Central Florida Greeneway (Highway 417) on which you head south. The slip-road on to this toll motorway is just under the fly-over on your LEFT, and you will need about $4.50 in total to reach Kissimmee or Walt Disney World or $3.75 to reach International Drive (via the Beeline Expressway, Highway 528).

You can avoid the tolls by staying on Lake Mary Boulevard for four

> BRIT TIP: The Beeline Expressway and Greeneway are both toll roads, so it's ESSENTIAL to have a few dollars' worth of change before you leave the airport, with some 25-cent coins, too, if possible.

> BRIT TIP: Watch out for one small hiccup on the Greeneway heading south. Just after Junction 34 it appears to split into two where it meets the East–West Expressway, Highway 408. Stay in the RIGHT lane to keep on the south-bound motorway.

miles until you hit Interstate 4, but you will encounter much more traffic this way and possibly hit the 4–6pm snarl-up through the city centre. The Greeneway is an excellent, easy-driving introduction to Orlando roads, even if it does cost an extra few dollars.

## Signposts and road names

Right, that gets you to your holiday base, but there are still a few other pitfalls, and it's best to be aware of them in advance. First and foremost, the Americans have invented a system of signposting and road-naming, the wisdom of which is known only to them. For instance, you cannot fail to find the main attractions, but retracing your steps back to the hotel afterwards can prove tricky because they often take you out of the parks a different way. Also, exits off the Interstate and other main roads can be on EITHER side of the carriageway, not just on the right as you would expect. This potential worry is offset, though, by the fact you can overtake in ANY lane on multi-lane highways, not just the outside ones. Therefore, you can happily sit in the middle lane and let the rest of the world go by until you see your exit. To get their own back at this

obviously unfair ploy by visiting tourists, American road signposters have another sneaky trick in that they don't give you much advance notice of turn-offs. You get the sign and then the exit in very quick succession. No nice, handy, 3-2-1 countdown as you get on our motorways. The local police also take a dim view of late and frequent lane-changing. But once again, the speeds at which you are travelling tend to minimise the dangers of missing your turn-off. Local drivers also tend to be courteous, so, if you signal properly, they will usually let you pull out. It is handy if your front seat passenger acts as navigator, though. Orlando has yet to come up with a comprehensive tourist map of its city streets and the maps supplied by the car rental companies tend to be rather simplified. It helps that none of the main attractions are off the beaten track, but the support of your navigator can be useful, especially while you are still getting your bearings in the first few days.

Around town, and in the main tourist areas like International Drive and Kissimmee, you will come across another way of confusing the unwary with the way road names are displayed. At every junction you will see a road name hung underneath the traffic lights, which are always suspended ABOVE the road. This road name is NOT the road you are on, but the one you are CROSSING. Once again there is no advance notification of each junction and the road names can be difficult to read as you approach them, especially at night, so keep your speed down if you think you are close to your turn-off so you can get in the correct lane. Don't worry, though, if you do miss a turning, as nearly all the roads are arranged in a simple grid system so it is usually easy to work your way back. Occasionally you will meet a crossroads where no right of way is obvious. This is a four-way stop, and here the priority goes in order of arrival, so when it's your turn you just indicate and pull out slowly (Americans don't have roundabouts, so this is the closest you will get to one).

Several major highways, notably the Beeline Expressway and Florida Turnpike and Greeneway, are also toll roads, so have some change handy in varying amounts from 25 cents to $1. They all do give change (in the GREEN lanes), but you will get through much quicker if you have the correct money (in the BLUE lanes).

As well as the obvious difference of driving on the 'wrong' side of the road in the first place (a particular hazard in car parks, some people find), there are also several differences in procedure of which it is handy to be aware. The most frequent British errors occur at traffic lights, where there are two variations to catch out the uninformed. At a red light it is still possible to turn RIGHT, providing there is no traffic coming from the left and no pedestrians crossing, unless otherwise specified (signs will occasionally indicate 'NO TURN ON RED'). Turning LEFT at the lights, you have the right of way with a green ARROW, but you have to give way to traffic from the other direction on a SOLID green light. The majority of accidents involving overseas visitors take place on left turns, so do take extra care here. There is also no amber light from red to green, but there IS an amber light from green to red.

## Speed limits and restrictions

Speed limits are always well marked with black numbering on white signs and, again, the police are pretty hot on speeding and on-the-spot fines

are steep: $57 for being stopped in the first place, plus $5 for every mile an hour you are over the limit. Limits vary from 55 to 70 mph on the Interstates (and can change frequently), where there is also a 40mph MINIMUM speed, to just 15 or 20mph in some built-up areas. Flashing orange lights suspended over the road indicate a school zone and you should proceed with caution, while school buses CANNOT be overtaken in either direction when they are unloading and have their hazard lights flashing. U-turns are forbidden in built-up areas and where a solid line runs down the middle of the road. It is also illegal to park within 10 feet of a fire hydrant or a lowered kerb, and NEVER park in front of a yellow-painted kerb – they are stopping points for emergency vehicles and you will be towed away. Never park on a kerb, either. Seat belts are also compulsory for all front seat passengers, while child seats MUST be used for children under four and can be hired from the car companies at around $3 a day. Children of four or five must either use a seat belt, whether sitting in the front or back, or have a child seat fitted. Florida has two additional quirks that should be noted. Firstly, you MUST put your lights on in the rain, and secondly you MUST park bonnet first. Reverse parking is frowned upon because number plates are often found only on the rear of cars and patrolling police cars like to be able to read them without the officers having to stop and walk round the car. If you park parallel to the kerb you must also be facing in the direction of the traffic. Disabled drivers should note their orange disabled badge IS recognised in Florida for parking in the well-provided disabled parking spaces. Also, a word on drinking and driving – don't do it! Florida has strict laws on driving under the influence of alcohol, with penalties of up to six months in prison for first-time offenders. The legal limit for the blood-alcohol level is lower than in Britain, so it is safer not to drink at all if you are driving. It is also illegal to carry open containers of alcohol in the car itself.

## Accidents

In the unlikely event of having an accident, no matter how minor, the police must be contacted before the cars can be moved (except on the busy I4). Car hire firms will insist on a full police report for the insurance paperwork. In the case of a break-down, there should be an emergency number for the hire company among their essential literature, or, if you are on a major highway, raise the bonnet of your car to indicate a problem and wait for one of the frequent police patrol cars to stop for you. Remember, also, always to carry your driving licence and your hire agreement forms with you in case you are stopped by the police at any time. Should you be pulled over, remain in your car with your hands on the wheel and be polite to the officer who comes over. Once they learn you are British, you MAY just get away with a ticking-off for a minor offence!

## Key routes

As already mentioned, the main route through Orlando is **Interstate 4** (or I4), a six- to eight-lane motorway linking the two Florida coasts. Interstates are always indicated on blue shield-shaped signs. For most of its length, I4 travels almost directly east–west, but, around Orlando, it swings annoyingly north–south. Annoying, because directions are still given either east or westwards, so be aware that in this case east means north in

real terms and a sign saying west means you are going south! All main motorways are prefixed I, the even numbers generally going east–west and the odd numbers north–south. Federal Highways are the next grade down, and are all numbered with black numerals on white shields, while state roads are known as Routeways (black numbers on white circular or oblong signs). All the attractions of Walt Disney World, plus those of SeaWorld and Universal Studios Escape, can be found and are well signposted from I4. Cypress Gardens is a 45-minute drive from central Orlando (south) west on I4 and Highway 27, while Busch Gardens is 75 minutes down I4 to Tampa. The Kennedy Space Center is a good hour's drive along the Beeline Expressway which intersects I4 at junction 28 and can also be joined by driving east on Sand Lake Road, an alternative route into the north of International Drive from the airport.

**International Drive** is the second key local roadway, linking as it does a seven-mile ribbon of hotels, shops, restaurants and some of the smaller attractions like Wet 'n' Wild, the Mercado Shopping Centre, The Pointe, Skull Kingdom, Wonder-Works, King Henry's Feast and Belz Factory Outlet shopping malls. (Be wary of a new section of I-Drive from Highway 192 north to the Osceola Parkway toll road in Kissimmee – this is NOT the main stretch.) From I4, take junctions 27A, 28, 29 or 30B. To the north, International Drive runs into Oakridge Road and then the South Orange Blossom Trail, which leads into downtown Orlando (junctions 38–41 off I4). International Drive is also bisected by Sand Lake Road and runs away into Epcot Drive to the south, which is another handy way to the attractions of Walt Disney World. It is a major tourist centre in its own right and makes an excellent

**Some of Florida's native inhabitants at Gatorland**

base from which to operate, especially to the south of Sand Lake Road, near to the Mercado Shopping Center, where you can actually enjoy a walk around on real pavement (and it's perfectly safe, too). It's a 20-minute drive from Walt Disney World's attractions and 10–15 minutes from Universal Studios and SeaWorld. However, I-Drive can become congested at peak times, especially at the junction with Sand Lake Road, so it can be better

> BRIT TIP: The new Osceola Parkway toll road which runs parallel to Highway 192 is a much handier route in to Walt Disney World from downtown Kissimmee and costs only $1.

to use I4 for north–south journeys. Universal Boulevard (formerly Republic Drive) is the new I-Drive link to Universal Studios Escape and is also a less congested alternative to I-Drive itself.

The other main tourist area is the town of Kissimmee to the south of Orlando and the south-east of Walt Disney World. It's an attraction in its own right, being the home of Water Mania, the Old Town

shopping complex, Gatorland, Green Meadows Farm, the Haunted Mansion and the Medieval Times, Arabian Nights, Wild Bill's and Capone's dinner shows, plus more hotels and restaurants. It is all grouped in a rather untidy straggle along a 12-mile stretch of **Highway 192** (The Irlo Bronson Memorial Highway), which intersects I4 at junction 25B, and is not much more than 10 minutes from Walt Disney World, 15 from SeaWorld and 25 from Universal Studios. The downtown area of Kissimmee (off

> BRIT TIP: The Kissimmee/St Cloud tourist information office on east Highway 192 has the best free map of the area, clearly indicating all the main routes and attractions.

Main Street, Broadway and Emmett Street) is much prettier and accessible by foot.

A long overdue but handy tourist addition to Highway 192 are a series of markers along its western tourist stretch from Splendid China (Number 4) to just past Medieval Times (Number 15). These striking and highly visible numbered signs make for accurate locators of many of the hotels, restaurants and attractions and, in time, will stretch the length of this long tourist corridor as the county and local businesses attempt to smarten up their act in keeping with much of the rest of the area's eye-catching development.

## Fuel

Finally, a quick word about re-fuelling your hire car at a typical American gas station (never 'petrol', remember). You will often have a choice of attendant or self-serve. You do not tip the attendant but you do pay a slightly higher price to cover the service. Most gas stations will also require you to pay in advance at night, i.e. before filling the car, and will require the exact amount in cash or your credit card. Some pumps also allow you to pay by credit card directly, without having to go in to the cashier's office. The American gallon is slightly smaller (by about a fifth) than the British version. Always use unleaded fuel and, to make American petrol pumps work, you must first lift the lever underneath the pump nozzle. As an additional tip, look out for RaceTrac petrol stations as they are usually the cheapest locally (for petrol *and* other sundries like soft drinks and cigarettes), although they can be cash ONLY operations (i.e. no credit cards).

## Local maps

While a lot of the freely distributed tourist maps of the Orlando area tend to be pretty sketchy, there are a couple which are better than others. For the best maps of Walt Disney World, International Drive and the main theme parks, get MapEasy's Guide to Orlando ($5.50 at Benjamin Books in Orlando International Airport) while AA members can also get hold of the most detailed road maps of Central Florida courtesy of the American version of their organisation, the AAA. Check with the AA before leaving home or visit the AAA in Orlando on East Colonial Drive in the Colonial Promenade shopping plaza (tel 407 894 3333) with your AA membership card and get their maps for Southern Metropolitan Orlando and Kissimmee (at $3 each). The Universal Map is almost as comprehensive and is available from most petrol stations, priced $2.50.

If, like me, you find a mobile phone essential to your well-being, you might like to know that there is a handy local firm who provide an ideal service. Phones rent from just $2.50 a day (plus $0.99/minute air time) and they will deliver to your hotel. Call All Cellular for details on 407 843 7716. They even rent pagers and small two-way radios for families who like to do their own thing but stay in touch.

Now, fully armed with the essential knowledge to be auto-mobile in Orlando, let's tell you a little more about what to expect from your holiday accommodation . . .

# Accommodation
*(or, Making Sense of American Hotels, Motels and Condos)*

To list all the various hotels, motels, holiday homes, guesthouses, condominiums, campsites and other forms of accommodation available in the Orlando area would fill up this book, so it is not the intention here to attempt a comprehensive guide. The metropolitan Orlando area can boast the highest concentration of hotels anywhere in the United States and more are being built all the time, with the number of rooms forecast to exceed 100,000 by 2000. The vast majority of British tourists will also have their accommodation arranged through the numerous package deals on offer, so the following detail is intended only as a general guide to the bigger, better or budget types.

## Hotels

The first thing to be aware of is that American hotels, particularly in the largest tourist areas like this, tend towards the motel type, even among some of the bigger and more expensive 'hotels'. This doesn't mean you will be short-changed as far as facilities and service are concerned, but you won't necessarily be located in one main building. The chances are that your room will be in one of several blocks, arranged around the other facilities such as the swimming pool, restaurant, etc. This is a significant distinction because of the safety aspects – it is possible for non-hotel guests to gain access to parts of a motel-style hotel, so it is important to be security-conscious in little matters like ensuring the room is locked and checking the ID of anyone who knocks at the door (although it is not something to be worried about. See also Chapter 11, Safety First). The size of rooms rarely alters, even between two-star and four-star accommodation. In general, it is the extra amenities of the hotel which give it extra star rating and not the size of the rooms themselves. A standard room usually features two double beds and will comfortably accommodate a family of four.

BRIT TIP: Few hotels have got round to providing hairdryers as standard in their rooms, although they can often be ordered from the front desk. If you bring your own, you will need a US plug adaptor (with two flat pins). Their voltage is also different, 110–120 AC, as opposed to our 220, so your hairdryer/electric razor will work rather sluggishly.

The other feature of motel-type accommodation which frequently takes British visitors by surprise is the lack of a restaurant in many cases. This is because the American hotel scene operates purely on a room-only basis – meals are always extra, and hence dining facilities are not always provided. This means you will often have to get out of your hotel/motel and drive to the nearest restaurant (of which there are a multitude – see Chapter 9) just for breakfast. Check the brochure carefully to see what dining facilities the various hotels provide if this would be a concern for you.

As a general rule, hotels in Orlando are big, clean, efficient and great value for money, even down to the provision of non-smoking rooms in many properties. However, one area where they do lag behind their British counterparts is in the provision of tea- and coffee-making facilities. At present there are few hotels that provide these as a matter of course, but they are slowly coming round to the demand. You will probably find that, in the absence of this facility, your tour rep will be able to sell you a handy tea-making kit for a nominal charge. What American hotels do all provide in abundance, however, are soft-drink and ice machines, with ice buckets in all the rooms (although you may find that you are paying well over the odds for a can of Coke, or whatever, from the machine at the end of your corridor).

All types of accommodation will also be fully air-conditioned and,

> BRIT TIP: Buy your soft drinks at the nearest supermarket, who will also be able to sell you a neat polystyrene cooler for about $4 that you can fill with ice from your hotel ice machine to keep your drinks cold.

when it is really hot, you will have to learn to live with the steady drone of the A/C unit in your room at nights. NEVER turn the air-conditioning off when you go out, even when it is cool in the morning because, by the time you return, the chances are your room will have turned into an oven.

Note also that the most expensive place to make a telephone call from is your hotel room! Nearly every hotel adds on a whacking 45–70 per

© Disney

**Disney's Wilderness Lodge Resort**

cent surcharge on every call (you can also be charged for a call even if no-one answers if it rings five or more times). A better way to make your calls is to buy a local phonecard, which even the holiday companies now sell, and use a normal payphone. There will be a 1–800 number to their central computer and you then punch in the special number on your card to bring up the dialling tone (give it plenty of time to connect – it can take up to 40 seconds before the dialling tone comes through in some instances). To call Britain from the USA, dial 011 44, then drop the first 0 from your area code.

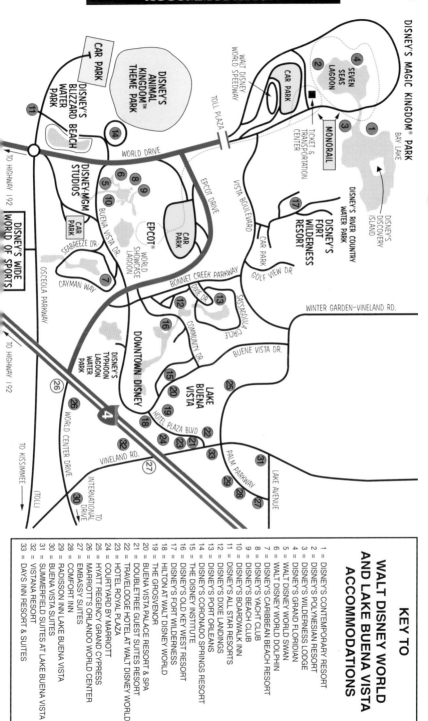

## KEY TO WALT DISNEY WORLD AND LAKE BUENA VISTA ACCOMMODATIONS

1 = DISNEY'S CONTEMPORARY RESORT
2 = DISNEY'S POLYNESIAN RESORT
3 = DISNEY'S WILDERNESS LODGE
4 = DISNEY'S GRAND FLORIDIAN
5 = WALT DISNEY WORLD SWAN
6 = WALT DISNEY WORLD DOLPHIN
7 = DISNEY'S CARIBBEAN BEACH RESORT
8 = DISNEY'S YACHT CLUB
9 = DISNEY'S BEACH CLUB
10 = DISNEY'S BOARDWALK INN
11 = DISNEY'S ALL STAR RESORTS
12 = DISNEY'S DIXIE LANDINGS
13 = DISNEY'S PORT ORLEANS
14 = DISNEY'S CORONADO SPRINGS RESORT
15 = THE DISNEY INSTITUTE
16 = DISNEY'S OLD KEY WEST RESORT
17 = DISNEY'S FORT WILDERNESS
18 = HILTON AT WALT DISNEY WORLD
19 = THE GROSVENOR
20 = BUENA VISTA PALACE RESORT & SPA
21 = DOUBLETREE GUEST SUITES RESORT
22 = TRAVELODGE HOTEL AT WALT DISNEY WORLD
23 = HOTEL ROYAL PLAZA
24 = COURTYARD BY MARRIOTT
25 = HYATT REGENCY GRAND CYPRESS
26 = MARRIOTT'S ORLANDO WORLD CENTER
27 = EMBASSY SUITES
28 = COMFORT INN
29 = RADISSON INN LAKE BUENA VISTA
30 = BUENA VISTA SUITES
31 = SUMMERFIELD SUITES AT LAKE BUENA VISTA
32 = VISTANA RESORT
33 = DAYS INN RESORT & SUITES

Remember also that hotel prices (both in this book and in Orlando) are always per room and NOT per person. Where they are listed here it is always at standard room rates (without local taxes) during PEAK season. This means they will be cheaper out of the main holiday periods, but prices are still likely to vary from month to month and with special deals offered from time to time. Always ask for rates before you book and check if any special rates apply during your visit (don't be afraid to ask for their 'best rate' at off-peak times which can be lower than any published rate). There can also be an additional charge ($5–$15 per person) for more than two adults sharing the same room. It pays to book in advance in high season because Orlando's additional popularity as a convention centre means it can get extremely busy.

About the best course of action, if you've just arrived and are looking for accommodation, is to head for one of the two official Visitor Centers in the area, one on International Drive just south of the Mercado Mediterranean Village (on the corner of Austrian Court and open every day from 8am–7pm) and the other at the eastern stretch of Highway 192 in Kissimmee (open from 8am–5pm), where they keep an updated list of all the hotels and their rates, with brochures on the latest special deals.

Alternatively, you can call the **Central Reservation Service** for a good choice of accommodations, often at discounted rates, on 407 740 6442 or toll-free in Orlando on 1-800 548 3311. They specialise in last-minute bookings in the price range and location you require, and there is no pre-charge or minimum stay requirement.

BRIT TIP: It is standard practice for American hotels to take a credit card imprint when you check in to cover any incidentals (phone calls, etc) during your stay. Make sure, therefore, you have plenty to spare on your credit card limit.

## Resort hotels for Walt Disney World® Resort

In keeping with the rest of this guide, a review of Orlando's hotels starts with Walt Disney World. With the convenience of being almost on the doorstep of the resort's main attractions, and linked by an excellent free transport system of monorail, shuttle buses and boats, Walt Disney World resort hotels, holiday homes and campsites are also all magnificently appointed and maintained. They range from the futuristic appeal of Disney's Contemporary Resort (the monorail travels right through the main building) to the wild west feel of Disney's Fort Wilderness Campground and Homes, and their landscaping, imagination and attention to detail are as good as the theme parks themselves. In all, there are more than 22,000 rooms throughout Walt Disney World's 40 square miles, while the 780-acre Disney's Fort Wilderness has 1,192 individual sites. However, all this grandiose accommodation comes at a price. A standard room at Disney's Grand Floridian Resort & Spa can cost up to $530 a night in high season, while a villa for six at the Disney Institute would set you back $390, and even the more budget-priced Disney's Caribbean Beach Resort can be more than $100 a night. Eating out in the hotels and resorts is not cheap, and you won't find many fast-food outlets as you do along International Drive and Highway 192.

However, there is now a budget choice for holiday-makers in Walt Disney World® Resort itself, and it is aimed specifically at the British market – the Disney's All Star Sports and Music Resorts (see below) and, new in 1999, the All Star Movie Resort. This means the convenience of being so close to some of Orlando's biggest attractions has been opened to a lot more holiday budgets, and it is worth a lot, especially in high season when the surrounding roads are packed.

Kids especially will love being a part of the Walt Disney World experience full-time, and there are first-class child-minding and babysitting services available at most Walt Disney World properties. Walt Disney World guests get to carry their own ID charge card with which you can charge meals, gifts, etc, to your room (and have them delivered there). There is exclusive early entrance to selected theme parks on various days up to an hour before the general public, while some Walt Disney World resorts feature meals with Disney characters. You also have the option of booking restaurants and dinner shows as soon as your reservation is confirmed, well ahead of other visitors. Additional perks to Walt Disney World-accommodated guests include free parking at the big theme parks (a saving of $5 a time) and guaranteed admission even if the public are being turned away in high season.

Around the Magic Kingdom® you will find four of Walt Disney World's grandest properties. The 15-storey **Disney's Contemporary Resort** boasts 1,050 rooms, a cavernous foyer and a recent $100 million renovation, as well as shops, restaurants, lounges, a real sandy beach, a marina, two swimming pools, six tennis courts, an electronic games centre and a health club – and magnificent views, especially from the highly-acclaimed hotel-top California Grill restaurant. The accent is on fun, fun, fun, and it is not the place for a quiet vacation! As with all Walt Disney World accommodation, rooms are large, scrupulously clean and extremely well furnished. Rates reach $325 in high season. **Disney's Polynesian Resort** is a real South Seas tropical fantasy brought to life with ultra-modern sophistication and comfort. Beautiful sandy beaches, lush vegetation and architecture cleverly disguise the fact that 853 rooms can be found here, built in film-set wooden longhouse style and all with balconies and wonderful views.

> BRIT TIP: Dine in wonderful South Seas style at the 'Ohana restaurant, but don't ask for the salt – unless you want to spark an amazing reaction!

Some excellent eating opportunities can also be discovered, along with canoe rentals, two popular kids' pools, a games room, shops and children's playground. Rates up to $445 in high season. **Disney's Wilderness Lodge** opened in 1994 and is one of the most picturesque places to stay. It is an imposing re-creation of a National Park lodge in amazing detail, down to the hot stream running through the massive wooden balcony-lined atrium lobby and out into the gardens, past the swimming pool (with hot and cold spas) and ending in Walt Disney World's own version of the Old Faithful geyser, erupting every hour! It offers authentic backwoods charm with five-star luxury but is connected to the Magic Kingdom® by boat and bus only. It also has two full-service

## KEY TO INTERNATIONAL DRIVE ACCOMMODATIONS

1 = PEABODY ORLANDO
2 = ORLANDO MARRIOTT
3 = RENAISSANCE ORLANDO RESORT
4 = UNIVERSAL TOWER & INN
5 = DELTA ORLANDO RESORT
6 = DAYS INN LAKESIDE
7 = INTERNATIONAL INN
8 = QUALITY INN INTERNATIONAL
9 = QUALITY INN PLAZA
10 = RAMADA INN PLAZA INTERNATIONAL
11 = GATEWAY INN

12 = LAS PALMAS HOTEL
13 = CLARION PLAZA HOTEL
14 = HOLIDAY INN EXPRESS
15 = ENCLAVE SUITES
16 = PARC CORNICHE
17 = RAMADA SUITES
18 = SUMMERFIELD SUITES HOTEL
19 = WESTGATE LAKES RESORT
20 = THE CASTLE
21 = OMNI ROSEN HOTEL
22 = HAWTHORN SUITES

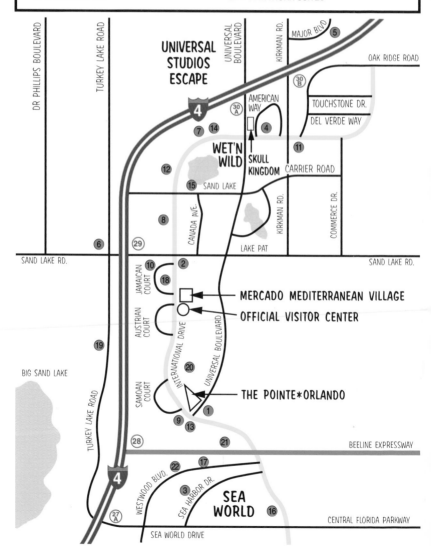

restaurants: the outstanding Artist's Point (for succulent wild game dishes and superb salmon, and a Pocahontas character breakfast) and the Whispering Canyon Cafe (for a lively breakfast and huge all-you-can-eat buffets), a snack bar and a pool bar. Rates around $330 in high season. **Disney's Grand Floridian** completes the quartet of Magic Kingdom® Park hotels, a hugely elaborate mock Victorian mansion with 900 rooms, an impressive domed and towered foyer and staff in Edwardian dress. The rooms are luxurious, hence the mega price range, and it is worth a look even if you are staying somewhere else. It also has six restaurants, including Walt Disney World's top-of-the-range establishment, Victoria and Albert's (where their set, six-course dinner with wine will set you back more than $100 per person), four bars and a comprehensive array of sporting and relaxation

**The lobby of Disney's Wilderness Lodge**

facilities. Rates begin at $294 and go as high as $1580 for a suite! Disney's Grand Floridian, Contemporary and Polynesian are all situated right on the monorail, the best and fastest system for getting into the Magic Kingdom® Park and Epcot®.

© Disney

**Disney's All Star Sports Resort room**

## Hotels at Epcot®

Across at Epcot® you have the choice of six hotels, including the 'entertainment architecture' of Walt Disney World Swan and Dolphin. These are either pastel-coloured concrete monstrosities or the best examples of how to make a hotel look fun, according to your point of view. **Walt Disney World Swan** is so named for the unmistakable 45-foot statue atop the hotel, which has 758 rooms, three restaurants, two lounge bars, eight tennis courts (shared with The Dolphin), swimming pool, shops, health club and a white sand beach. If you appreciate room lamps shaped like pineapples, this is the place for you, but again it isn't cheap: high season rates start at $275 and 80% of its business tends to be convention-orientated. Sister hotel **Walt Disney World Dolphin** features a 27-storey pyramid with two giant 'dolphin' statues on the top. A massive 1,510 rooms (the second most of any one-building hotel in Orlando) indicate that here is another seriously busy hotel (especially with conventions) although the service is first class. Seven restaurants, three bars, swimming pool and grotto fun-pool, fitness club, games room and some tasty shops (especially for chocolate lovers!) can be found here, with rates from $275. Both hotels are privately

4

run but still have to conform the Walt Disney World® Resort's exacting standards for appearance, style and service. Transport to the theme parks and other amenities is by boat and bus.

The 45-acre **Disney's BoardWalk Inn and Villas** resort is the most extravagant property in Walt Disney World, featuring a 378-room Inn, 532 villas, four themed restaurants, a TV sports club and two nightclubs, plus an impressive array of unique shops, sports facilities and a huge, free-form swimming pool with a 200-foot water-slide, all situated on a re-created semi-circular boardwalk around Crescent Lake. The overall effect is stunningly pretty, and the attention to detail in the rooms is quite breathtaking. Outstanding features are the summer-cottage style villas, Mediterranean restaurant Spoodles (for arguably the best buffet breakfasts in Orlando) and the Big River Grille & Brewing Works for a magnificent array of beers. Top of the range is the expensive but magnificent seafood restaurant, the Flying Fish café. Even if you are not staying here, it is a delightful resort to visit for a meal, the night-life or just a wander along the boardwalk. Once again it is not a cheap option – high-season rates kick in at $279.

**Disney's Caribbean Beach Resort** is one of the largest resort-type hotels anywhere in America, with 2,112 rooms and the accent on budget price and value for money. The rooms tend to be smaller and plainer (although they still comfortably house a family of four, and include mini-bars and coffee makers), but the facilities in the form of restaurants, bars and outdoor activities (including a lakeside recreation area with themed waterfalls and slides) are as good as anywhere else in the resort. Transportation from the five Caribbean 'villages' that make up the resort to the theme parks is by bus,

and rates start at $139 peak season. Going up-market again, the refined, almost intimate, **Disney's Yacht Club** has 635 rooms designed with nautical themes, all set around an ornamental lake. For a hearty breakfast, the Yacht Club Galley (one of three restaurants and two bars) also offers some of the most satisfying fare in Walt Disney World. Sister hotel **Disney's Beach Club** completes the Epcot® line-up. With 580 spacious rooms set along a man-made white sand beach, it's like a tropical island paradise. You can go boating or catch a water-shuttle service to Epcot®, while other theme park transportation is provided by tram and bus. Water fun is provided at the shared Stormalong Bay, a heated two-and-a-half-acre recreation area with water slides and a sandy-floored lagoon. Standard rooms at both start at $295 during high season.

## Walt Disney World budget accommodation

The recently opened **Disney's All Star Resorts** are Disney's first serious venture into capturing a big share of the budget accommodation market, particularly with us Brits, who typically tend to stay outside Walt Disney World. Here, for just $74–$89 a night year round, you can stay in one of the five sports-themed blocks (Surfing, Basketball, Tennis, Baseball and American Football) centred around a massive food court, two swimming pools, a games arcade and shops, or the music-themed version (Jazz, Rock, Broadway, Calypso and Country). Both centres, which have a total of 3,840 rooms, have pool bars, shops, laundry facilities and a pizza delivery service, and, while their bright, almost garish decor lacks the refined touches of other resorts and rooms tend to be a lot smaller than their higher-priced counterparts, they are well-designed for budget-conscious families who still want to enjoy all the Walt Disney World conveniences. Transportation to other areas of Walt Disney World® Resort is provided free by bus. Being added in 1999 are the 1,920 rooms of the All Star Movie Resort to boost this Brit-popular option.

## Downtown Disney Resorts

The other main accommodation centre within Walt Disney World is the area surrounding the Downtown development, which is just off to the right as you drive in along Epcot Drive. Here you will find: **Disney's Dixie Landings Resort**, a 2,048-room resort which has a steamboat as a reception area, a wonderful cotton mill-style food court in addition to a Cajun-themed full-service restaurant and an old-fashioned general store (i.e., gift shop). Rooms are either *Gone With The Wind*-style mansionesque (surrounded by grand staircases and columns) or rural Bayou backwoods (decorated with wooden and brass fittings). It also has Ol'Man Island, a three-and-a-half-acre playground, incorporating swimming pool, kids' area and a fishing hole! Transportation is by boat and bus, and rates up to $154. **Disney's Port Orleans Resort** by comparison adopts the atmosphere of the French quarter of New Orleans for its 1,008 rooms. Turn-of-the-century-style fittings and a Mardi Gras feel make this one of the most pleasantly imaginative hotels, with full-service dining at Bonfamilles café plus the Sassagoula Floatworks and Food Factory court, two bars, a games room, shopping arcade and a fun pool, Doubloon Lagoon. Again, rates hit $154 at high season and transportation is by bus to all the other entertainment facilities. **Disney's Old Key West Resort** is partly a holiday ownership scheme

set-up of five-star proportions, but the one-, two- or three-bedroomed studios in a magnificent Key West setting can also be rented out on a nightly basis (up to $885) when not in use by club members. Additional

> BRIT TIP: There's also the new **Disney Institute** resort area – so much more than just accommodation. Full details are on pages 152–3.

facilities include swimming pools, tennis courts, games room, shops and fitness centre. **Disney's Fort Wilderness** offers an impressive array of camping facilities and chalet-style homes that can house up to six people. Two 'trading posts' supply fresh groceries, while there are two bars and cafés and a range of on-site activities, including the thrice-nightly Hoop-Dee-Doo Musical Revue, campfire programme, films, sports, games and a prime position from which to view the nightly Electrical Water Pageant. Buses and boats link the campsites with other Walt Disney World areas, with sites from $64 and homes up to $214.

The newest hotel is the eye-catching **Disney's Coronado Springs Resort**, which can be found on Buena Vista Drive en route to Disney's Blizzard Beach Water Park and the Animal Kingdom™ Theme Park. Themed on the American south-west with Spanish overtones, this 1,967-room complex is spread over more than 130 acres and offers hacienda-style accommodation blocks set around a 15-acre lake and beach. There are four elaborately-landscaped pools, including one with a large slide, three restaurants, including the full service Maya Grill which features an open wood-fire

## KEY TO HIGHWAY 192 ACCOMMODATIONS

1 = RAMADA RESORT MAINGATE
2 = COMFORT INN MAINGATE
3 = RADISSON INN MAINGATE
4 = HOLIDAY INN SUNSPREE RESORT
5 = HOLIDAY INN HOTEL & SUITES
6 = HOLIDAY INN MAINGATE WEST
7 = KINGS HOTEL
8 = CASA ROSA INN
9 = PARK INN INTERNATIONAL
10 = BROADWAY INN
11 = KNIGHTS INN MAINGATE
12 = SHERATON INN LAKESIDE
13 = HAMPTON INN MAINGATE
14 = HILTON GATEWAY
15 = HYATT ORLANDO
16 = DAYS SUITES
17 = LIFETIME OF VACATIONS RESORT
18 = VILLAGES AT MANGO KEY
19 = QUALITY SUITES
20 = HOMEWOOD SUITES
21 = BRYAN'S SPANISH COVE
22 = ISLE OF BALI
23 = ORBIT ONE
24 = PARKWAY INTERNATIONAL
25 = ORANGE LAKE RESORT
26 = FLORIDA GULF APARTMENTS
27 = ALEXANDER HOLIDAY HOMES (OFFICE)
28 = TROPICAL PALMS
29 = PHENIX PROPERTIES
30 = ADVANTAGE VACATION HOMES
31 = BRIGADOON HOLIDAY HOMES
32 = HOLIDAY VILLAS
33 = PREMIER VACATION HOMES
34 = WESTGATE VACATION VILLAS
35 = UNICORN INN
36 = CARIBE ROYALE RESORT & SUITES
37 = COMFORT SUITES HOTEL

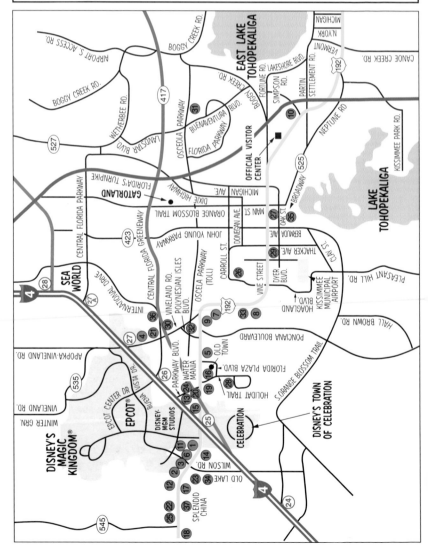

grill, a bar/lounge, health club and 95,000 square foot convention centre – so it's not a quiet resort. Transportation by bus, and rates at $149. To make a reservation at any of Walt Disney World's properties, simply call 407 (from outside Orlando) 934 7639.

## Disney Hotel Plaza

In addition to the official Walt Disney World hotels, there are another seven 'guest' hotels inside Walt Disney World® Resort itself at the Disney Hotel Plaza on the doorstep of Downtown Disney. These benefit from Disney's efficient free bus service to the attractions and guaranteed admission to the theme parks, and you can make reservations for shows and restaurants before the general public, but they are almost without exception more expensive than similar hotels outside Walt Disney World. Top of the list (for service, mod cons and price) is the 814-room **Hilton at Walt Disney World Village** (tel 407 827 4000, high-season rates up to $365). Also fairly expensive are the **Grosvenor** (626 sumptuously-appointed rooms, exceptional service, colonial decor, rates at $220, tel 407 828 4444), **Buena Vista Palace** (a bustling, 27-storey cluster of mirrored towers housing 1,014 rooms, many with a grandstand view of Epcot's Spaceship Earth, plus a European-style spa, three heated pools, tennis courts and a marina with boat rentals, tel 407 827 2727, rates at $224) and the **Doubletree Guest Suites Resort** (229 family-sized suites offering every conceivable in-room convenience and great kids' facilities, tel 407 934 1000, rates at $269). More modest (from $139 at peak periods) are the **TraveLodge Hotel** (325 rooms, good views over the Marketplace, in-room coffee makers, two restaurants, cocktail lounge and nightclub, tel 407 828 2424), and the **Courtyard by Marriott** (323 rooms in a 14-storey tower and six-storey annex featuring glass-walled lifts, three pools and rates up to $179, tel 407 828 8888). The current *Brit's Guide* favourite for this area, though, is the recently refurbished (at a cost of almost $20m) **Hotel Royal Plaza**, with a lovely, welcoming aspect, 394 wonderfully spacious and well-equipped rooms and 22 suites, a neat, full-service diner-restaurant and relaxing lounge bar, a landscaped pool area, four tennis courts, a health club and a Disney gift shop. Like all the hotels in the Boulevard, it is well positioned for a stroll to Downtown Disney's attractions and features free bus transport and guaranteed access to the parks, plus preferred tee times at all five Disney golf courses (high-season rates at $215, tel 407 828 2828).

**Kidsuite at the Holiday Inn Sunspree**

## Other Orlando accommodation

As you move further away from Walt Disney World the prices tend to moderate somewhat. This is a round-up of what's on offer.

# Lake Buena Vista

You can still spend a small fortune at the **Hyatt Regency Grand Cypress** in Lake Buena Vista, for example, which is considered to be Orlando's top hotel. This 1,500-acre resort offers three nine-hole and one 18-hole golf course (all designed by Jack Nicklaus), a swimming pool with waterfalls and slide, 21-acre boating lake, tennis complex, health club and equestrian centre. Rates START at $200, but the 750 rooms and suites are magnificently appointed (it also has five restaurants, three lounges and a poolside bar, tel 407 239 1234). Nearby is **Marriott's Orlando World Centre**, another *Brit's Guide* favourite and an impressive landmark as you approach Walt Disney World® Resort, set as it is in 200 landscaped acres and surrounded by another golf course. An elaborate lobby, Chinese antiques and the sheer size of the hotel (1,503 rooms, 85 suites, seven restaurants, four pools and a health club) put it in the expensive range (rates from $229 per room, tel 407 239 4200), but it is very conveniently situated and it possesses one of the most stunningly picturesque pool areas, complete with waterfalls and palm trees, in Orlando, plus the whizziest glass-fronted lifts anywhere! It does, however, get very busy, especially with convention business. Extra facilities include a separate wading pool for kids, an indoor pool, a sports pool, four whirlpool spas, a golf school, tennis centre, five shops and a well-organised kids' programme. Similarly, but on more budget lines, the **Holiday Inn Sunspree Resort at Lake Buena Vista** (507 rooms from $105, tel 407 239 4500) and **Holiday Inn Hotel and Suites** (670 rooms from $95, tel 407 396 4488) are both excellent for kids, with a highly-rated supervised childcare programme, a good range of pools, restaurants and other facilities. All rooms feature mini-kitchenettes. Both properties also feature the trademark 'Kidsuites' which offer an attractive novelty for families – a private playhouse/bedroom built into the hotel room, equipped with its own TV, cassette player, video game player, clock, fun phone, table and chairs. They are all done in different themes and offer a refreshing alternative to normal hotel family accommodation – right down to the separate check-in facilities for the youngsters. The Sunspree Resort is slightly handier for Walt Disney World, but the Hotel and Suites at Maingate East is almost next door to Old Town offering more facilities, and both feature free Disney transport. Sunspree has recently added a 2,100 square-foot Cyber Arcade, with access to the World Wide Web and other high-tech elements, while both also have the extra option of 50 two-room suites for more family comfort. Outside of Disney, these have to be the best family-equipped hotels anywhere in Orlando. Kids 12 and under eat free, as they do at the smart **Holiday Inn Maingate West** with its tropical courtyard, free-form heated pool and kiddie pool (287 rooms at $99, tel 407 396 1100). **The Sheraton Lakeside Village**, also on west Highway 192, is surprisingly good value for a big-name group, especially with three pools, tennis courts, kids' play-grounds, mini-golf, paddleboats and two restaurants. Kids 10 and under eat breakfast and dinner free with a paying adult and there is free transportation to Walt Disney World (651 rooms at $130, tel 407 396 2222). Likewise, the smaller **Hampton Inn Maingate**, again only one-and-a-half miles from Walt Disney World at the junctions of I4 and Highway 192, offers great value at just $99 in high-season, with a heated outdoor pool, free local phone calls, continental breakfast and shuttle service (164 rooms, tel 407 396 8484), as does the **Hilton Inn Gateway**, just west of I4, with a kids-eat-free programme, free morning coffee, two pools, a restaurant, deli and fitness centre (501 rooms from just $65, tel 407 396 4400). The **Hyatt Orlando** also looks as if it should be more expensive with its 922 rooms, three restaurants, four pools and kiddie pools, spas, playgrounds and other recreational facilities. Situated right on the junctions of I4 and Highway

> BRIT TIP: When booking one of the chain hotels, make sure you have its full address – it is easy to end up at the wrong Holiday Inn or Howard Johnson!

192 it could not be more convenient, yet its year-round rates start at just $89 (tel 407 396 1234).

A novel choice is the wonderfully African-themed **Wyndham Safari Resort**, which boasts the Python water slide, heated pool and kids pool, with free transport to Disney's theme parks and 'kids eat free' with parents at Casablanca's restaurant. Rooms are extremely well-equipped, with hairdryers, coffee makers and ironing boards, all this within walking distance of the Crossroads shopping centre and close to Downtown Disney Marketplace (489 rooms and 96 suites at $130, tel 407 239 0444).

## Kissimmee

Moving out along Highway 192 (the Irlo Bronson Memorial Highway) into Kissimmee, you will find the biggest choice of budget accommodation in the area. Facilities generally vary very little and what you see is what you get. All the big hotel chains can be found along this great tourist sprawl, and rates can be as low as $25 per room off-peak, or $35 for room with a kitchenette (what the Americans call an 'efficiency'). Be prepared to shop around for a good rate (discounts may be available at off-peak times), especially if you cruise along Highway 192 where so many hotels advertise their rates on large neon signs. As a general rule, prices drop the further you go from Walt Disney World. Don't be afraid to ask to see inside rooms before you settle on your holiday base. Take into consideration how much time you'll have to use extra facilities.

## Chains

Among the leading chains are **Best Western** (all with pools, family orientated but large, in the budget $40–$80 range), **Days Inn** (rather characterless and some without restaurants, but always good value – $50–$85 in most cases – and convenient, with some rooms available with kitchenettes), **EconoLodge** (see under Best Western, but slightly more expensive), **Howard Johnson** (also a bit dearer, but with more spacious rooms and a free continental breakfast), **Quality Inn** (sound, popular chain, and from as little as $39), **Ramada** (rates can vary more widely between hotels in the $60–$100 range, some offer free continental breakfast) and **TraveLodge** (another identikit group, but also on the budget side). The **Fairfield Inns** are the budget version of the impressive Marriott chain, while the **Budgetel** group also rate highly for hotel security as well as lower prices. **The Holiday Inn** chain varies so widely in both price and service, I have picked out only individuals worthy of note.

**Doubletree** hotels and suites are another up-market chain with excellent facilities, as are the **Radisson** group (both in the $100–$150 range).

## Independent organisations

In addition, there are literally dozens of smaller, independent outfits who offer special rates from time to time in order to compete with the big boys. Look out in particular for offers of 'Kids Eat Free' as this can save you quite a bit. Of the non-chain operators, the **Casa Rosa Inn** offers simple, relatively peaceful Mediterranean-style hospitality (on west Highway 192, tel 407 396 1060, rates at $89. The **Park Inn International** (same location, tel 407 396 1376) also has one of the better lake-front locations to go with its budget rates (up to $69), and some of its rooms have kitchenettes. For pure budget price **The Broadway Inn** east on Highway 192 to Simpson Road is hard to beat (200 rooms from $39, tel 407 846 1530), as is the **Knights Inn Maingate**, just a mile west of Disney's main entrance on Highway 192 (96 rooms and 24 efficiences at $59, tel 407 396 4200).

## International Drive

Further away from Walt Disney World, but handily situated for Universal Studios Escape, SeaWorld and closer to downtown Orlando is the final main tourist area of International Drive. For overall location and value for money I-Drive is hard to beat. It is more thoughtfully laid out, some attractions are within walking distance, and the hotels and motels tend to be slightly more attractive. Top of the range for quality is the **Peabody Orlando**, a luxurious, 891-room tower block with every possible facility you could wish for, including an Olympic-size pool,

> BRIT TIP: For an attraction with a difference, don't miss the Peabody Hotel's twice-daily Duck March, which sees their trademark ducks take up residence from 11am–4pm in the huge lobby fountain! It's a fascinating sight and a great place for afternoon tea. Just sit and watch them roll out the red carpet for the resident mallards!

health club, four tennis courts with professional coaching available and some of the best restaurants in Orlando, notably the exclusive gourmet cuisine of Dux and the amazing B-Line Diner (see Eating Out, Chapter 9). Service is superb and the whole atmosphere is a cut above normal tourist fare. Check out the Royal Duck Palace on the tennis deck if you don't believe me. However, rates are also suitably impressive (in excess of $200 per room per night) and, if there are any large conventions in town, don't

**The Peabody Orlando**

expect a quiet stay (tel 407 352 4000). The **Orlando Marriott** (1,054 rooms from $119, tel 407 351 2420) is similarly extravagant, with three swimming pools in its beautifully landscaped grounds (kids aged 11 and under eat free with their parents), as is the magnificently appointed **Renaissance Orlando Resort** (on Sea Harbour Drive, 780 rooms from a mere $215, tel 407 351 5555), claiming the world's largest atrium lobby and with some enormous rooms and suites, an Olympic-size swimming pool, tennis courts, fitness centre including sauna and steam room, five restaurants and special kids' activities. Back on more budget lines, the **Universal Tower and Inn** (302 rooms from $79, tel 407 351 2100) is a sound family-orientated establishment, superbly located for Universal Studios and Wet 'n' Wild, while worthy of particular British note is the **Delta Orlando Resort** (800 rooms from $99, tel 407 351 3340), which also benefits from being slightly off the main drag (on Major Boulevard). The 25-acre Delta is a highly popular hotel with several tour operators, notably Thomson, and goes out of its way to provide home-from-home touches, like coffee makers and bottled water in the rooms, English beer in the lively Studio 70 disco-bar and real bacon and baked beans with the food court's breakfast buffets. Facilities are above average for this price range, including three pools, a hot tub grotto, saunas, mini-golf, floodlit tennis, free year-round kids' club and playground, a babysitting service and a refreshing full-service restaurant, Mango's, where kids 12 and under eat free with their parents. There is also a free shuttle to Universal Studios Escape, SeaWorld and Wet 'n' Wild, and it all adds up to a *Brit's Guide* highly-commended resort. The **Days Inn Lakeside** on Sand Lake Road is also worth seeking out (609 rooms, tel 407 351 1900) for its excellent all-round facilities and lakeside location (the Days Inn chain offer free meals for kids under 12 when accompanied by their parents in their hotels that have restaurants), as well as the **Quality Inn International** (728 rooms, in the heart of I-Drive, kids under 12 eat free, tel 407 351 1600), and **Quality Inn Plaza** (a massive 1,020 rooms in multiple blocks with multiple pools and another kids-eat-free restaurant, high-season prices from $59 but as low as $29, tel 407 345 8585). If personal safety is

> **BRIT TIP:** The Quality Inn International and Plaza are consistently British favourites for their location and sheer good value.

paramount to you, the recently extensively refurbished **Clarion Plaza Hotel** has a state-of-the-art security system, as well as a pool with jacuzzi and waterfall, three restaurants, a 24-hour deli and a nightclub (810 rooms from $125, tel 407 352 9700).

New on I-Drive is the fanciful **Castle Doubletree**, just behind Austin's and Café Tu Tu Tango restaurants. It is a nine-storey fantasy palace based on the Magic Kingdom® Park's castle and features tower and turret rooms, a grand outdoor heated pool with a 12-foot fountain, hot tub, pool bar and grill, and a children's play area. Its overall impression is a bit garish, but the rooms are all immaculately furnished and, at around $99–$125, a lot cheaper than many comparable hotels (216 rooms, tel 407 345 1511).

The other eye-catching property on I-Drive is the monolithic **Omni Rosen Hotel**, the third largest hotel in Orlando, right next to the Beeline Expressway and therefore ideally located for getting around the whole area. While it caters primarily for the convention trade (it is right next door to the massive Convention Center), it also offers excellent tourist facilities with its 1,334 rooms and 80 suites featuring state-of-the-art security, a huge swimming grotto, an exercise centre, tennis courts, three excellent restaurants and two bars. Rates from $165, call 407 354 9840 for more details.

## Off the beaten track

Getting slightly off the beaten track might bring you to the up-market suburb of Winter Park to the north of the city, where the **Park Plaza Hotel** offers a smaller, more European style of hotel from just $80. It has an award-winning restaurant and is right in the middle of the exclusive Park Avenue shopping district (27 rooms, tel 407 647 1072). Another little Winter Park gem is the friendly, family-run **Langford Resort Hotel**, just two blocks off Park Avenue on New England Avenue. It boasts a slightly old-fashioned charm from its 50s and 60s hey-day as an ultra-exclusive haven for the rich and famous, but now affords great value in a peaceful location, especially with its tropically set Olympic-sized pool, health spa (offering saunas, steam baths and facials) and inviting bar area. The amenities of Park Avenue are wonderfully convenient and the Langford also features some excellent live entertainment on Tuesdays to Saturdays (220 rooms at $95 in high season, tel 407 644 3400).

## Suites & holiday homes

Finally, to round off this helter-skelter trip through places to stay, here is a quick look at a fast-growing area of accommodation in Orlando – that of suites hotels and holiday homes. These are extremely popular with Americans and beginning to catch on with us Brits as a neat way of larger family groups or friends staying together and cutting the cost of their stay both by doing much of their own cooking and the extra value of sharing. Typically, the homes, whether they come in the form of individual houses, collections of houses, resorts or condominiums (holiday apartment blocks), all usually have access to excellent facilities in the form of swimming pools and recreation areas, and are fully equipped with all mod cons like microwaves, TVs and washer-dryers. For these, you MUST be prepared to use a hire car to get around, but the savings for, say, a group of eight staying together are obvious. A three-bedroomed house sleeping eight can cost as little as $150 a night, or just $19 per person. Provided you are happy with the idea of doing your own cooking and washing-up, holiday homes definitely represent good value for money. Once again, the following can be only a representative selection of the properties on offer.

Basically, the choice is between what the Americans call suites – apartments built in hotel-like blocks around communal facilities but lacking some hotel features like bars, room service and lounges – or out-and-out holiday homes, some in private residential areas and others in estate-type developments, most of which have their own pools and tend to work out slightly cheaper. Prices where listed are per WEEK and will specify how many can share that apartment or house, but rates can vary according to special deals and price increases.

## Budget suites

Suites hotels are a rapidly-expanding Orlando accommodation type, with the four versions of the **Embassy**

**Suites** the prime example (with rates from $763–$1,323 a week, they are ideal for large families, tel 407 352 1400 or 239 1144). Typically, a suites hotel gives you the extra benefit of your own mini-kitchen, including microwave and all cutlery and crockery, while many now provide a complimentary continental breakfast. Starting off with the suites in budget territory, the **Enclave Suites** on Carrier Drive, off Kirkman Road, offer de luxe studios that sleep four from $483/week and two-bed, two-bath studios sleeping six from $845 (tel 407 351 1155). They feature two outdoor and one indoor pool, a fitness room, jacuzzi, games room and restaurant. Kids eat free with their parents and there is complimentary continental breakfast and free local phone calls. **Days Suites**, next door to Old Town on Highway 192, has 604 one- and two-bedroomed suites, the largest of which can sleep 6–10 people (tel 407 396 7900). Rates start at $343/week and kids under 12 eat free at their restaurant. Three pools, a cafeteria and barbecue area and kids' playground make for a full range of amenities. Next to Splendid China at the west end of Highway 192 is the **Grand Lake Resort**, a motel/condominium complex with 50 units that sleep four and 50 that sleep six (tel 407 396 3000). High-season rates start at $630, and their features include a heated pool, tennis, boating and fishing facilities, shuffleboard, kids' playground, free breakfast on Mondays and a free barbecue every Wednesday. In a similar location, the new **Comfort Suites Maingate Resort** offer some of the smartest facilities at an excellent price. Their 150 spacious one-room suites sleep up to six and offer free continental breakfast daily and free transport to the theme parks (tel 407 390 9888, rates from $700/week).

For an equally well-equipped new resort the **Buena Vista Suites**, on International Drive not far from Exit 27 of I4, also offer a taste of luxury. On top of a dazzling range of facilities, including a heated outdoor pool, jacuzzi and fitness centre, they offer a full, free breakfast and free transport to Walt Disney World® Resort parks. Their two-room rates (that sleep 4–6) start at $833 in high season (tel 407 239 8588). The **Villages at Mango Key** are smart new town houses masquerading as a suites resort on Lindfields Boulevard, just off Highway 192 past Splendid China heading west (tel 407 397 2211). Their beautifully designed two-bedroomed houses sleep six from $770 a week, while the three-beds sleep eight from $945, and there is a 10 per cent discount for second and third weeks. There is also a large, heated pool, jacuzzi, tennis courts and volleyball court. The **Parc Corniche** condominium suite hotel is a similarly luxurious property on Parc Corniche Drive off International Drive, just south of SeaWorld (tel 407 239 7100). Surrounded by an 18-hole championship-quality golf course, it also has a heated pool, whirlpool and kiddie pool, playground, games room and full-service restaurant and lounge, with a free continental breakfast and local phone calls. Rates for a one-bedroomed suite start at $1,050 in high season and $1,225 for a two-bed suite. In a similar range are the **Quality Suites** at Maingate East, one mile east of I4 on Highway 192 (tel 407 396 8040). Their two-bedroomed suites can sleep up to 10 from $1,050/week and their magnificent courtyard area that houses two pools, a poolside bar, whirlpool spa and patio is the equal of any top-quality hotel. Kids under 10 eat free with their parents, and there is a free continental breakfast. The **Ramada Suites** by SeaWorld, near International Drive, has 160 two-bed, two-bath suites that sleep up to six from $763–$903/ week. There is a special Kids' Club that is free to guests, plus free breakfast to add to their splendid facilities that consist of three jacuzzis, two pools, an exercise gym, video games room and paddleboats (tel 407 239 0707).

## Deluxe

Moving into the deluxe range you find the handy **Homewood Suites** on Parkway Boulevard next to Highway 192, just one-and-a-half miles from the main entrance of Walt Disney World® Resort. Their 156 suites sleep up to six from $973/week, but rates go as low as $553 out of season. Two pools and a jacuzzi, free breakfast and evening

**The Clarion Plaza Hotel**

social functions are their main features, while each room has two colour TVs and a video player (tel 407 396 2229). **Hawthorn Suites** score highly for their location (on Westwood Boulevard, just behind SeaWorld), excellently furnished rooms and value for money that includes free breakfast daily, a free shuttle service to Walt Disney World attractions, two TVs in every room, a free health club and little details like the provision of an iron

and ironing board. Rates vary from $1,103 for a 1-bed suite sleeping four to $1,295 for a 2-bed sleeping six, and they have already proved popular with British guests (tel 407 351 6600). Galaxy Group Management have no less than four luxurious resort properties all within a few miles of Walt Disney World's attractions and boasting first-rate facilities. The **Isle of Bali** offers spacious two-bed, two-bath villas in a South Seas style, with the resort also offering swimming pool, spa bath, tennis courts and fishing and boating on their own lagoon. High-season rates $1,015/week. **Bryan's Spanish Cove** features 116 lakefront villas sleeping six in a Treasure Island setting. Water activities abound, along with a scenic swimming pool, kids' playground and games room. High season at $1,050/week. **Orbit One** has another 116 villas, again two-bed, two-bath (the master bathroom having a huge Roman tub!) in a picturesque landscaped garden setting less than two miles from Walt Disney World. Two large pools, one for kids, water slides, tennis, shuffleboard, putting green and a free continental breakfast all add up to great amenities, with high season rates at $1,050. Top of the range are the 144 **Parkway International** villas in a mock-jungle setting and with safari decor (but five-star facilities). The villas are all stunningly furnished, and extra amenities include a nature trail, café, huge swimming pool, kids' pool and playground and free continental breakfast. For all Galaxy Group villas, call 407 239 5000.

The all-new **Caribe Royale Resort Suites** is one of the largest suites hotels in the world, with 1,218 spacious two-room suites set in three tower blocks around a tropically-landscaped pool area and with a truly immense reception lobby. The whole site exceeds 30 acres and some incredibly detailed thought has gone into features like security, ensuite amenities and extra provisions like a massive (free!) buffet breakfast and a poolside bar and grill. There are supervised kids' activity programmes plus free transport to Walt Disney World® Resort, for which it is conveniently located at the southern end of International Drive, right on the Central Florida Greeneway to and from the International Airport. There is also a free shuttle bus service to the new Lake Buena Vista Factory Stores just a mile away (tel 407 238 8000, rates from $1,390).

## Exclusive

Continuing the exclusive theme is the **Summerfield Suites Hotel** on International Drive (tel 407 352 2400) and at Lake Buena Vista (tel 407 238 0777). At $1,883/week high season it's not easy on your wallet, but the 146 one- and two-bedded rooms are magnificently furnished with every conceivable mod con. Stand-out features include the 24-hour video rental and shop facilities, the courtyard pool and bar areas, the excellent free daily breakfast and the sheer spaciousness of the two-bed suites, which sleep up to eight. Three TVs mean there is no fighting for the remote control, and the kitchen is superbly equipped – plus there is a delivery service from several local restaurants. **Orange Lake Resort**, four-and-a-half miles west of Walt Disney World's main Highway 192 entrance, is another golfers' paradise, with 27 challenging holes and a driving range, on top of the Olympic-size pool, jacuzzis, saunas, 80-acre sandy beach lake, watersports, children's playground, two restaurants, cinema and video games room. Rates are in keeping: up to $1,575/week for a two-bed, two-bath villa (tel 407 239 0000). The jewel in the crown, however, has to be the **Vistana**

**Resort**, again in the Lake Buena Vista area (tel 407 239 3100). You almost never need set foot outside its wonderful family-orientated confines as the Vistana possesses five pools, seven jacuzzis, 13 tennis courts, basketball, shuffleboard, fitness centres with steam and sauna rooms, an 18-hole mini-golf course, five kids' pools and playgrounds, video games rooms, general store and deli, two restaurants and bars and even a video library, as well as its own 24-hour security. Their amazingly spacious villas, in six differently themed areas, sleep up to eight, but wait for the price: up to $1,925/week!

## Holiday homes

Turning to holiday homes, **Welcome Homes USA** are one of the foremost operators for condos, villas and private homes in the Kissimmee area, with some of the smartest properties (especially their fully-fitted designer-decorated kitchens) at a broad range of prices from $490–$1,400/week. Their full-

**Delta Orlando Resort**

size houses come with communal or private pools and the whole operation features British office staff. Homes are all no more than 10 or 15 minutes drive from Walt Disney World® Resort, in proper residential areas, and feature everything from dishwashers to teaspoons (but not hairdryers). For details, call 407 933 2233. For great value and excellent properties, **Alexander Holiday Homes** (tel 407 932 3683), also in Kissimmee, have 170 detached two-, three- and four-bedded homes all with pools and immaculately furnished, within 15 minutes of Walt Disney World with rates from $455 to $1,365 (although the majority are now snapped up by tour operators like Unijet). From fully-fitted kitchens to walk-in wardrobes and private pools, these are a great way to enjoy a bit of Florida freedom on your holiday.

## More luxurious

For an even more luxurious touch, in four locations around Orlando and Kissimmee, **Orlando Resorts** offer one-, two-, three- and four-bed villas and homes in convenient, spacious privacy. Not all have private pools, but there are central facilities that include pools, jacuzzis, tennis, fishing, boating and fitness centres as well as 24-hour security. Rates from $965/week in high season (tel 407 260 8989). **Brigadoon Holiday Homes** in Cypress Lakes, Kissimmee, have some extremely spacious three- and four-bed homes from $504/week (tel 407 847 6466). All homes have screened, solar-heated pools, cable TV and free local phone calls, and babysitting services are also available, with discounts for senior citizens and stays of more than two weeks. **Best Orlando Vacation Services** offer a smart condo complex opposite the Florida Mall that comes at budget

prices. It has two pools and is within walking distance of the Mall facilities, while being only a five-minute drive from I-Drive. Rates vary so call 407 933 2889. One of the largest operators, **Advantage Vacation Homes**, have 271 two-, three- and four-bedroomed homes, most with private pools, in west Kissimmee, sleeping up to 10 people (tel 407 396 2262 or 0800 895 613 in the UK). Weekly rates are from $791–$1,750 and they offer golfing packages and senior citizen discounts.

New operator **All Star Vacation Services** have a range of specially selected and luxuriously appointed homes in the Kissimmee area, all conveniently situated for local attractions and with private pools. They can also fix up car hire, attraction tickets and even cruises, but rates weren't fixed as we went to press, so call 407 933 2004 for details. **Master Management** are proving popular for their 35 executive homes at the western end of Highway 192, just south of Lindfields Boulevard, which provide a welcome touch of peace and quiet while being barely 15 minutes from Walt Disney World (up to $1,575, tel 407 932 0515).

## CFI Resorts

Finally, **CFI Resorts**, who operate the five-star Hotel Royal Plaza in Walt Disney World Village, also run four similarly top-quality villa resorts around Orlando. **Westgate Lakes Resort** is located just off I4 on Turkey Lake Road and is set among 97 acres of tropical splendour with lake frontage and watersports. Here, 340 spacious one- and two-storey villas sleep up to eight, and the first-class central facilities include a huge free-form swimming pool, jacuzzis, private beach, tennis courts, a guest laundry room, health club and children's playground and Kids' Club programme, as well as three restaurants and bars and nearby golf. It doesn't come cheap, however: high-season rates hit $945 for a one-bed villa and $1,890 for a two-bed (tel 407 351 2460).

**Westgate Vacation Villas**, all 1,000 of them, in Kissimmee, are set among 187 acres around three lakes and offer free breakfast and cheese and wine parties with live entertainment. Villas are one-, two- or three-bedded and some have jacuzzis, while there are also tennis courts, eight pools, six kids' pools, a sauna, playground, fishing, paddleboats and a video games room, as well as snack bar, minimarket and gift shop. Rates peak at $2,800 a week, but the villas are the most luxurious you will find (tel 407 396 8523). Additionally, UK-based **Something Special Holidays** are the biggest operator in Florida for *named* accommodation, and they can offer an all-inclusive service or accommodation only. They have 87 hand-picked villa properties in Kissimmee in 1999 and their direct-sell staff all have first-hand knowledge of the area and the ability to tailor your booking to two or more centres. For a copy of their glossy brochure or to book, call 01992 557700.

## Bed & breakfast

Once again, you can see there is no shortage of choice, and you will even find a few places offering bed and breakfast. However, these are a long way removed from a traditional British B&B with one notable and laudable exception. **The Unicorn Inn**, on the corner of Orlando Avenue and Emmett Street in downtown Kissimmee, opened in '95 and is run by a Yorkshire couple who have lavished a small fortune on turning a ramshackle building into a luxurious but homely bed and breakfast inn that really caters for

the individual. Rates start at just $65 per night, and there are discounts for stays of one week or longer on their eight individually-styled rooms. They keep a few pushchairs and high-chairs for parents with young children and can arrange babysitting for you. They even provide their own personalised maps of the area with up-to-the-minute advice on local events and bargains. Their location is ideal for walking around the prettier parts of town and you can be sure of a decent cup of tea for a change! Call Don or Fran for more information on this little gem on 407 846 1200.

## Babysitting

For folks keen to give themselves an evening off from parenthood and take advantage of Orlando's many night-time opportunities, babysitting is a ready option. Both Airtours (KinderCare) and Virgin Holidays (Anny's Nannys) run babysitting or child minding services, all Walt Disney World® Resort hotels have babysitting as a regular feature and several larger hotels also offer it as an extra, notably the Delta Orlando, Buena Vista Palace, Caribe Royale Suites, Clarion Plaza, Embassy Suites, Grosvenor Resort, Hawthorn Suites, Hilton at Walt Disney World, Holiday Inn Maingate East and Holiday Inn Sunspree Resort. Additionally, an independent company with an excellent local reputation are **SuperSitters**, who can provide babysitters at any hotel or villa. All their sitters are screened, bonded and have CPR and Red Cross training, and their rates start at $8 an hour with a 4-hour minimum stay. Extra children are $1 per hour per child. To book a SuperSitter, call 407 382 2558.

Right, that's enough planning and preparation for now, it's time to HIT THE THEME PARKS …

# 5 The Theme Parks – Disney's Fab Four

*(or, Spending the Day With Mickey Mouse and Co.)*

**B**y now you should be prepared to deal with the main business of any visit to Orlando: Walt Disney World® Resort and the other main theme parks of Universal Studios Escape, SeaWorld and Busch Gardens.

If you have only a week in the area this is where you should concentrate your attention. Seven days is barely enough to sample the main theme parks, and even then you may decide Busch Gardens is a bridge too far. If you have less than a week you should concentrate on seeing as much of Walt Disney World as possible. However, once Universal's **Islands**

**of Adventure** is up and running in summer 1999, the demands on your time (and money) will be immense

© Disney

**Camp Minnie-Mickey at Disney's Animal Kingdom® Theme Park**

## ADVENTURELAND
1 JUNGLE CRUISE
2 SWISS FAMILY TREEHOUSE
3 PIRATES OF THE CARIBBEAN
4 THE ENCHANTED TIKI BIRDS

## FRONTIERLAND
5 BIG THUNDER MOUNTAIN RAILROAD
6 COUNTRY BEAR JAMBOREE
7 THE DIAMOND HORSESHOE
8 SPLASH MOUNTAIN
9 TOM SAWYER ISLAND

## LIBERTY SQUARE
10 HALL OF PRESIDENTS
11 THE HAUNTED MANSION
12 LIBERTY SQUARE RIVERBOAT
13 MIKE FINK KEELBOATS

## FANTASYLAND
14 CASTLE STAGE
15 LEGEND OF THE LION KING
16 PETER PAN'S FLIGHT
17 IT'S A SMALL WORLD
18 SNOW WHITE'S ADVENTURES
19 MR TOAD'S WILD RIDE
20 MAD TEA PARTY

## MICKEY'S TOONTOWN FAIR
21 BARNSTORMER
22 MINNIE'S COUNTRY HOUSE
23 MICKEY'S COUNTRY HOUSE
24 TOONTOWN HALL OF FAME

## TOMORROWLAND
25 TOMORROWLAND SPEEDWAY
26 SPACE MOUNTAIN
27 SKY-WAY TO FANTASYLAND
28 ASTRO ORBITER
29 THE EXTRATERRORESTRIAL ALIEN ENCOUNTER
30 THE TIMEKEEPER
31 WALT DISNEY'S CAROUSEL OF PROGRESS
32 TOMORROWLAND TRANSIT AUTHORITY
33 BUZZ LIGHTYEAR'S SPACE RANGER SPIN
34 WALT DISNEY WORLD RAILROAD
35 LAUNCH TO DISCOVERY ISLAND & FORT WILDERNESS

MAGIC KINGDOM® PARK

5

and a week will simply not suffice. Two weeks will be the basic requirement for all first-timers to the area, and even then you will struggle to say you have Done It All.

When it comes to price, be aware you can always save money on the regular prices of all the non-Disney attractions. Nearly all the local tourist publications will have money-off vouchers, while the official **Visitor Center** on International Drive (tel 407 363 5872) sells discounted tickets for all the theme parks and other attractions, even if it is only a couple of dollars off in some instances. Your **tour operator's** Orlando reps will also usually be able to offer attractively priced tickets as they buy in bulk and benefit from special offers from time to time. **Universal Studios Escape** have ticket booths in some of the shopping malls that give several dollars off all tickets except Disney ones, while **Know Before You Go** in central International Drive and on Highway 192 by the Haunted Mansion (or tel 407 396 5400 or toll free in the US on 1-800 749 1993) offer some of the most attractive seasonal discounts (for example, in spring 1998, $5 off Disney-MGM Studios, $4 off Church Street Station and $10 off many dinner shows). Hopefully, this underlines the message about not buying all your attraction tickets back home. It is all too easy when you are sitting in the travel agent's office to pre-book everything they offer, but you CAN save money by shopping around and you should avoid the pitfall of buying more tickets than you have time for.

## Ratings

All the rides and shows are judged on a unique rating system that splits them into the Thrill Rides or Shows and the Scenic or Aaah ones (as in 'Aaah, isn't that nice!'). Thrill rides earn T ratings out of five (hence a TTTTT is as exciting as they get) and scenic rides get A ratings out of five (an AA ride is likely to be over-cute and missable). Obviously it is a matter of opinion to a certain extent, but you can be fairly sure that a T or A ride is not worth your time, a TT or AA is worth seeing only if there is no queue, a TTT or AAA should be seen if you have time, but you won't have missed anything essential if you don't, a TTTT or AAAA ride is a big-time attraction that should be high on your list of things to do, and finally a TTTTT or AAAAA attraction should not be missed out at any cost. The latter will have the longest queues and, hence, you will probably want to plan your visit around these rides. Some rides are also restricted to children over a certain height and are not advisable for people with back, neck or heart problems, or for pregnant women. Where this is the case I have just noted 'Restrictions, 3ft 6in', and so on. Where families have small children under the height restriction, but mum and dad still want to try the ride, you DON'T have to queue twice. When you get to the front of the queue, tell the operator you want to do a Baby Swap. This means mum can ride while dad looks after junior, and, on her return, dad can ride while mum does the babysitting.

# Magic Kingdom® Park

Irrespective of how much time you have to devote here, the starting point for any visit has to be **Magic Kingdom®** at Walt Disney World® Resort, the park that best encompasses and embodies the spirit of utter delight that Walt Disney World bestows on all its visitors. It's the original Walt Disney World development that sparked the tourist explosion of Orlando from the late 1970s. In comparative terms, the Magic Kingdom® is closest to Disneyland Paris, Disneyland in Los Angeles and the Japanese version in Tokyo. Outside those three, it has no equal as an enchanting and exciting day out for all the family.

What I will now attempt to do is steer you through a typical day at the Magic Kingdom®, with a guide to all the main rides, shows and places to eat, how to park, how to avoid the worst of the crowds (and the Magic Kingdom® really DOES get busy) and how much you should expect to pay.

Magic Kingdom®, open since 1971, takes up just 100 of Walt Disney World's 28,000 acres but attracts almost as many visitors as the other 27,900 put together! It has seven separate 'lands', like slices of a large cake centred on the most

## The Magic Kingdom® Park at-a-glance

| | |
|---|---|
| **Location** | Off World Drive, Walt Disney World® Resort |
| **Size** | 100 acres in 7 'lands' |
| **Hours** | 9am–7pm off peak; 9am–10pm Washington's Birthday, spring school holidays; 9am–midnight high season (Easter, summer holidays, Thanksgiving and Christmas) |
| **Admission** | Under 3-free, 3–9, $34 (1-day ticket), $151 (5-Day Park Hopper), $219 (7-Day All-in-One Hopper); adult (10+) $42, $189, $274. |
| **Parking** | $5 |
| **Lockers** | Yes; under Main Street Railroad Station; $5 ($2 refund) |
| **Pushchairs/** | $6 (Stroller Shop to right of main entrance, $1 deposit refunded) |
| **Wheelchairs** | $6 ($1 deposit refunded) or $30 ($10 deposit refunded) (Main Ticket Centre or Stroller Shop) |
| **Top Attractions** | Splash Mountain, Space Mountain, Alien Encounter |
| **Don't Miss** | Disney's Magical Moments Parade, SpectroMagic and evening fireworks (not off peak) |
| **Hidden Costs** | **Meals** Burger, chips and coke $6.20<br>Three-course dinner $19.25 (Liberty Tree Tavern) |
| | **Kids' meal** $2.99 |
| | **T-shirts** $16–$30 |
| | **Souvenirs** $1–$285 |
| | **Sundries** Mickey Mouse Hat (with ears!) $16 |

famous landmark of all Florida, Cinderella Castle. There are almost 40 attractions packed in here, not to mention numerous shops and restaurants (although the eating opportunities are less impressive than Epcot® and Disney-MGM Studios). It's easy to get lost or overwhelmed by it all, especially as it does get so busy (even the fast-food restaurants have serious queues in high season), so study the notes and plan your visit around what most takes your fancy.

## Location

It is located at the innermost end of the vacation kingdom, with its entrance toll plaza three-quarters of the way along World Drive, the main entrance road off of Highway 192. World Drive runs north–south through Walt Disney World® Resort, while the Interstate 4 entrance, Epcot Drive, runs basically east–west. As you drive into the World, you can tune your car radio to 810 AM and hear Walt Disney World's own radio station telling you all about the delights in store for your visit! Unless you are staying at one of the hotels at Walt Disney World you will have to pay your $5 parking fee at the toll plaza and that brings you to the Magic Kingdom®

BRIT TIP: It is essential when you park to note on your parking ticket exactly what area you are parked in and the row number, e.g. Mickey, Row 30. All the sections are named after Disney characters, and if you don't note where you are parked you could have difficulty relocating your hire car!

Park car park (or parking lot), an enormous stretch of tarmac that can accommodate more than 10,000 cars (there are security gates at all resorts so you need a car pass). The majority arrive between 9.30 and 11.30am, so the car parks can become pretty jammed then, which is another good reason to get here EARLY. If you are not here by 8am during peak periods you might want to wait until after 1pm, or even later in the day when the park is open late into the evenings (as late as midnight at the height of summer and at Christmas).

To give you another idea of the size of the operation, a system of motorised trams carries you from the car park to the Ticket and Transportation Centre at the heart of the Magic Kingdom's operation. Unless you already have your ticket (which will save you valuable time if you have), you will have to queue up at the ticket booths here to go any further. Once you have ticket in hand, you pass the booths to several turnstiles which give access to either the monorail or ferryboats, and it is only these methods of transport that will finally bring you to the doorstep of the Magic Kingdom® itself. Of course, if you are staying on a Walt Disney World property, you can also catch the monorail directly or one of the trams or buses that make up Walt Disney World's free transport system. If you're at the head of the queue and can get straight on, the monorail (dead ahead of you) is slightly quicker in reaching the Magic Kingdom®. Otherwise, if you have to queue for the monorail, it is usually better to bear left and take the ferryboats which may be slightly slower but involve less queuing.

One final note, in all the main theme parks you may well find one or two attractions closed for refurbishment, even in high season, to mark the constant process of keeping everything as fresh and new as possible. However, you'll never be short of things to do!

## Main Street, USA

Right, we've finally reached the park itself … but not quite. Hopefully you've paid heed to the need to arrive early and you're among the leading hordes aiming to swarm through the main entrance. The published opening times may say 9am, but the gates to Magic Kingdom® Park are quite likely to open anything up to 45 minutes before then. This will bring you into **Main Street, USA**, the first of the seven lands. Immediately on your right is **Emporium**, a fascinating shop featuring original cartoon cels and prints. On your left is **City Hall**, from where you can pick up a park map and entertainment schedule of the day's events, if you haven't been given them at the toll plaza, and make reservations for the main restaurants. Ahead of you is **Town Square**, where you can take a one-way ride down Main Street, USA on a horse-drawn bus or fire engine. The Street itself houses some of the best shopping in the Magic Kingdom® as well as the **Main Street Cinema**, which shows continuous classic silent films, and the **Walt Disney World Railroad**, the park's Western-themed steam train that runs the full circumference of the Magic Kingdom® and is one of the better attractions when the queues are at their longest elsewhere. You can eat breakfast, lunch and dinner at Tony's Town Square Restaurant, a full-service diner specialising in Italian meals, The Plaza Restaurant (lunch and dinner, sandwiches, salads and sundaes), The Crystal Palace (breakfast, lunch and dinner, buffet-style food), the Main Street Bake Shop (delicious pastries, tea and coffee), Casey's Corner (hot dogs

and soft drinks), or the Plaza Ice Cream Parlor.

Look out for the **Guest Information Board** at the top of Main Street USA that gives waiting times for all the attractions through the day.

Unless you are a late arrival, give Main Street, USA no more than a passing glance for the moment and head for the end of the street where you will find the real entrance to the park. This is where you will have to wait for the final opening hour to arrive, the famous 'Rope drop', and you should adopt one of three tactics here, each aimed at doing one or two of the most popular rides before the crowds build up and queues become substantial (queues of an hour for Splash Mountain are not unknown on the busiest days). One: if you fancy heading straight for the five-star log-flume ride Splash Mountain, keep left in front of The Crystal Palace and the majority of the crowd here will head for the same place. Two: if you have young children who can't wait to ride on Cinderella's Golden Carrousel or the other very popular rides of Fantasyland, stay in the middle and head directly through the castle. Three: if the excitement and thrills of the new ExtraTERRORestrial Alien Encounter and the indoor roller-coaster Space Mountain appeal to you first, move to the right by the Plaza Restaurant and you'll get straight into Tomorrowland.

© Disney

**Main Street, USA**

5

Now you'll be in pole position for the opening rush to the main attractions (and it will be a rush – have your running spikes ready!).

## Adventureland

If you head for the first option, to the left (effectively going clockwise around the park), you will first come to **Adventureland**. If you are heading for Splash Mountain, with the rest of the early-morning queue-beaters, you will pass the Swiss Family Treehouse on your left and bear right through an archway (with restrooms on your right) into Frontierland, where you bear left and Splash Mountain is dead ahead. Stopping to admire Adventureland, however, these are the attractions you will encounter.

> BRIT TIP: If you are determined to get the most from your day, make sure you have a good breakfast BEFORE you arrive to give you plenty of energy and save time once the park is open!

**Swiss Family Treehouse**: this recently refurbished imitation Banyan tree is a clever replica of the treehouse from Disney's 1960 film *Swiss Family Robinson*. It's a walk-through attraction where the queues (rarely long) move steadily if not quickly, providing a fascinating glimpse of the ultimate treehouse, complete with kitchen, rope bridges and running water! AAA.

**Jungle Cruise**: it's not so much the scenic, geographically-suspect boat ride (where the Nile suddenly becomes the Amazon) that is so amusing here as the patter of your boat's captain, who spins a non-stop

yarn about your jungle adventure that features wild animals, tropical plants, hidden temples and sudden waterfalls. Great detail but long queues, so visit either early morning or late afternoon (evening queues are shortest, but you'll miss some of the detail in the dark). AAAA.

**Pirates Of The Caribbean**: one of Walt Disney World® Resort's most impressive attractions that involves the use of their pioneering work in audio-animatronics, life-size figures that move, talk and, in this instance, lay siege to a Caribbean island! Your underground boat ride takes you through a typical pirate adventure and the wizardry of the special effects is truly amazing. This is worth several rides, although it may be a bit spooky for very young children. Queues are rarely long here and almost non-existent late in the day and evening. AAAAA.

**The Enchanted Tiki Room**: one of the original, rather tired audio-animatronics ventures is due for a humorous, up-beat new style as Iago (from Aladdin) and Zazu (The Lion King) lead a cast of colourful parrots, macaws and other animated birds in a 16-minute revue of appeal mainly to younger children. The main plus points are that queues are rarely very long and you do get to sit down in air-conditioned comfort. AAA.

Additional entertainment is provided by a steel drum band, and the best of the shopping is the House of Treasure as you come out of the Pirates ride. For food, you have the choice of Aloha Isle, for yoghurt and ice-cream, El Pirata Y el Perico (Mexican snacks, hot dogs and salads), Sunshine Tree Terrace (for fruit snacks, yoghurt, tea and coffee) and The Oasis (more snacks and drinks).

## Frontierland

Passing through Adventureland brings you to **Frontierland**, the target of many of the park's early birds. This Western-themed area is one of the busiest parts of the Magic Kingdom and is best avoided from late morning to late afternoon.

**Splash Mountain**: based on the 1946 classic Disney cartoon *Song Of The South*, this is a watery journey into the world of Brer Rabbit, Brer Fox and Brer Bear. The first part of the ride is all magnificent cartoon scenery and jolly fun with the main characters and a couple of minor downward swoops in your eight-passenger log-boat. The conclusion, a five-storey plummet at an angle of 45 degrees into a mist-shrouded pool will make you convinced you are falling off the edge of the world! A huge adrenalin rush, but very busy at nearly all times of day (try it first thing or during one of the main parades to avoid the worst of the queues). You will also get VERY wet! Restrictions, 3ft 6in. TTTTT.

**Big Thunder Mountain Railroad**: when Disney do a roller-coaster they make it one of the classiest, and here it is, a runaway mine train that swoops, tilts and plunges through a mock abandoned mine filled with clever props and spectacular scenery. You'll need to ride it at least twice to appreciate all the fine detail, but again queues are heavy, so go first thing (after Splash Mountain) or late in the day. Restrictions, 3ft 4in. TTTT.

**Country Bear Jamboree**: now here's a novelty, a 16-minute musical revue presented by audio-animatronic bears! It's a great family fun show with plenty of novel touches (watch out for the talking Moose-head). Again, you'll need to beat the crowds by going early morning or early evening. AAAA.

**'The Diamond Horseshoe Saloon Revue'**: after all the audio-animatronic gadgetry here's an honest-to-goodness Western saloon show performed by real people! You no longer have to book, just turn up a little in advance, and if you fancy a slapstick song-and-dance routine featuring can-can girls, corny comedy and audience participation, this is for you. Snacks and drinks are available before the show. AAA.

**Frontierland Shootin' Arcade**: apart from the Penny Arcade in Main Street, USA, this is the only other attraction that will cost you a few extra cents, 50c for five shots at a series of animated targets. TT.

**Frontierland Stunt Show**: your daily schedule will tell you when to watch out for this regular peak period feature as the Good Guys shoot it out with the Bad Guys over the rooftops of Frontierland. AAA.

**Tom Sawyer Island**: take a raft over to this overgrown playground, complete with mysterious caves, grottos and mazes, rope bridges and Fort Sam Clemens, where you can fire air guns at passing boats. A good get-away in early afternoon when the crowds are at their highest, while Aunt Polly's Dockside Inn is a refuge within a refuge for snacks and soft drinks. TT.

Shops here sell cowboy hats, guns and badges as well as Indian and Mexican handicrafts, while for food try Pecos Bill Café (salads, sandwiches and burgers), Westward Ho Refreshments (soft drinks, snacks and yoghurt) or the Turkey Leg Wagon (tempting, smoke-grilled turkey legs).

## Liberty Square

Continuing the clockwise tour of the Magic Kingdom® brings you next into **Liberty Square**, Walt Disney World's homage to post-Independence America. A lot of the historical content here will go over the heads of British visitors, but it

© Disney

**Frontierland – Splash Mountain**

still has some great attractions.

**Liberty Belle Riverboat**: cruise America's 'rivers' on an authentic paddle steamer, be menaced by Indians and thrill to the tales of the Old West. This is also a good ride to take at the busiest times of the day, especially early afternoon. AAA.

**Mike Fink Keelboats**: a Davy Crockett journey along the same waters as the Riverboat, encountering the same dangers and escaping the same crowds! AA.

**The Haunted Mansion**: a very clever delve into the world of ghost train rides that is neither too scary for kids nor too twee for adults. Not so much a thrill ride as a scenic adventure, hence AAAA. Watch out for the neat touch at the end when your car picks up an extra 'passenger'. Longish queues during the main part of the day, however.

**The Hall of Presidents**: this is the attraction that will mean least to us, a two-part show that is first a film about the history of the Constitution and then an audio-animatronic parade of all 42 American presidents. Epcot's American Adventure does this better for overseas visitors. AA.

Shopping here is of a more antique-orientated nature, while eating opportunities offer the full-service Liberty Tree Tavern (which serves hearty soups, steaks and traditional dishes like meatloaf and pot roast), Columbia Harbour House (for counter-service fried chicken and shrimp and chips) or Sleepy Hollow (a picnic area serving snacks, drinks and vegetarian meals).

## Fantasyland

Exiting Liberty Square you walk past Cinderella Castle and come into **Fantasyland**, the spiritual heart of the Magic Kingdom® Park and the area with which young children are most fascinated. The attractions here are all designed with kids in mind, but some of the shops are quite sophisticated in their wares, while Cinderella's Royal Table is a must for a fun family meal.

**'It's A Small World'**: this could almost be Walt Disney World® Resort's theme ride, a family boat trip through the different continents, each represented by hundreds of dancing, singing audio-animatronic dolls in delightful pageants of colourful set-pieces. It sounds horribly twee, but it actually creates a surprisingly striking effect, accompanied by Walt Disney World's annoyingly catchy theme song. Crowds are steady and peak in

BRIT TIP: When you are faced by more than one queue for an attraction, head for the left-hand one. Almost invariably this will move slightly quicker than that on the right (it's the psychological effect of driving on the right-hand side of the road, they say).

early afternoon. AAAA.

**Dumbo The Flying Elephant**: parents hate it, kids love it and all want to do this two-minute ride on the back of a flying elephant that swoops in best Dumbo style, even if the ears do not flap. Do this one early or expect to queue. TTT.

**Mad Tea Party**: again the kids will insist you take them in these spinning, oversized tea-cups that have their own 'steering wheel' to add to the whirling effect. Actually, they're just a heavily-disguised version of many similar fairground rides. Again, go early or expect serious crowds. TT.

**Mr Toad's Wild Ride**: here's a good, fun runaway car ride for all the family as Mr Toad's jalopy takes you on a helter-skelter journey through fields, barns and his own ancestral manor, avoiding haystacks and other obstacles along the way. Very busy from mid-morning to late afternoon. TTT.

**Snow White's Adventures**: a completely revamped ride in 1995, but still similar to Mr Toad's, it tells the cartoon story of Snow White with a few ghost train effects that may scare small children. Good fun, though, for parents and kids. Again, you will need to go early or late (or during the main afternoon parade) to beat the queues. TTT.

**Cinderella's Golden Carrousel:** the centre-piece of Fantasyland shouldn't need any more explanation other than it is a vintage carousel ride that the kids all adore. Particularly, there are long queues here during the main part of the day. TT.

**Legend of the Lion King**: children will also love this cleverly-staged version of the recent Disney cartoon, using puppets, actors and special effects to tell the story of the young lion cub born to be King. It is a bit of a test of endurance, though, as queues are long and then there is a pre-show you have to stand

through before taking your seat in the air-conditioned theatre. AAAA.

**Peter Pan's Flight**: don't be fooled by the long queues at this one, it is a rather tame ride by Magic Kingdom® standards, although it is still a big favourite with kids. Its novel effect of flying up, up and away with Peter Pan quickly wears off, but there is still a lot of clever detail as your 'sailing ship' journeys over the roofs of London and into Neverland. AAA.

**Skyway to Tomorrowland**: this one-way cable-car ride provides a terrific aerial view of the Magic Kingdom® that is even more impressive at night. AAA.

In addition to the main rides, there are also different musical shows daily on the Castle Forecourt Stage in front of Cinderella Castle and the Fantasyland Character Festival behind Dumbo, while you can meet some more Disney characters (and watch the kids get wet) at **Ariel's Grotto**. Eating opportunities are at The Pinocchio Village Haus (salads, burgers and hot dogs), Hook's Tavern (beverages and shakes), Lumière's Kitchen (for children's meals) and the Enchanted Grove and Mrs Potts' Cupboard (for ice creams and sundaes). Cinderella's Royal Table is THE place, however, for a Magic Kingdom® meal, be it breakfast, lunch or dinner (and you need to make reservations for all three). The majestic hall,

© Disney

**The Barnstormer at Goofy's Wiseacre Farm**

5

waitresses in period costume and well-presented food make for a memorable dining experience, with the food consisting of salads, seafood, roast beef, prime rib and chicken. Expect to pay around $30 for a three-course dinner.

## Mickey's Toontown Fair

In the top corner of Fantasyland (just past the Mad Tea Party) is the shrub-lined entrance to the smallest and newest Land, **Mickey's Toontown Fair**, which replaced the old Mickey's Starland in 1996. It is easy to miss, but it does have its own station on the railroad. Its primary appeal is to children, and they won't want to miss out on the chance to meet their favourite Disney characters, including Mickey himself. It is exceptionally kid-friendly and beautifully landscaped and designed, and features a huge new merchandising area, the County Fair, so wallets beware!

**Mickey's Country House:** here is a walk-through opportunity to see the world's most famous mouse at home and have your picture taken with him in the Judge's Tent afterwards. AAAA.

**Minnie's Country House:** this is a chance to view Minnie's home and 'unique memorabilia', all designed in a Country and Western theme style. AAA.

**Toontown Hall of Fame:** here there are three opportunities to meet a host of other Disney favourites. The Villains Room features the likes of Captain Hook and Jafar, Mickey's Pals lets you meet Goofy, Pluto, Minnie and Co., and Famous Faces introduces characters such as Cinderella, Snow White and Pocahontas. TTTTT (for kids!).

**The Barnstormer at Goofy's Wiseacre Farm:** this is an all-new mini roller-coaster just for the young 'uns (although possibly a bit too

much for the under 5s) and is another masterpiece of design as it swoops through the barn, even if it is a pretty short ride for all the queuing. Watch out for the chance to meet Goofy in person! TTT.

**Donald's Boat:** parents beware, your youngsters could get very wet here. If you have already encountered the dancing fountains at Epcot® between Future World and World Showcase, prepare for more watery delights here as this boat-themed fountain spouts off in all sorts of unlikely ways. AAA.

## Tomorrowland

Continuing down from Fantasyland finally brings you into the last of the seven Lands, **Tomorrowland**, which has undergone a facelift to smarten up its façades and spice up the attractions. It now boasts a cartoon-like space-age appearance guaranteed to appeal to youngsters, and has some of the Magic Kingdom® Park's more original shops.

**Space Mountain**: this is one of the three most popular attractions, with Splash Mountain and the ExtraTERRORestrial Alien Encounter, and its reputation is quite deserved. It is a fast, tight-turning roller-coaster completely in the dark save for occasional flashes as you whizz through 'the galaxy'. Don't do this one after you've just eaten! The only way to beat the almost non-stop crowds here is to go either first thing, late in the day or during one of the parades or the fireworks show. Restrictions, 3ft 8in. TTTTT.

**Tomorrowland Speedway**: despite the long queues, this is a rather tame ride on supposed race tracks that just putt-putts along on rails with little real steering required. Restrictions, 4ft 4in. TT.

**Astro Orbiter**: this is a jazzed-up version of the flying Dumbos in Fantasyland, just a bit faster and higher and, instead of an elephant, you are 'piloting' a rocket. Large, slow-moving queues are another reason to give this one a miss. TT.

**Walt Disney's Carousel Of Progress**: this one will surprise, entertain and amuse, all at the same time. It is a 100-year journey through the development of modern technology and how it affects our lives, with audio-animatronics and a revolving theatre that reveals different stages in that development. Its 22-minutes are rarely threatened by crowds. AAA.

**Tomorrowland Transit Authority**: like the Astro Orbiter, this is an old attraction which was revamped during Tomorrowland's facelift. It provides an elevated view of the area, including a glimpse inside Space Mountain, in electro-magnetically-powered cars. If the queues are short, which they usually are, give it a go. AAA.

**ExtraTERRORestrial Alien Encounter**: this new attraction draws some HUGE queues (go early if you can) to its clever, high-tech preamble and awesomely scary show, a 'teleportation' demonstration that goes seriously wrong and brings an Alien to life in the middle of the audience. The fear factor adds a new dimension to the Magic Kingdom® Park, but it will be too strong for most kids (and anyone scared of the dark!). TTTT.

**The Timekeeper**: formerly the Transportarium, this 360° film show has become an amusing time-travel 'experiment', with comedian Robin Williams providing the voice of robot operator Timekeeper, who guides his assistant Nine Eye backwards and forwards in time. AAAA.

You can also catch the Skyway cable car here to Fantasyland, while the Galaxy Palace Theater hosts live musical productions featuring Disney characters and talent shows, at various times throughout the day.

For food, Cosmic Ray's Starlight Cafe has burgers, chicken and salads, The Plaza Pavilion does pizza, subs and salads, Auntie Gravity's (ouch!) Galactic Goodies serves up frozen yoghurt and fruit juice and The Launching Pad at Rockettower Plaza offers hot-dogs, snacks and drinks.

**Buzz Lightyear's Space Ranger Spin**: this was due to open late in 1998 and sees guests join an interactive space fantasy, defending Earth's supply of batteries from evil Emperor Zurg in best Toy Story style. AAAA (expected).

## Other events

Having come full circle around the Magic Kingdom® Park you are now back at Main Street, USA, and you should return here in early afternoon if you want to get away from the crowds and have a better look at the impressive array of shops or take in the Main Street Cinema. Watch out for the Dapper Dans, a strolling barbershop quartet, who perform regularly.

In addition to the permanent attractions, the Magic Kingdom® Park also has several other daily events which should not be missed. Watch out in particular for **'character greetings'** around the park of various Disney cartoon characters, who will quite happily pose for photographs. The imaginative detail of the architecture and gardens is not bettered anywhere else: such intricate touches as themed rubbish bins for each of the Lands and re-naming rest-rooms for 'Princes' and 'Princesses' makes this one of the great achievements in the entertainment world.

Watch out, too, for the show-stopping **Disney's Magical Moments** parade every day at 3pm. It goes from Main Street, USA up to the Castle Forecourt, then left into Liberty Square and Frontierland (or vice versa). It features a host of

**5**

**Tomorrowland**

colourful floats and characters from Disney films like Cinderella, Aladdin and The Lion King in a terrific, interactive cavalcade that will captivate the children and use up several rolls of film! And, if you think the park looks pretty good during the day, prepare to be amazed at how wonderful it looks at night when some of the lighting effects are truly astounding. When the park is open in the evenings (during the main holiday periods), there is also the twice-nightly **'SpectroMagic'** Parade (wait for the second one to beat the crowds), a mind- and eye-

**The Magical Moments Parade**

boggling light and sound extravaganza that has cornered the market in glitter and razzamatazz. It's difficult to do it justice in words, so make sure you see it. Evening hours are also highlighted by **'Fantasy in the Sky'** firework show over the Castle which is sparked off every night by Tinkerbell (seeing is believing!). Be warned, however, people start staking out the best spots to see the parades well in advance, up to an hour in some cases for the kerbs along Main Street, USA. At Christmas and Easter there are special Santa Claus and Easter Bunny parades. You can also breakfast with your favourite Disney characters at The Crystal Palace and Cinderella's Royal Table ($14.95 for adults, $7.95 for three to 11s) or

BRIT TIP: You can book one of Disney's character meals (there are 20 within Walt Disney World® Resort) up to three years in advance on 407 939 3463.

have dinner with them at the Liberty Tree Tavern ($20.50 and $10.95).

With the crowds typically being so heavy here, it is well worth remembering you CAN escape them by leaving the park in early afternoon (not forgetting to get a hand-stamp for re-admission and keeping your car park ticket which is valid all day) and returning to your hotel for a few hours' rest or a dive into the water parks. Disney's Discovery Island, a walk-through mini zoo and aviary, is also handy for a quiet few hours.

Finally, one of the park's best-kept 'secrets' is the Keys to the Kingdom, a four-hour guided tour of many backstage areas, including the service tunnel under the park, and entertainment production buildings. It costs an extra $45, call 407 939 8687 for details.

# Epcot®

Amaze and annoy your friends by revealing that Epcot® stands for Experimental Prototype Community Of Tomorrow, once you have marvelled at the double-barrelled entertainment value of this 260-acre future world playground. Actually, it is not so much a vision of the future as a look at the world of today, with a strong educational and environmental message which children in particular are quick to pick up on.

At more than twice the size of the Magic Kingdom® Park it is more likely to require a two-day visit (although small children will find it less entertaining than the Magic Kingdom®) and your feet in particular will notice the difference!

## Location

Epcot® is located on Epcot Drive and the parking fee is again $5 as you drive into its main entrance (there is a separate entrance for guests of Disney's Yacht and Beach Club Resorts, Disney's BoardWalk Inn and Villas and the Walt Disney World Swan and Dolphin Hotels). It opened in October 1982 and its giant parking lot is big enough for 12,000 vehicles, so again a tram takes you from your car to the main entrance (although if you are staying at another of the Walt Disney World® Resort's hotels you can catch the monorail or bus service to the front gate). Once you have your ticket, you wait by the turnstiles for the opening moment (often accompanied by a Disney character or two) and are then admitted to the central plaza area, surrounded by the two Innoventions centres.

Epcot® is divided into two distinct parts arranged in a figure of eight and there are two tactics to avoid the worst of the early morning crowds. The first or lower half of the '8'

**Monorail to Future World**

consists of **Future World**, seven different pavilions arranged around Spaceship Earth (the giant 'golfball' that dominates the Epcot® skyline) and Innoventions. The second part, or the top of the '8', is **World Showcase**, a potted journey around the world via 11 internationally-presented pavilions that feature a taste of their culture, history, shopping, entertainment and cuisine. Once you are through the gates, start by heading for the Future World pavilions to your left (Universe of Energy, Wonders of Life, Horizons and the new Test Track) and then continue up into World Showcase. This way you will visit some of the best rides in Epcot® ahead of the main crowds. Alternatively, if the rides don't appeal quite so much as a visit to such diverse cultures as Japan and Morocco, spend your first couple of

**Test Track in Future World at Epcot®**

## Epcot® at-a-glance

| Location | Off Epcot Drive, Walt Disney World® Resort |
|---|---|
| Size | 200 acres in Future World and World Showcase |
| Hours | 9am–9pm off peak; 9am–10pm (Washington's Birthday, spring school holidays; 9am–midnight high season (Easter, Summer holidays, Thanksgiving and Christmas) |
| Admission | Under 3-free, 3–9, $34 (1-day ticket), $151 (5-Day Park Hopper), $219 (7-Day All-in-One Hopper); adult (10+) $42, $189, $274. |
| Parking | $5 |
| Lockers | Yes; to left underneath Spaceship Earth and International Gateway; $5 ($2 refund) |
| Pushchairs/ Wheelchairs | $6 (to right underneath Spaceship Earth and International Gateway, $1 deposit refunded) $6 ($1 deposit refunded) or $30 ($10 deposit refunded) (same location) |
| Top Attractions | Spaceship Earth, Body Wars, Honey I Shrunk The Audience, Test Track, Maelstrom, Universe of Energy, American Adventure |
| Don't Miss | IllumiNations, dinner at any one of the many fine restaurants |
| Hidden Costs | **Meals** Burger, chips and coke $7.05<br>Three-course dinner $24.99 (Restaurant Marrakesh) |
| | **Kids' meal** $3.25 |
| | **T-shirts** $16–$32 |
| | **Souvenirs** $2.25–$200 |
| | **Sundries** Kid's Tigger suit $30 |

hours in the Innoventions centres (which are very popular from mid-morning), then head into World Showcase as soon as it opens at 11am and you will be ahead of the crowds for several hours. If you time your journey around the Showcase (which is a full one-and-a-half-mile walk) to arrive back in Future World by late afternoon, you will find the worst of the milling throng will have passed through.

The other thing you will want to do early on is book a table for lunch or dinner at one of the many fine restaurants. The best reservations go fast, but there are three different locations where you can make your booking. These are called Worldkey Information Satellites and are clever audio-visual terminals which give you access to Walt Disney World hosts and hostesses who deal with all the information about Epcot®. They will give you advice on where and when to eat and will take your booking. The three Satellites are located to the left of the Guest Relations office, which is situated at the lower end of Innoventions East on your left hand side as you walk in; just to the north of the two Innoventions centres; and in front of the German pavilion of World Showcase.

## Future World

Here is what you will find in Future World.

### Universe of Energy

There is just the one attraction here but it is a stunner as you are taken on a 45-minute show-and-ride in the company of American comedienne Ellen DeGeneres that explores the creation of fuels from the age of dinosaurs to their modern day usages. The film elements convince you that you are in a conventional theatre, but then your seats suddenly rearrange themselves into 96-person solar-powered cars and you are off on a journey through the sights, sounds and even smells of the prehistoric era. The dinosaurs are very convincing! Queues are steady but not overwhelming throughout the day from mid-morning. AAAAA.

### Wonders of Life

This is one of Future World's most popular pavilions, hence you need to be here either early or late in the day. **Body Wars** is a terrific simulator ride through the human body as in the films *Fantastic Voyage* or the more recent *Inner Space*. It is quite a violent adventure, too, hence it is not recommended for people who suffer from motion sickness, anyone with neck or back injuries or pregnant women. TTTT. **Cranium Command** is a hilarious theatre show set in the brain of a 12-year-old boy, showing how he negotiates a typical day. It is both audio-animatronic and film-based. See how many famous TV and film stars you can name in the 'cast'. AAAA. **The Making of Me** is a sensitive film on

the creation of human life and will therefore require parental discretion for children as it has its explicit moments, although not without humour. AAA. **AnaComical Players** and **Goofy About Health** are both theatre shows, one live, the other animated, aimed at amusing and educating the youngsters, while the **Fitness Fairground**, with hands-on exhibits like exercise bikes, gives you the chance to see just how far all the holiday fun has taken its toll on your body! You can also assess your golf/tennis/baseball swing in **Coach's Corner**, complete a health survey with the **Met Lifestyle Revue** and test your senses in the **Sensory Funhouse**. The Pure and Simple restaurant offers delicious – and nutritious – alternatives to the usual burgers and chips.

### Horizons

This is another one-ride pavilion that takes you through different visions of the future on land, sea and space, including some that have already been overtaken by modern science. The 15-minute ride also features a simulated fast-moving conclusion that can be mildly disconcerting for those who suffer from travel sickness. Queues fluctuate throughout the day, notably when the larger Universe of Energy has just disgorged its audience. It has recently been revamped with some up-to-the-minute touches. AAAA.

### Test Track ✶

The newest attraction at Epcot® (due to open late in '98 after a long delay) should be a stunner, a 5½ minute whirl along the Walt Disney World Resort's longest and fastest track to date. **Test Track** starts with a pre-show into the world of General Motors' quality and safety techniques, preparing riders for first-hand experience of vehicle

5

**FUTURE WORLD**

1 SPACESHIP EARTH
2 INNOVENTIONS EAST
3 UNIVERSE OF ENERGY
4 WONDERS OF LIFE
5 HORIZONS
6 TEST TRACK
7 ODYSSEY CENTER
8 JOURNEY INTO IMAGINATION
9 THE LAND
10 INNOVENTIONS WEST
11 TTHE LIVING SEAS

**WORLD SHOWCASE LAGOON**

12 MEXICO
13 NORWAY
14 CHINA
15 GERMANY
16 ITALY
17 THE AMERICAN ADVENTURE
18 JAPAN
19 MOROCCO
20 FRANCE
21 INTERNATIONAL GATEWAY
22 UNITED KINGDOM
23 CANADA

EPCOT®

testing. The way the cars whizz around the *outside* of the building (at up to 60mph) gives you just a glimpse of what's in store. The reality is far more thrilling as you are taken on a thorough tour of a GM proving ground, including a hill climb test, suspension test (hold on to those fillings!), brake test, environment chamber, barrier test (remember those crash test dummies?) and the steeply-banked high-speed finale. For those who manage to regain their breath, there is a post-show area with interactive equipment, a multimedia film and the chance to view the latest GM models. Yes, it is a touch commercial, but, with a ride as spectacular as this, who cares! Go first thing to beat the anticipated (long) queues. TTTTT (expected).

The next door **Odyssey Center** offers baby-care and first aid facilities, telephones and restrooms.

### Journey Into Imagination

The three different elements here lead on one from another, so start with **Journey Into Imagination** in the company of the inventive Dreamfinder and his baby dragon pal Figment. It's unfailingly and wonderfully silly with some hugely imaginative images that will either make you laugh out loud or groan. AAA. From the ride you go up into the **Image Works** which is essentially a series of hands-on exhibits for kids ranging from electronic paintbrushes and musical instruments to the Rainbow Corridor full of variously coloured neon tubes. Go back down the stairs and out of the building to your right and you come to the **Magic Eye Theater** and the 3-D film *Honey, I Shrunk The Audience* with Rick Moranis. If you have already seen *Muppets 3-D* at Disney-MGM Studios you might have an idea what to expect. Special effects and moving

seats add to the entertainment that makes you feel you have been miniaturised. And beware the sneezing dog! AAAAA. Outside, kids are always fascinated by the Jellyfish and Serpentine Fountains that send water squirting from pond to pond, and there is always one who tries to stand in the way and 'catch' one of the streams of water. Have your cameras and camcorders ready!

### The Land

This pavilion features four elements that combine to make a highly entertaining but educational experience on food production and nutrition. **Living with the Land** is an informative 14-minute boat ride that is worth the usually long queue. This journey through various types of food production sounds a pretty dull idea, and it may not appeal much to younger children, but adults and school-age kids will sit up and take notice of the three different ecological communities, especially the greenhouse finale. AAAA. Having ridden the ride you can also walk the walk on a guided tour through the greenhouse complex

**5**

© Disney

**'Honey, I Shrunk the Audience' is an outstanding Epcot® attraction**

and learn even more about Walt Disney World's horticultural projects. It takes an hour, but you have to book up in person at the desk near the Green Thumb Emporium. **Food Rocks**, just to the right as you exit the ride, is easy to overlook, but don't! This musical tribute to nutrition, presented by Food Rapper (what a great name!) and featuring Pita Gabriel (ouch!) is a hilarious 12-minute skit that will amuse kids and adults alike. AAAA. **The Circle of Life** is a 15-minute live-action/animated story that explains environmental concerns, easily digestible for kids. Queues not a problem here, either. AAA.

The Sunshine Season food court offers the chance to eat some of the Walt Disney World® Resort's own produce, and again there are healthy alternatives to the usual fast food fare, while the Garden Grill Restaurant is a slowly revolving platform that offers more traditional food, including pasta, seafood and delicious rotisserie chicken. Mickey and friends also turn up here for character breakfasts ($8.95 for kids 3–11 and $15.95 for adults), lunch and dinner ($10.95 & $17.95), but book early.

### The Living Seas

This pavilion does for the sea what the Land Pavilion does for the land. There is a three-minute trip around the man-made 5.7 million gallon aquarium that takes you to Sea Base Alpha, the main attraction. This two-level development takes visitors through six modules that present stories of undersea exploration and marine life. Crowds build up substantially through the day, so go either early or late. AAAA.

The pavilion also includes the highly-recommended Coral Reef restaurant that serves magnificent seafood, as well as providing diners with a grandstand view of the massive aquarium. Dinner for two will cost around $60, which isn't cheap, but the food is first class.

### Spaceship Earth

This ride spirals up the 18 storeys into the 'golfball', telling the story of communication from early cave drawings to modern satellite technology. This is easily the most popular ride in the park, largely because of its visibility and location, hence you need to do it either first thing or late afternoon when the crowds have moved on from Future World into World Showcase. The highlight is the depiction of Michelangelo's painting of the Sistine Chapel, which will be lost on small kids, but it's an entertaining 15-minute journey all along. AAAA. As you exit the ride you come into the Global Activity Center, presented by AT&T, with a host of interactive educational exhibits.

### Innoventions East and West

These two centres of hands-on exhibits and computer games include a glimpse of Walt Disney World's latest investigations into virtual reality entertainment, and other demonstrations of current and future technologies, especially the Internet, by companies like Honeywell, Hammacher Schlemmer, Apple, Motorola and Silicon Graphics. The kids will automatically gravitate to the free **Sega Game Center** and they may take a bit of moving along! Worth trying also is the Sega grand prix simulator which offers you the chance to 'race' other visitors (but for $4 extra). Alternatively it's just as entertaining to watch those involved. **Epcot® Discovery Center** is full of educational ideas and will answer all your questions about the park, while musical entertainment is provided periodically by the Future Corps Band and other innovative live acts. Food outlets include the counter service Electric Umbrella Restaurant for lunch and dinner (sandwiches, burgers and salads), the Pasta Piazza Ristorante, which offers tempting pizzas and pasta, and the Fountain View Espresso and Bakery for tea, coffee and pastries. You'll also find the huge shopping plaza **Centorium** in Innoventions East, featuring stacks of quality Epcot® and Disney souvenirs.

## World Showcase

If you found Future World a huge experience, prepare to be amazed also by the more down-to-earth but equally imaginative pavilions around the World Showcase Lagoon. Each features a glimpse of the host country in dramatic settings. Several have either amusing rides or films that show off the tourist features of the countries, while in nearly every case the restaurants offering national fare are some of the best in Orlando.

### Mexico

Starting at the bottom left of the circular tour of the lagoon and moving clockwise, your first encounter is the spectacular pyramid that houses **Mexico**. Here you will find the amusing boat ride along **El Rio del Tiempo**, the River of Time, which gives you a potted nine-minute journey through the people and history of the country. Queues here tend to be surprisingly long from mid-morning to late afternoon. AAA. The rest of the pavilion is given over to a range of shops in the **Plaza de los Amigos** that vary from

> BRIT TIP: The Cantina is a great spot from which to watch the nightly IllumiNations fireworks and laser show.

pretty tacky to sophisticated, the **Reign of Glory – a Celebration of Mexico's Pre-Columbian Arts** exhibition, and the **San Angel Inn**, a dimly-lit and romantic full-service diner offering traditional and tempting Mexican fare. Outside, on the lagoon, is the **Cantina de San Angel**, a fast-food counter for tacos, chili and burgers, while, as with all World Showcase pavilions, there is live entertainment and music at various times (advertised on the daily schedule).

### Norway

Next up is **Norway**, which features probably the best of the rides in World Showcase, the Viking-themed **Maelstrom**. This 10-minute longboat journey through the history and scenery of the Scandinavian country features a short waterfall drop and a North Sea storm, and attracts longish queues during the day, so again the best tactic is to go either early on or in the evening. TTT. **The Puffin's Roost** offers Norwegian shopping (clothing, trolls, toys and glasswork), while there are periodical Norwegian-themed exhibits in the reconstruction **Stave Church**. The pavilion also contains a clever reproduction of Oslo's Akershus fortress. **Restaurant Akershus** offers lunch and dinner buffets featuring Norwegian dishes and the **Kringla Bakeri Og Kafe** serves open sandwiches, pastries and drinks.

### China

The spectacular architecture of **China** is well served by the pavilion's main attraction, the stunning **Wonders Of China**, a 20-minute, 360-degree film in the circular Temple of Heaven. Here you are surrounded by the sights and sounds of one of the world's most mysterious countries in a special cinematic production, the

5

**Video Game Chairs at the Hammacher Schlemmer exhibit**

technology of which alone will leave you breathless. If you were ever tempted to pay a visit to the country itself, this film will convince you. Queues build up to half an hour during the main part of the day. AAAA. **Land of Many Faces** is a new exhibit introducing China's ethnic peoples. Two restaurants, the **Nine Dragons** (table service, first class) and the **Lotus Blossom Café** (counter service, fairly predictable spring rolls and stir-fries) offer tastes of the Orient, while the **Yong Feng Shangdian Department Store** is a virtual department store of Chinese wares and gifts. Don't miss the periodic shows of Oriental music and acrobatic acts on the plaza in front of the Temple.

The **Village Traders Outpost** between China and Germany features hut-style shops and snacks, with musical entertainment. If and when Disney add a new pavilion, it is almost certain to go in here.

### Germany

**Germany** offers more in the way of shopping and eating than it does entertainment, although you will still find strolling players, courtyard musicians and a lively **Biergarten**, with its brass band. It also offers hearty portions of German sausage, saurkraut and rotisserie chicken. The **Sommerfest** is fast-food

German-style (bratwurst and strudel), while this pavilion boasts the highest number of shops of any Epcot® pavilion, including chocolates, wines, china, crystal, toys and cuckoo clocks.

### Italy

Similarly, **Italy** has pretty, authentic architecture (including a superb reproduction of St Mark's Square in Venice), lively music and amusing Italian folk stories, three tempting gift shops (enter Delizie Italiane's choice of chocolates, biscuits and candies in the open-air market at your peril!), and its restaurant, **L'Originale Alfredo di Roma Ristorante**. It's a touch expensive, but the atmosphere, decor and singing waiters (!) add extra zest to the meals, which include world famous fettucine, chicken, veal and seafood. Expect a three-course meal to cost you about $30.

### America

At the top of the lagoon and dominating World Showcase is **The American Adventure**, not so much a pavilion as a celebration of the country's history and constitution. A colonial fife and drum band add authentic sounds to the 18th-century setting, overlooked by a faithful reproduction of Philadelphia's Liberty Hall. Inside the Hall you will find the spectacular **American Adventure Show**, a magnificent

**Innoventions – Alec Tronic**

film and audio-animatronic® production lasting half an hour which details the country's struggles and triumphs, its presidents, statesmen and heroes. It's a glossy, patriotic performance, featuring outstanding audio-animatronic special effects, and, while some of it will leave foreign tourists fairly cold, it is difficult not to be impressed by the overall sense of pride and achievement inherent in so much American history. It doesn't pull any punches on the subject of Native American issues, either. Avoid at mid-day for the queues. AAAA. Outside, handcarts offer touches of American nostalgia and antiques, while the **Liberty Inn** offers some fairly predictable fast-food fare for lunch and dinner. The **America Gardens Theatre** facing the lagoon presents regular musical performances from worldwide artists which vary seasonally.

### Japan

Next up on the clockwise tour is **Japan**, where you will be introduced to typical Japanese gardens and architecture, including the breathtaking Chi Nien Tien, a round building one-half scale reproduction of a temple, some magnificent art exhibits, musical performances and live entertainment like kite-making. For a different dining experience, the **Teppanyaki Dining Rooms** and **Tempura Kiku-Sushi** both offer a full, table-service introduction to Japanese cuisine while **Yakitori House** is the fast-food equivalent and the **Matsu No Ma Lounge** features sushi and speciality drinks. The restaurants are hosted by Mitsukoshi, as is the superb department store.

### Morocco

**Morocco**, as you would expect, is a real shopping experience, with artfully-crafted bazaars, alleyways and stalls selling a well-priced array of carpets, leather goods, clothing, brass ornaments, pottery and antiques (seek out that Magic Lamp!). All of the building materials were faithfully imported and hand-built to give Morocco an outstanding degree of authenticity, even by the World Showcase's high standards, and will keep you gazing at its clever detail around the winding alleyways to the **Nejjarine Fountain** and gardens, which can be enjoyed on a guided walking tour. **Restaurant Marrakesh** offers a full Moroccan dining experience, complete with traditional musicians and a belly dancer. It's slightly pricey ($49.95 for the Moroccan feast for two) but the atmosphere is always lively and VERY different.

### France

**France** is predictably overlooked by a replica Eiffel Tower, but the smart streets, buildings and the sheer cleanliness of it all is a long way removed from modern-day Paris! This is a pre-World War I France, with official buskers, comedy street theatre and mime acts adding to the rather dreamy atmosphere. Don't miss **Impressions de France**, another stunning big-film production that serves up all the grandest sights of France to the accompaniment of the music of Offenbach, Debussy, Saint-Saëns and Satie. Crowds get quite heavy from mid-morning to early evening but it is a stunning performance (although kids might feel left out). AAAA. If you are looking for a gastronomic experience this is also the pavilion for you as there is the choice of four restaurants, of which **Chefs De France** and **Bistro de Paris Restaurant** are both major discoveries. The former is an award-winning, full-service and therefore expensive establishment featuring top quality French cuisine created by

French chefs on a daily basis, while the latter offers more intimate bistro dining, still with an individual touch and plenty of style. Alternatively, the **Boulangerie Patisserie** is a sidewalk café offering more modest fare at a more modest price. Shopping here is suitably chic, notably the Plume et Palette and La Signature.

## United Kingdom

Coming next to the **United Kingdom** will be something of a disappointment to British visitors. Sad to say, but this is the dullest of all the 11 international pavilions, certainly with little to entertain those of us who have been inside a traditional pub before or shopped for Royal Doulton or Pringle goods. That really is the sum total on offer here. The **Rose and Crown Pub** is a fairly authentic pub, but you can certainly get better food and drink (steak and kidney pie $12, cottage pie $11 and a pint of Bass, Harp Lager or Guinness for a whopping $4.50) at these prices. Entertainment includes live music, the World Showcase Players (a street theatre) and a traditional herb garden and maze. Other shops are The Tea Caddy, The Magic of Wales, The Queen's Table, The Lords and Ladies (perfumes, tobacco, family trees) and The Toy Soldier (traditional games and toys).

## Canada

**Canada** completes the World Showcase circle, with its main features being **Victoria Gardens**, based on the rightly world famous Butchart Gardens on Vancouver Island, some spectacular Rocky Mountain scenery, a replica French gothic mansion, the Hotel du Canada, and another stunning 360-degree film, **O Canada!** As with China and France, this beautifully showcases the country's sights and scenery, and serves as a terrific, 17-minute advertisement for the Canadian Tourist Board. It gets

busiest from late morning to late afternoon. AAA. **Le Cellier Steakhouse** is a modestly-priced cafeteria offering seafood, chicken, soup and salads for lunch and dinner. Try their fresh poached salmon or bread custard with maple syrup.

If you plan a two-day visit to Epcot® it makes sense to spend the first day in World Showcase, arriving early and heading there while most of the rest of the morning crowds linger in Future World, booking your evening meal around 5.30pm, and then lingering around the lagoon for the evening's **IllumiNations** show, which is half an hour before closing every day. This epic firework and laser show features a soaring soundtrack and a mind-boggling display of pyrotechnic effects. It will certainly be etched on your memory for a long time to come. Try to put a price on how much money has just gone up in smoke before your eyes – it runs into thousands of dollars EVERY night! For your second visit, try arriving in late afternoon and then doing Future World in more leisurely fashion than is the case in mid-morning to mid-afternoon. Queues at most of the pavilions are almost non-existent for rides like Universe of Energy, Body Wars, Horizons and Living With The Land, although Spaceship Earth (and probably Test Track) stays busy nearly all day (except for the evening, when everyone is out around the lagoon for IllumiNations). You CAN do Epcot® in a day – if you arrive early, put in some speedy legwork and give some of the peripheral detail a miss. But, of all the parks, it is a shame to hurry this one. In the shops (almost 70 in all), try to save your browsing for the busiest times when most people will be packing out the rides. The Innoventions Centres are also busiest from mid-morning to late afternoon, and relatively uncrowded in the evening.

# Disney-MGM Studios

Welcome to Hollywood! Well, the Walt Disney World® Resort's version of it. When it opened in May 1989, Michael Eisner, Chairman of the Walt Disney Company, insisted it was 'the Hollywood that never was and always will be'. Sounds double Dutch? Don't worry, all will be revealed in your day-long tour of this real-life combination of theme park and working TV and film studio. It's the most common question about Disney-MGM Studios, and yes, there really are genuine film and TV productions going on even while you're riding around the park peering into the backstage areas.

Rather bigger than the Magic Kingdom® Park at 154 acres but substantially smaller than Epcot® at 260, Disney-MGM Studios is a different experience yet again with its combination of rides, spectacular shows (including the unmissable Indiana Jones™ Epic Stunt

## Disney-MGM Studios at-a-glance

| | |
|---|---|
| **Location** | Off Buena Vista Drive or World Drive, Walt Disney World |
| **Size** | 110 acres (more than half as studio backlot) |
| **Hours** | 9am–7pm off peak; 9am–10pm high season (Easter, Summer holidays, Thanksgiving and Christmas) |
| **Admission** | Under 3-free, 3–9, $34 (1-day ticket), $151 (5-Day Park Hopper), $219 (7-Day All-in-One Hopper); adult (10+) $42, $189, $274. |
| **Parking** | $5 |
| **Lockers** | Yes; next to Oscar's Super Service, to right of main entrance; $5 ($2 refundable) |
| **Pushchairs/ Wheelchairs** | $6 (from Oscar's Super Service, $1 deposit refunded) $6 ($1 deposit refunded) or $32 ($10 deposit refunded) (same location) |
| **Top Attractions** | Twilight Zone™ Tower of Terror, Star Tours, Great Movie Ride, Muppet Vision 3-D |
| **Don't Miss** | Mulan Parade, evening fireworks (high season only), Indiana Jones™ Stunt Spectacular, new Fantasmic! show |
| **Hidden Costs** | **Meals** Burger, chips and coke $6.20 Three-course dinner $19.95 (Sci-Fi Dine-In Theater) |
| | **Kids' meal** $3.25 |
| | **T-shirts** $22–$40 |
| | **Souvenirs** $1.50–$95 |
| | **Sundries** Music of Disney CD $19.98 |

5

# DISNEY-MGM STUDIOS

1 MULAN PARADE ROUTE
2 SUPERSTAR TELEVISION
3 INDIANA JONES™ EPIC STUNT SPECTACULAR
4 ABC SATURDAY MORNING SOUND STUDIO
5 STAR TOURS RIDE
6 HUNCHBACK OF NOTRRE DAME MUSICAL ADVENTURE
7 JIM HENSON'S MUPPET*VISION 3-D
8 'HONEY, IS SHRUNK THE KIDS' MOVIE SET ADVENTURE
9 CATASTROPE CANYON 'SPECIAL EFFECTS' ON BACKLOT OUR
10 AMERICAN FILM INSTITUTE SHOWCASE COSTUMES & PROPS
11 DISNEY-MGM STUDIOS BACKLOT TOUR
12 THE GREAT MOVIE RIDE
13 VOYAGE OF THE LITTLE MERMAID 'ARIEL'S WONDERFUL STORY'
14 BACKSTAGE PASS TO '101 DALMATIANS'
15 THE MAGIC OF DISNEY ANIMATION
16 THE TWILIGHT ZONE™ TOWER OF TERROR
17 BEAUTY & THE BEAST – LIVE ON STAGE
18 GUEST INFORMATION BOARD
19 WALT DISNEY THEATRE
20 TOY STORY PIZZA PLANET
21 FANTASMIC!
22 ROCK 'N' ROLLER COASTER (1999)

MAIN ENTRANCE

Spectacular!), street entertainment, film sets and smart gift shops. Like the Magic Kingdom® Park, the food on offer won't win awards, but some of the restaurants (notably the Sci-Fi Dine-in Theater and 50s Prime Time Café) have superbly imaginative settings that will keep everyone amused. New for spring 1999 will be the **Copperfield Magic Underground** restaurant which promises a dazzling 'world of illusion' dining experience created by top illusionist David Copperfield. Disney-MGM Studios also has rather more to keep the attention of smaller children than the education-orientated Epcot®, but you can still easily see all it has to offer in a day, and, if you make an early start, you can safely say you have 'done' it by 5pm unless the crowds are really heavy.

**Hollywood Boulevard**

## Location

The entrance arrangements will be fairly familiar if you have already visited either the Magic Kingdom® or Epcot®. Disney-MGM Studios are located on Buena Vista Drive (which runs between World Drive and Epcot Drive) and the parking fee is $5. Look out for the landmark 130-foot water tower adorned with Mickey Mouse ears and dubbed – wait for it – the **Earffel Tower**! Again, make a note of where you park before you catch your tram to the main gates, where you must wait for the official opening hour. If the queues build up quickly, the gates will again open early, so be ready to jump the gun and get a running start!

Once through the gates you are into Hollywood Boulevard, which is a street of mainly gift shops, and you have to decide which of the three main ride attractions to head for first as these are the ones where the queues will be heavy nearly all day. Try to ignore the lure of the shops as

it is better to browse in the early afternoon when the queues build up at the rides. Incidentally, if you thought Walt Disney World® Resort had elevated queuing to an art form in their other two parks, wait until you see the clever ways they are arranged here! Just when you think you have got to the ride itself there is another twist to the queue you hadn't seen or an extra element to the ride which holds you up. The latter are called 'holding pens' and are merely an ingenious way of making it seem like you are being entertained instead of queuing. Look out for them in particular at the Great Movie Ride and Jim Henson's Muppet*Vision 3-D. An up-to-the-minute check on queue times at all the main attractions is kept on a Guest Information Board on Hollywood Boulevard, just past its junction with Sunset Boulevard, where you can also book for one of the feature restaurants.

Disney-MGM Studios is laid out in rather more confusing fashion than its two main counterparts, which all have neatly packaged Lands or pavilions, so you need to consult your maps frequently to

5

make sure you are going in the right direction. It is easier to get sidetracked here than in any of the other main theme parks.

## Three main rides

Having said that, the opening-gate crowds will all surge in one of three directions which will give you a pretty good idea of where you want to go. By far the biggest attraction in MGM is 'The Twilight Zone™ Tower of Terror', a magnificent haunted hotel ride that culminates in a 13-storey drop in a lift – not once, but twice! It's not for the faint-hearted, but it is a huge thrill, and the queues build up here like nowhere else, up to two hours at peak periods. Consequently, if the Tower appeals to you, do it FIRST! Head up Hollywood Boulevard then turn right into Sunset Boulevard and it is at the end of the street, looming ominously over the rest of the park. The second major attraction, the space-flight simulator **Star Tours**, is at the opposite side of the park. Go up Hollywood Boulevard, and turn left and past Superstar Television. When it first opened, this was the bee's knees for adventure rides and it is still, for my money, one of the cleverest rides you will encounter. If you dash straight out of Star Tours, you can head back to the top of Hollywood Boulevard for the third main attraction, **The Great Movie Ride**, where queues again touch an hour at peak times. Here you ride through a potted history of classic films into some elaborately re-created scenes.

However, this pattern is likely to change when the park's big new attraction, the **Rock 'n' Roller Coaster** opens later in 1999. This will be the first Disney attraction to feature a high-speed launch and multiple, complete inversions, with a synchronised rock soundtrack

resonating from speakers in each vehicle. Expect it to draw some significant crowds when it opens.

Here's a full run-down of all the current attractions in more detail, working around the park in a clockwise direction.

## Great Movie Ride

**The Great Movie Ride**: this faces you as you walk in along Hollywood Boulevard and is a good place to start if the crowds are not too serious. An all-star audio-animatronics® cast recreate a number of box office smashes, including Jimmy Cagney's *Public Enemy*, Julie Andrews in *Mary Poppins*, Gene Kelly in *Singing in the Rain* and many more masterful set pieces as you ride through on your conducted tour. Small children may find the menace of the Alien a bit too strong, but otherwise it has fairly universal appeal and features some live twists it would be a shame to spoil by revealing. AAAA.

**SuperStar Television**: this 30-minute audience participation show features American TV shows like *General Hospital, Cheers, The Golden Girls* and *The Johnny Carson Show*. About a dozen 'volunteers' are chosen from the front of the queue before you enter the 1,000-seat theatre, and they will all feature in re-creating scenes from the various TV programmes. With the assistance of Walt Disney World® Resort's own 'production director' it can often be a hilarious show, and queues are rarely long. AAA.

**ABC Saturday Morning Sound Studio:** specially designed to appeal to kids is this interactive sound effects studio featuring the new animated series 101 Dalmatians. Again, the 'producer' is the real star of the show and it can be highly amusing for adults. The show exits into the excellent, hands-on SoundWorks studio where you can try your hand at making your own sound effects. AAA.

**Indiana Jones™ Epic Stunt Spectacular!**: consult your park map for the various times during the day when this rip-roaring stunt cavalcade hits the stage. A specially-made movie set creates three different backdrops for Indiana Jones's stunt men and women to put on a dazzling array of clever stunts, scenes and special effects from the Harrison Ford film epics. Again there is an audience participation element and some amusing sub-plots I won't reveal. Queues for the near-45-minute show begin to form up to half an hour before showtime so be prepared for a wait here, but the auditorium holds more than 2,000 so everyone usually gets in. TTTTT.

## Star Tours

**Star Tours**: anyone remotely amused by the *Star Wars* film trilogy will enjoy just queuing up for this ride, a breathtaking seven-minute spin in a Star Speeder. The elaborate walk-in area is full of Star Wars gadgets and gizmos that will completely take your attention away from the fact you often have to wait in line here for up to an hour. From arguing robots C3PO and R2D2 to your robotic 'pilot', everything has a brilliant sense of space travel, and the ride won't disappoint you! Restrictions, no children under three. TTTTT.

**Jim Henson's Muppet*Vision 3-D**: the 3-D is crossed out here and 4-D substituted in its place, so be warned some strange things are about to happen! A wonderful 10-minute holding pen pre-show takes you in to the specially-built Muppet Theater for a 20-minute experience with all of the Muppets, 3-D special effects and much more. When Fozzie Bear points his squirty flower at you, prepare to get wet! It's a gem,

and children in particular will love it. Queues are substantial through the main parts of the day, but Walt Disney World® Resort's queuing expertise always makes them seem shorter than they actually are. AAAAA.

**Honey, I Shrunk The Kids Movie Set Adventure**: this adventure playground for kids gives youngsters the chance to tackle gigantic blades of grass that turn out to be slides, crawl through caves, investigate giant mushrooms and more. However, some may turn round and say 'Yeah. A giant ant. So what?' and head back for the rides. There can be long queues here, too, so arrive early if the kids demand it (and bring plenty of film). TTT. (Kids only).

**BACKSTAGE PASS to '101 Dalmatians'**: the first element of a three-part sequence takes you behind the scenes of Disney film-making. This 25-minute section showcases the recent remake of *101 Dalmatians* starring Glenn Close, with a look inside the clever animal animation, a glimpse of Disney-MGM Studios soundstages and their current productions and finally a full-scale set-up of the world of Cruella De Vil. It is a fascinating tour, but it won't hold the attention of small children and you will find it hard-going with pushchairs. AAA.

**Disney-MGM Studios Backlot Tour**: part two, which takes 35 minutes, starts with some more special effects (including a brave audience 'volunteer' who gets torpedoed and deluged with gallons of water) before you board the special trams for a look at the off-limits part of the Studios. You are introduced to the production backlot, famous 'houses' and props before visiting **Catastrophe Canyon** for a demonstration of special effects that try both to drown you and blow you up! AAA (plus TTTT!).

5

**The Twilight Zone™ Tower of Terror**

You exit into the **American Film Institute Showcase** of costumes, props and set-pieces from recent films like *George of the Jungle*.

**Walt Disney Theater:** The latest film release is featured here with a 25-minute 'The Making Of' show on that epic. Recent features have been *Evita*, *Armageddon* and *Hunchback of Notre Dame*. AAA.

**Voyage of The Little Mermaid**: this 17-minute live performance is primarily for children who have seen and enjoyed the Disney cartoon. Like Legend of the Lion King in the Magic Kingdom® Park it brings together live actors, animation and puppetry to re-create the highlights of the film. Parents will still enjoy the special effects, but queues tend to be surprisingly long so go either early or late. Those in the first few rows may get a little wet. AAA.

**The Magic of Disney Animation**: an amusing and entertaining 45-minute tour through the making of cartoons. It's up to you how you pace the walk-through tour, but don't miss Robin Williams in a special cartoon, *Back To*

*Neverland*, with Walter Cronkite, and the fascinating view of some of Disney's animators at work. It concludes with a film of some of the highlights of Disney's many animated classics, and you will be amazed at how much you have learned in the course of your tour (although small children might be a bit lost by it all). Queues are rarely serious here, so it's a good one for the afternoon. AAAA.

**Fantasmic!:** due to debut in late 1998, this promises to rival IllumiNations at Epcot® as a tour de force of lights, lasers and very special effects. Staged twice a night in a 6,900-seat amphitheatre behind the Tower of Terror, it features the 'dreams' of Mr M Mouse, portrayed as the Sorcerer's Apprentice, through films such as *Pocahontas*, *The Lion King* and *Snow White*, but hijacked by various Disney villains, leading to a tumultuous battle, with Our Hero emerging triumphant in a sparkling finale. Dancing waters, shooting comets, animated fountains, swirling stars, balls of fire and more combine in a truly breathtaking presentation – just watch out for the giant, fire-breathing dragon! AAAAA.

## Tower of Terror

**The Twilight Zone Tower of Terror™**: the tallest landmark in Walt Disney World® Resort (at 189 feet) invites you to experience another dimension in this mysterious Hollywood hotel that time forgot. The exterior is intriguing, the interior is fascinating, the ride is scintillating and the queues are mind-blowing! The only unfortunate aspect of this really thrilling attraction, which is so much more than just the advertised 13-storey free-fall, is the fact that the majority of queuing time is outside in the sun, and, when it is hot, you

© Disney

are almost melting by the time you reach the air-conditioned inner sanctum of the spooky hotel. Typically, just when you think you have got through to the ride itself, there is another queue, but the inner detail is so clever you can spend the time inspecting how realistic it all is – before you enter the Twilight Zone itself. You have been warned! Restrictions, 3ft 6 in. TTTTT.

**'Beauty and the Beast Live On Stage'**: a live performance of the highlights of this recent Disney classic will entertain the whole family for 20 minutes in the nearby Theater of the Stars. Check the daily schedule for showtimes. AAA.

## Parades

Another popular show is **'Disney's The Hunchback of Notre Dame – A Musical Adventure'**, a clever 32-minute musical and animated/puppetry show that highlights the key elements of the Disney film. It is staged five times a day in the Backlot Theater and features a wonderfully elaborate stage setting. AAA. Have your cameras handy in this area for the **Backlot**, a collection of clever façades that give the appearance of city scenery, which you can wander around on foot. In the best Disney tradition, there is also a daily parade of the company's 36th full-length animated feature, **Mulan**, providing a fabulous festival of the film's music, magic and fun that kids adore. AAAA. During peak periods, the **'Sorcery in the Sky'** Fireworks Show presents a dazzling conclusion to the evening. Best viewing point is in front of the Great Movie Ride as a certain mouse makes an appearance at the grand finale.

## Food and shops

While the choice of food may not be wide-ranging, there is always plenty of it and at a reasonable price. **The Hollywood Brown Derby** offers a full-service restaurant in fine Hollywood style (reservations necessary – special Early Evening Value meals from 4–6pm), while **Mama Melrose's Ristorante**

BRIT TIP: I always recommend the Sci-Fi Diner or 50s Prime Time Café to make your main meal here a bit different. There are plenty of ice cream, drinks, popcorn and hot-dog stalls around the park to keep you going as well.

**5**

**Italiano** is a similar table-service Italian option. The **Sci-Fi Dine-In Theater Restaurant** is a big hit with kids as you dine in a mock drive-in cinema, complete with cars as your 'table', waitresses on roller-skates and a big film screen showing corny old black-and-white science fiction clips. The **50s Prime Time Café** is another hilarious dining experience as you sit in mock stage sets from American 50s TV sitcoms and eat meals 'just like Mom used to make'. Watch out for the waiters, who all claim to be your brother and warn you to take your elbows off the table, etc. Reservations are also necessary. Otherwise, choices of fast-food eateries consist of the **ABC Commissary**, **Backlot Express**, **Hollywood & Vine**, **Rosie's Red-Hot Dogs** or the **Soundstage Restaurant** and **The Catwalk Bar** for various counter-service options, from sandwiches and salads to pizza, pasta and fajitas. Disney character meals are also available at the Soundstage Restaurant for breakfast and lunch ($13.95 and $14.95 for adults, $7.95 and $9.95 for 3–11s) but you need to book first thing for these.

There are also 18 gift and speciality shops to be investigated, 7 of them along Hollywood Boulevard which are worth checking out in early afternoon between the morning and evening crowds. Look out for **Sid Caheunga's One-Of-A-Kind** (just to the right of the main entrance gates as you look out) which stocks rare movie and TV items, including many celebrity autographs, the **Legends of Hollywood** (on Sunset Boulevard) for a rather different range of souvenirs and **It's A Wonderful Shop** (in the Backlot) for Christmas gifts and collectibles. **Keystone Clothiers** (at the top of Hollywood Boulevard) offer some of the best Disney apparel in any of the parks. Otherwise all the main rides and film attractions have their own shops.

# Walt Disney World® Resort at Christmas

While Walt Disney World is a wonderfully exciting place to visit at any time of the year, its theme parks (and the big resort hotels) take on extra character over the Christmas and New Year period. And, if you can visit prior to the seriously busy days from just before Christmas Day to New Year's Day, you get the benefit of all the added decorations and atmosphere and none of the overwhelming crowds.

Each of the three parks takes on a suitably festive character, with the addition of artistic artificial snow, Xmas lights and a huge, magnificently decorated fir tree.

**Disney-MGM Studios** also features an eye-popping extravaganza of original exterior house decorations on the Backlot Tour that actually adorned a family home before becoming an attraction in their own right. Don't try to count the lights – there are more than 2 million!

**The Magic Kingdom® Park** turns Main Street into its Christmas extravaganza, with the 60-foot tree dominating the seasonal scene. There is also the unmissable Mickey's Very Merry Xmas Parade, which replaces the 3pm Disney's Magical Moments Parade in December. This is a positive delight for its lively music and eye-catching costumes, full of Disney characters like Mickey, Minnie, Goofy and Chip 'n' Dale, and the action and excitement will easily keep the attention of the whole family for its 20-minute duration. Another seasonal extra is the Twas The Night Before Xmas Show at the Galaxy Palace Theater, with lots of lively singing and dancing from various Disney characters and the Kids of the Kingdom group, a well-choreographed and highly enthusiastic bunch who really make the show come alive with plenty of Xmas spirit.

**Epcot®** is the jewel in the Christmas crown, though, with two outstanding extra features which really serve to light up the Yule scene, almost literally. At 6pm, the elaborate daily Christmas tree lighting ceremony is quite breathtaking as the rest of the park lights go out and then the World Showcase bridge and the tree itself are illuminated in dramatic stages to some grand musical accompaniment. This is followed by the twice-nightly Candlelight Procession in the American Gardens Theater. This is another large-scale production, featuring a 200-strong choir who file on to the stage carrying battery-powered candles, to join a full orchestra and guest narrator to sing traditional carols and tell the Biblical story of the very first Christmas. It is tasteful, dramatic and eye-catching, but you should arrive EARLY for a seat as people start queueing two hours in advance!

# Disney's Animal Kingdom™ Theme Park

Disney's newest, smartest and most radical theme park opened its gates for the first time in April 1998 to huge public acclaim. For my money, once the final area of Asia is fully open in early 1999, it represents an outstanding and completely different park experience from anything Disney have so far attempted. With its emphasis on nature and conservation, it largely avoids the non-stop thrills and attractions which mark out the other three parks and instead offers a change of pace, a more peaceful and relaxing motif, as well as Disney's usual seamless entertainment style – plus two serious thrill rides!

The number of attractions are relatively few, just three out-and-out rides, plus two scenic journeys, two elaborate nature trails, five shows, including the hilarious 3-D film It's Tough to be A Bug! and the full-blown theatre of Festival of the Lion King, an elaborate adventure playground, petting zoo and Disney character greeting area. It's a far cry from the intense hustle-bustle of the Magic Kingdom® Park, and it carries

**5**

## Disney's Animal Kingdom™ Theme Park at-a-glance

| | |
|---|---|
| **Location** | Directly off Osceola Parkway, also via World Drive and Buena Vista Drive. |
| **Size** | 500 acres divided into 6 'lands' |
| **Hours** | 7am–7 or 8pm |
| **Admission** | Under 3-free, 3–9, $34 (1-day ticket), $151 (5-Day Park Hopper), $219 (7-Day All-in-One Hopper); adult (10+) $42, $189, $274. |
| **Parking** | $5 |
| **Lockers** | Yes; either side of Entrance Plaza; $5 ($2 refundable) |
| **Pushchairs/** | $6 ($1 refundable) at Garden Gate Gifts, through entrance on right) |
| **Wheelchairs** | $6 ($1 refund) and $40 ($10 refund), same location |
| **Top Attractions** | Countdown to Extinction, Kilimanjaro Safaris, It's Tough To Be A Bug, Tiger River Rapids (in 1999), Festival of the Lion King |
| **Don't Miss** | Gorilla Falls Exploration Trail, Conservation Station, dining at Rainforest Café |
| **Hidden Costs** | **Meals** Burger, chips and coke $7.40 |
| | **Kids' meal** $3.49 |
| | **T-shirts** $16–$36 |
| | **Souvenirs** $3–$50 |
| | **Sundries** Mickey Mouse safari hat $16 |

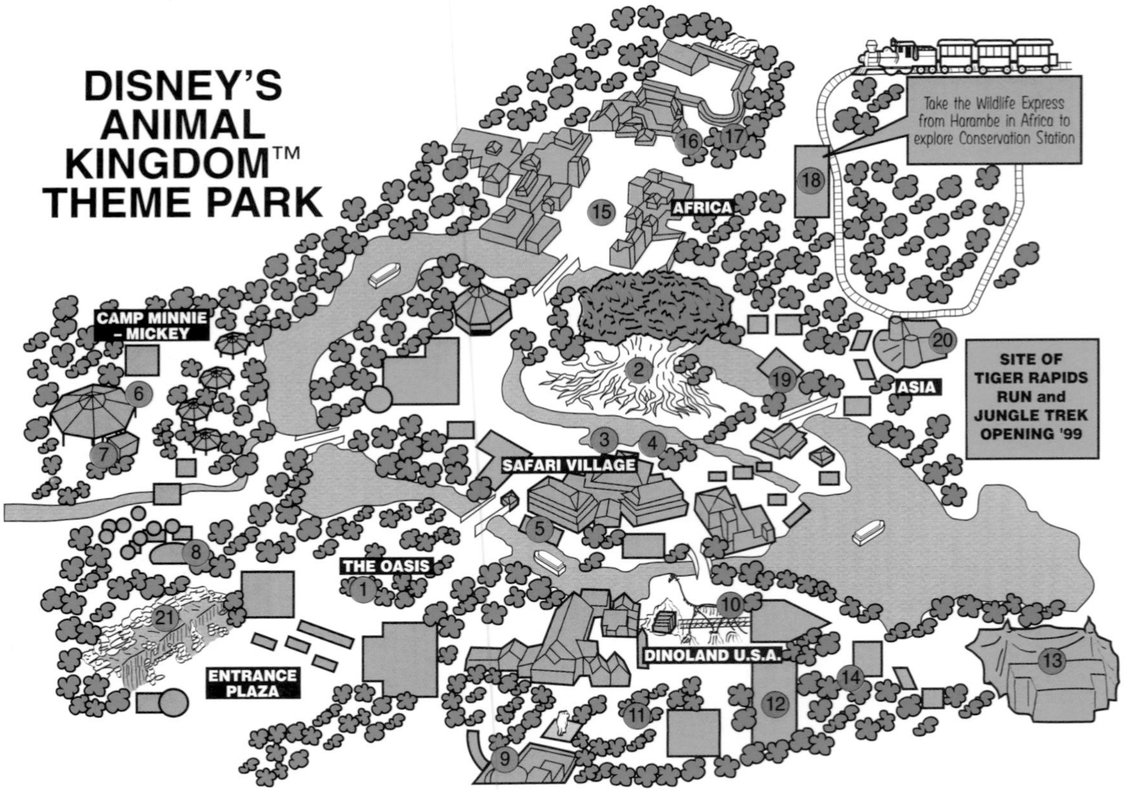

**THE OASIS**

1  THE OASIS TROPICAL GARDEN

**SAFARI VILLAGE**

2  THE TREE OF LIFE

3  THE TREE OF LIFE GARDEN

4  IT'S TOUGH TO BE A BUG!

5  DISCOVERY RIVER BOATS AT
   SAFARI VILLAGE

**CAMP MINNIE-MICKEY**

6  CHARACTER GREETING AREA

7  FESTIVAL OF THE LION KING

8  GRANDMOTHER WILLOW'S GROVE

**DINOLAND USA**

9  COUNTDOWN TO EXTINCTION

10 THE BONEYARD

11 CRETACEOUS TRAIL

12 DINOSAUR JUBILEE

13 JOURNEY INTO JUNGLE BOOK

14 FOSSIL PREPARATION LAB

**AFRICA**

15 HARAMBE

16 KILIMANJARO SAFARIS

17 GORILLA FALLS

18 WILDLIFE EXPRESS

**ASIA**

19 DISCOVERY RIVER BOATS AT
   UPCOUNTRY LANDING

20 FLIGHTS OF WONDER

21 RAINFOREST CAFÉ

DISNEY'S ANIMAL KINGDOM™ THEME PARK

Take the Wildlife Express from Harambe in Africa to explore Conservation Station

SITE OF TIGER RAPIDS RUN and JUNGLE TREK OPENING '99

**Discovery River Boat trip**

a strong environmental message that aims to create a greater understanding of the world's ecological problems. School-age children should find it quite educational, though younger kids may be a little left out. It is outrageously scenic, notably with the 145-foot Tree of Life and the Kilimanjaro Safaris, but it won't overwhelm you with Disney's usual sense of grand style. Rather, it is a chance to experience a part of the world that is both threatened and threatening in a safe, secure manner. It is obviously not the Real Thing in nature terms, but it does open up a vital taste of some of the world's most majestic areas to people who would otherwise never have the chance to see them. Ultimately, this is where ecology and Disney's commercial touch meet and find a peaceful co-existence.

The most conclusive word on Disney's first full-blown animal adventure goes to professor David Bellamy, who said: 'This park has been designed and looked after by the best animal welfare people you can think of. Bad zoos are bad news and should be closed down, but good zoos are good news and the only hope for keeping about 500 species of animals alive in the future'. And that's good enough for me.

## Getting there

If you are staying in the Kissimmee area, Disney's Animal Kingdom™ Theme Park is the easiest to find. Just get on the (toll) Osceola Parkway and follow it all the way to the toll booths, where the parking fee is $5. Alternatively, coming down I4, take Exit 26 for Epcot® and follow Epcot Drive as far as Buena Vista Drive, which leads on to Osceola Parkway. From the western end of Highway 192,come in on World Drive and then Osceola Parkway.

If you arrive early (which is advisable), you will be able to walk up to the Entrance Plaza. Otherwise, the usual tram system will take you in, so make a note of the area in which you park (e.g. Unicorn, row 67). The Plaza is overlooked by the mountainous Rainforest Café with its 65-foot waterfall, which is a must for an (early) lunch or dinner. The park's scheduled opening time is 7am to allow the animals the earliest opportunity to roam their habitats

**Some of the cast at Disney's Animal Kingdom™ Theme Park**

(they return to secure pens at night). With Orlando getting so hot through the summer months, this early start also gives visitors the best chance to view the animals before they seek shade.

Again, if the queues build up significantly before 7am, opening may well be brought forward – on its first day, April 22, 1998, the huge crowds required a 6am opening, and the gates were closed to new arrivals 75 minutes later when the capacity had been reached!

> BRIT TIP: The early start is especially advised for the Kilimanjaro Safaris. You will see far more in the first few hours of the day than during the afternoon.

For the early birds, here is your best plan of campaign. Once through the gates, animal lovers should head first for Kilimanjaro Safaris, through the Oasis, Safari Village and into Africa. From there, head straight into Pangani Forest Exploration Trail and you will have experienced two of the most satisfying animal encounters in the park. Alternatively, thrill-seekers should turn right in Safari Village and head for DinoLand USA, where Countdown to Extinction is the big attraction. With that one safely under your belt before the serious crowds arrive, head back through the Village to Asia and Tiger River Rapids raft ride (once this area is fully open), the other five-star ride. Right, those are your main tactics, here is the full rundown of what's on offer.

## The Oasis

This is a gentle, walk-through introduction to the park, a rocky, tree-covered area featuring several animal habitats and studded with streams, waterfalls and lush plant life. Here you will meet miniature deer, macaws, parrots, iguanas, sloths and tree kangaroos in a wonderfully understated environment that leads you across a stone bridge and brings you out into the main open park area. AAA.

## Safari Village

This hugely colourful 'village' is the hub of the Animal Kingdom, from which the other four lands radiate. Its theme is a tropical artists' colony, with animal-inspired artwork everywhere, four main shops and two eateries.

**Tree of Life:** this 145ft-high arboreal edifice is the centrepiece of the park, an awesome creation that seems to give off a different perspective from wherever you view it. The 'trunk' and 'roots' are covered in 325 animal carvings representing the Circle of Life, from the dolphin to the lion. Paths lead round the Tree, interspersed with more natural animal habitats that showcase flamingos, otters, ring-tailed lemurs, macaws, axis deer, tamarin monkeys, cranes, storks, ducks and tortoises. For stats lovers, the Tree canopy spreads 160ft wide, the trunk is 50ft wide and the roots spread out 170ft in diameter. There are 103,000 leaves (all attached by hand) on more than 8,000 branches! AAAA.

**It's Tough to be A Bug!:** winding down among the Tree's roots brings you 'underground' to a 430-seat theatre and another example of Disney's artistry in 3-D films and special effects. This hysterically funny eight-minute show, a homage to 80% of the animal world, features grasshoppers, beetles, spiders, stink bugs and termites (beware the 'acid' spray!) as well as a number of tricks I couldn't possibly reveal. Queues build up from midday onwards, but they do move quite steadily. AAAAA.

**Discovery River Boats:** this one-way trip to Asia is surprisingly busy during the main part of the day. Surprising because it is a fairly gentle scenic ride, rather like a tamer, grown-up version of the Jungle Cruise at Magic Kingdom® Park, providing a circular journey around the Village and its peculiar collection of sights, such as steaming geysers and yet more exotic animals. Your boat host will also introduce you to some smaller members of the park along the way (tarantulas, anyone?). AAA.

Safari Village also features the innovative **March of the ARTimals** twice a day, a procession of 'living art' that is an eye-catching showcase of the talents of the local costume designers, stilt-walkers, sculptors, basket-makers and weavers, the **Safari Village Band**, who combine music with the sounds of nature, and Animal Tales, Disney storytellers in native dress who combine mime, puppetry and acting.

Shopping is at a premium here, too, with a huge range of merchandise, souvenirs and gifts (notably in **Disney Outfitters** and **Island Mercantile**), while the two counter-service restaurants, **Pizzafari** and **Flame Tree Barbecue**, are possibly the best of the park's rather average eating options (with the exception of the Rainforest Café). Indeed, provided it is not too hot, the Flame Tree Barbecue offers quite a relaxing and picturesque experience, set among some pretty gardens, pools and fountains on the edge of Discovery River.

## Camp Minnie-Mickey

This woodland retreat features gently winding paths and some more of Disney's typically clever scenery, like the benches, lighting and the gurgling stream, with Donald Duck

and his nephews hiking down the side, that develops into a series of kid-friendly squirt fountains.

**Character Greeting Areas:** here, four trails lead to a series of jungle encounters with Disney characters like Mickey and Minnie (naturally), Winnie the Pooh and Tigger, Chip 'n' Dale, Baloo and King Louie, Timon and Rafiki. AAAAA (for kids).

**Festival of the Lion King** at Lion King Theater: not to be missed, this high-powered 40-minute production brings the hit film to life in quite spectacular fashion with giant, moving stages, huge animated figures, singers, dancers, acrobats and stilt-walkers. All the well-known Lion King songs are given an airing in a coruscation of colour and sound, and it serves to underline the quality Disney bring to their live production shows. Its quality is matched only by its popularity – people begin queuing a good 30 minutes in advance for the 1,000-seater amphitheatre. Try to take in either the first show of the day or the last. AAAA.

**'Friends from the Animal Forest' at Grandmother Willow's Grove**, based on characters from the Disney classic *Pocahontas*, this 15-minute show sees various animals – racoons, rabbits, cranes, a skunk, armadillo and porcupine – interacting with the central live actress and Mother Willow in the question of who can save the forest. It doesn't seem to do much for small children, there is not much shade in the summer and it is standing room only once the 350 seats have been filled. AAA.

## DinoLand USA

Rather at odds with the natural theming of the rest of the park, DinoLand is a full-scale palaeontology exercise, with this

© Disney

**The Festival of the Lion King**

mock 'town' taken over by a university fossil dig. Energetically tongue-in-cheek (the 'students' who work in the area have the motto 'Been there, dug that' and you enter under a mock brachiosaurus skeleton, the Oldengate Bridge – ouch!), it still features some genuine and fascinating glimpses into dinosaur research at the **Fossil Preparation Lab** and the **Dinosaur Jubilee** mini-museum of artefacts (if it is retained beyond 1998).

**Countdown to Extinction:** here is the park's main claim to fame for thrill ride fans, a mind-blowingly realistic journey back to the end of the Cretaceous Period and the giant meteor that put paid to dinosaur life. You enter the high-tech Dino Institute, 'a discovery center and on-going research lab dedicated to uncovering the mysteries of the past', to be presented with a multi-media show of dinosaur history that leads you in to a briefing room. Here you learn your 'mission', to go back 65 million years for a glimpse of Cretaceous life. However, one of the institute's scientists hijacks your journey for his own project, to capture a dinosaur just before the fateful meteor's arrival, and you are sent careering through the sights, sound and even smells of a sunless, prehistoric jungle in your 12-passenger Time Rover. The menace of a carnivorous carnotaurus, the unpredictable lurching of your vehicle and the impending threat of the meteor add up to a breathtaking whizz through a stunning environment. You will need to ride at least twice to appreciate all the clever details, but queues build up quickly, so go either first thing or late in the day. Expectant mothers and anyone who suffers from heart, back or neck problems or motion sickness are advised not to ride, while the height restriction is 46 inches as it is likely to terrify young children. TTTT plus AAAAA!

> **BRIT TIP:** The best ride in your Time Rover is at the front left of the car for maximum effect of the twists and turns and the dinosaur menace.

**The Boneyard:** a hugely imaginative adventure playground, it offers kids the chance to slip, slide and climb through the 'fossilised' remains of triceratops and brontosaurs, explore caves, dig for bones and splash through a mini-waterfall. The amusing signage will go over the heads of most kids, but it is ideal for parents to let their young 'uns loose for up to an hour (although not just after the neighbouring Jungle Book show has finished). TTTT (kids only).

**'Journey into Jungle Book'** at Theater in the Wild: another highly theatrical musical presentation, with actors in elaborate costumes and innovative puppetry in a faithful recreation of the film and its songs. Arrive a good 15–30 minutes early on busy days as the 1,500-seater

**The Boneyard adventure playground**

amphitheatre fills up quickly. AAAA.

**Cretaceous Trail:** landscaped, walk-through animal encounter featuring lush, tropical forest and 'living' dinosaurs like soft-shelled turtles and Chinese crocodiles. AA.

Dining options include the **Restaurantosaurus**, counter-service burgers and hot dogs (presented by McDonald's, so you get McDonald's fries, Chicken McNuggets and Happy Meals but no Big Macs) and two snack bars, while shopping is centred on **Chester and Hester's Dinosaur Treasures**, the 'Fossiliferous Gift Store' with groan-inducing slogans like Merchandise of Extinction, Prehistoric Prices and Last Stop for 65 Million Years!

> BRIT TIP: Restauranto-saurus also features Donald's Prehistoric Breakfastosaurus from 7am–10.30am with Donald Duck and other character favourites. It costs $14.95 for adults and $8.95 for 3–11s.

## Africa

The largest land in Disney's Animal Kingdom™ Theme Park, it recreates the forests, grasslands and rocky homelands of equatorial Africa's most fascinating residents in a richly landscaped setting that is part run-down port town setting and part endless savannah. The outside world seems thousands of miles away and there is hardly a glimpse of Walt Disney World® Resort (there is one, but I'm not telling!).

**Harambe**, a reconstruction Kenyan port village, complete with white-coral walls and thatched roofs, is the starting point for your African adventure. The Arab-influenced Swahili culture is depicted in the native tribal costumes and architecture. Here you will find two more shops, including the **Mombasa Marketplace Ziwani Traders**, where you can suit up safari-style, and the counter-service **Tusker House Restaurant** for spit-roasted prime rib, rotisserie and fried chicken and salads as well as four snack and drink outlets. Themed

5

**Kilimanjaro Safaris**

entertainment, with the African Contemporary Band, adds spice to the location and whets the appetite for the attractions in store.

**Kilimanjaro Safaris**: the queuing area alone earns high marks for authenticity, preparing you for the sights and sounds of the 110-acre savannah beyond. You board a 32-passenger truck, with your driver/guide relaying information about the flora and fauna on view and a bush pilot overhead relaying stats on the wildlife, including the dangers threatening them in the real world. Hundreds of animals are carefully spread out in various habitats, with no fences in sight – the ditches and barriers are all well concealed – as you splash through fords and cross rickety bridges (will one of them collapse?), and you are likely to get a close-up view of rhinos, elephants,

BRIT TIP: The best (and most jolting) ride is at the back of the truck, while the Safari is best avoided from midday to late afternoon when many animals take a siesta.

giraffes, zebras, lions, baboons, antelope, ostriches and hippos. Half way round, your journey becomes a grim race to stop elephant poachers, although the outcome is fairly obvious. Once again, the authentic nature of everything you see (okay, so some of the tyre 'ruts' and termite mounds are concrete and the baobab trees are fake) is quite awesome with the spread of the vegetation and the landscaping, and the only drawbacks are the lack of photo stops along the route (and the ride can be pretty bumpy), while you are not guaranteed to see some of the animals as they are free to roam over quite a large area and can

disappear from view. The ride is not recommended for anyone with back or neck problems or expectant mothers. AAAA.

**Pangani Forest Exploration Trail**: as you leave the Safari you turn into an overgrown nature trail that showcases gorillas, hippos, meerkats, rare tropical birds and naked mole rats(!). You wander the trail at your own pace and visit several research stations where you can learn more about the animals on display, including the swarming, ant-like colony of naked mole rats (see, I wasn't making it up), the underwater view of the hippos (check out the size of a hippo skull and those teeth!) and the savannah overlook, where giraffe and antelope graze and the amusing meerkats frolic. The walk-through aviary gives you the chance to meet the carmine bee-eater, pygmy goose, African green pigeon, ibis and brimstone canary, among others, but the real centrepiece of the Trail is the Silverback gorilla habitat, in fact, two of them. The family group can often be seen just inches away from the giant plate-glass window, while the bachelor group further along can prove more elusive. Again, the sheer natural aspect of the Trail is breath-taking and it provides a host of good photo opportunities. It is best to visit early in the day to see the animals at their most active. AAAAA.

**Wildlife Express to Conservation Station**: the clever little train journey here, with its peek into some of the back-stage areas, is just the preamble to the park's interactive and educational exhibits, including the **Affection Section**, the petting zoo of lambs, goats, donkeys, sheep and guinea hogs. The main part of Conservation Station is quite educational, though, and aimed at children with enquiring minds. The first exhibits are interactive information stations about the environment and ecological dangers in **Song of the Rain Forest**, and the story progresses through endangered species like the manatee at the **Mermaid Tales Theater** to a self-guided tour of the park's back-stage areas on interactive screens and the work of the world's eco-heroes, who can also be quizzed on screen. Finally, you can look into the wildlife tracking centre, the animal hospital, bird hatchery and neonatal care centre. You could easily spend an hour here as the environmental message sinks home, along with that of Disney's Wildlife Conservation Fund.

## Asia

The final land of the park was still in developmental stage at the end of 1998, awaiting its full opening as the gateway to the imaginary south-east Asian city of Anandapur, with its temples, ruined forts, landscape and wildlife.

**'Flights of Wonder' at Caravan Stage:** another wildlife show, this one showcases the talents and traits of a host of birds, built into a production of mythical proportions as a treasure-seeking student encounters Phoenix, the birds' guardian, in a crumbling, fortified town. Vultures, eagles, toucans, macaws and many other feathered friends take a bow as Phoenix reveals the treasure of the avian world. Unfortunately, the Caravan Stage where all this takes place lacks any shelter from the sun and is fiendishly hot in summer. AAA.

**Discovery River Boats:** this is the other half of the journey from Safari Village and again draws quite long queues through the day. AAA.

**Tiger Rapids Run:** due to open early in 1999, this should be the park's other serious thrill ride, a bouncing, threatening, watery raft journey that also reveals the ecological dangers of wholesale clear-cut burning of the forests. Watch out for the scenic delights of the Painted Pavilion and the Tiger Temple along the way, as well as the logging truck that threatens to fall on your raft! You will also get quite wet, which is not something you want to do first thing in the day during the winter months. TTTTT (expected).

**Maharajah Jungle Trek:** Asia's version of the Gorilla Falls Trail, a walk-through encounter past decaying temple ruins, with Komodo Dragons, an aviary with bats and flying foxes, extensive tiger enclosure, gibbon towers and hoof-stock overlook. AAAAA (expected).

Asia plans also promise a new restaurant, and the area's completion should make for a satisfying experience for all park visitors.

Finally, returning to the front entrance gives you the chance to sample or just visit (and shop at) the **Rainforest Café**, the second in Walt Disney World® Resort. If you haven't seen the one at Downtown Disney Marketplace, you should definitely call in here to sample the amazing jungle interior with its audio-animatronic animals, waterfalls, thunderstorms and unique bar area. A three-course meal would set you back about $23 (kids meals at $5.99), but the setting alone is worth it and the food is way above average.

## We want to hear from you

Now, that is the current Brit's Guide view after visits in both April and June 1998, but the park is still taking shape and YOU can play a part in our research by passing on any tips and observations to the address at the back of the book.

# Four More of the Best
## (or, Expanding Orlando's Universe)

It is finally time to leave wonderful **Walt Disney World®** behind and venture out into the rest of central Florida's great choice of attractions. And, believe me, there is still a terrific amount in store.

For a start, they don't come much more ambitious than Universal Studios Escape. The area that used to consist of just the one theme park, Universal Studios Florida®, is fast developing into a fully-fledged resort of similar scope to Walt Disney World. A second dynamic theme park, Universal's Island of Adventure, opens in 1999, hot on the heels of the 30-acre CityWalk entertainment district. The first resort hotel, the Portofino Bay, opens later in 1999, followed by the

Hard Rock Hotel in 2000 and at least three more by 2005. At the same time, the whole site will feature its own transportation systems of water carriages, ferries, trams and motor coaches as well as walking and biking thoroughfares, in addition to their 20,000-vehicle car parks. There are also plans for a golf course.

The marketing alliance with SeaWorld, Busch Gardens and Wet 'n' Wild has proved another success, with the 7- and 10-day FlexTickets being seen as excellent value. The opening of Universal's Islands of Adventure will add a 3-day Studios Islands pass for about £65 (3–9s £52) and a 3-day Plus that adds admission to the live music clubs at CityWalk for £79 (adults) and £65 (3–9s).

**Universal's famous rotating globe marks the entrance to the Studios**

1 KONGFRONTATION
2 TWISTER
3 ISLANDS OF ADVENTURE PREVIEW CENTER
4 HERCULES & XENA PRODUCTION SPECIAL
5 PRODUCTION CENTRAL
6 HITCHCOCK'S 3-D THEATER
7 NICKELODEON STUDIO TOUR
8 TERMINATOR 2 3-D
9 THE FUNTASTIC WORLD OF HANNA-BARBERA
10 LUCY: A TRIBUTE
11 THE BONEYARD
12 EARTHQUAKE – THE BIG ONE
13 JAWS
14 BEETLEJUICE'S GRAVEYARD REVUE
15 THE WILD, WILD, WILD WEST STUNT SHOW
16 DYNAMITE NIGHTS STUNTACULAR
17 BACK TO THE FUTURE . . . THE RIDE
18 ANIMAL ACTORS SHOW
19 FIEVEL'S PLAYLAND
20 ET ADVENTURE
21 THE GORY, GRUESOME & GROTESQUE HORROR MAKE-UP SHOW
22 AT & T AT THE MOVIES
23 A DAY IN THE PARK WITH BARNEY
24 THE BLUES BROTHERS

# Universal Studios Florida®

Universal opened its Florida park in June 1990 (it has had its original Los Angeles site open to the public since before World War II) and quickly became a serious competitor to Disney. The two are currently going head-to-head with all their new attractions and, for the visitor, it means a consistently high standard and good value in everything on offer (although the choice is beginning to be utterly bewildering!). Also, if you have already been to the LA Universal Studios, this one is better.

The obvious question to ask here is whether you need to go to Disney-MGM Studios as well as Universal, and the answer is an emphatic YES! Universal is a very different kettle of fish to Disney-MGM Studios, with a more in-your-face style of entertainment that goes down well with older kids and younger adults. Younger children are also well catered for in Fievel's Playland and the A Day In The Park With Barney show. Universal can require more than a full day in high season. As with Disney's parks, the strategies for a successful visit are the same. Arrive EARLY (i.e. up to

## Universal Studios Florida® at a glance

| | |
|---|---|
| **Location** | 1000 Universal Studios Plaza, off Kirkman Road and Turkey Lake Road (Junction 30B off I4) |
| **Size** | 444 acres in 6 themed areas |
| **Hours** | 9am–7pm off peak; 9am–10pm high season (Washington's Birthday, Easter, Summer holidays, Thanksgiving, Christmas) |
| **Admission** | Under 3-free; 3–9, $34 (1-day ticket), $52 (2-day ticket), $82.95 (7-day Flex Ticket), $107.95 (10-day Flex Ticket); adult (10+) $42, $62, $99.95, $129.95 |
| **Parking** | $6 |
| **Lockers** | Yes; opposite Guest Relations in Front Lot; 4 × 25c |
| **Pushchairs/ Wheelchairs** | $6 (next to First Union Bank) to right of main entrance $6 and $30 (same location) |
| **Top Attractions** | Jaws, Back To The Future, ET, Earthquake, Kongfrontation, Terminator 2 3-D, Twister |
| **Don't Miss** | Dynamite Nights Spectacular, dining at Hard Rock Café |
| **Hidden Costs** | **Meals** Burger, chips and coke $6.58<br>Three-course dinner $19.15 (Hard Rock Café) |
| | **Kids' meal**    $3.99 |
| | **T-shirts**    $16.95–$24.95 |
| | **Souvenirs**    $2.95–$189.95 |
| | **Sundries**    Universal Studios PAL video $19.95 |

45 minutes before the official opening time), do the main rides first, avoid main meal times if you want to eat, and step out for a few hours in the afternoon (try shopping or dining at CityWalk) if the crowds get too much.

Highlights are the new Twister attraction, Terminator 2 3-D show, five-star simulator ride Back To The Future (state of the art technology here), the Jaws ride, the Funtastic World of Hanna-Barbera (another simulator, slightly toned down for young children) and the other two blockbuster rides of King Kong and Earthquake. Queues at all of these top an hour at peak periods, and even the smaller attractions get seriously busy.

## Location

Universal Studios Florida® is sub-divided into six main areas, set around a huge, man-made lagoon, but there are no great distinguishing features between many of them so keep your map handy to steer yourself around. The main entrance is found just off the new exit to I4 or by the Universal Boulevard link from International Drive by Wet 'n' Wild. Parking costs $6 in their massive new multi-storey car park (one of the largest in the world) and there is quite a walk (with some moving walk-ways) to the front gates. Once through with the madding crowd, your best bet is to turn right on to Rodeo Drive, along Hollywood Boulevard and Sunset Boulevard and into Expo Center for Back to the Future … The Ride. From there, head straight across the bridge to Jaws, then go back along the Embarcadero for Earthquake and into New York for Twister and Kongfrontation. This will get most of the main rides under your belt early on before the crowds really build up, and you can then take it a bit easier by putting your feet up for

a while at one of the several shows. Alternatively, try to be among the early birds flocking to the blockbuster Terminator show at the entrance to Hollywood Boulevard to avoid the queues that build up very quickly for this much-publicised attraction, then head for Back to the Future.

Here's a full blow-by-blow guide to the Studios.

## The Front Lot

Coming straight through the gates brings you into **The Front Lot**, which is basically the administrative centre, with a couple of large gift stores (have a look at these in mid-afternoon) plus The Fudge Shoppe and the Beverly Hills Boulangerie (sandwiches, pastries and tea and coffee). Call at Guest Services here for written guides for disabled visitors, TDD and assisted listening devices, as well as to make restaurant bookings. First aid is available here and on Canal Street between New York and San Francisco, while there are facilites for nursing mothers at Family Services by the bank through the gates on the right.

## Production Central

Ahead and to the left is **Production Central**, and this brings you into the main business of the park.

**Hitchcock's 3-D Theater**: this tribute to the film-making genius of the late Alfred Hitchcock is a touch over-long for most children at 40 minutes, although it has three separate elements to keep you guessing at 'What Happens next?' The 3-D effects from his horror film *The Birds* come to the rescue of the first section, which is basically just a series of clips from his 53 films for Universal Studios. Next up is a re-creation of the famous shower scene from *Psycho*, with an audience 'volunteer' and a neat twist at the

**The five-storey tornado at Twister**

end, and finally some more special effects from *The 39 Steps* are explained with film techniques. Queues build up quickly here after opening time, so save it for late in the day. It also advises parental discretion for children under 13, but few seem put off by the horror elements, which are fairly tame by modern standards. TTT.

**Nickelodeon Studios**: a lot of this American kids' TV series will be lost on us Brits (although it's now on satellite TV in Britain) as visitors are taken behind the scenes into the production set. All kids will be able to identify, however, with the chance to get gunged in green slime by the Gakmeister! And they'll love the rest rooms which feature green slime 'soap' and sirens when you flush the loo. Long queues build up quickly, though. AAA.

**The Funtastic World of Hanna-Barbera**: this is one of Universal's simulator rides that is always a big hit with kids. It involves a cartoon chase of the funniest order, with your seats becoming jet-propelled in the bid to save an all-star cartoon cast. Humongous queues, so go either first thing or late. Expectant mothers, those with heart, back or neck problems and children under

3ft 4in must use the stationary seats. TTTT.

The **Bone Yard** is now a rather depleted area reserved for famous old props after they were discarded by the films in which they starred. AA.

Next door to the Bone Yard, **Production Central** is a temporary seasonal exhibit offering a close-up

> **BRIT TIP:** The interactive do-it-yourself cartoon world as you exit the ride (in the Hanna-Barbera Store) is also a great place for parents to unleash the kids for half an hour (or when it rains).

look at props and scenery from recent Hollywood film blockbusters like *The Lost World* and *Jurassic Park*. AAA.

**Hercules and Xena – Wizards of the Screen:** This replaced the old Murder She Wrote show in 1997 and features the two TV heroes in full action mode. It goes behind the scenes to explain how the programmes are produced and

**The Great White Shark**

**Six tons of howling fury awaits visitors in Kongfrontation**

blends specially-created 'live' action, with stunt actors and clever film and sound effects, with audience volunteers helping out when the latest episode goes awry. Experience exotic creatures, evil gods and true, sword-wielding heroism, then buy the T-shirt! TTT.

The main eating outlet here is the **Studio Stars Restaurant**, which features an all-you-can-eat buffet plus a full à la carte menu with tempting seafood, pizza, pasta and sandwiches. Shopping includes the Hanna-Barbera Store, Jurassic Park Visitors' Center and Bates Motel Gift Shop.

## New York

From Production Central you head on to **New York** and some great scene-setting in the architecture and detail of the buildings and streets.

It's far too clean to be authentic, but the façades are first class and worth a closer look.

**Twister:** newly-opened in 1998, this experience, based on the hit film, breaks new ground in live special effects as audiences are brought 'up close and personal' with the awesome destructive forces of a tornado. The five-storey terror will shatter everything in its path, building to a shattering crescendo of

**Beetlejuice's Graveyard Revue**

destruction (watch out for the flying cow!). The noise is quite stunning, but it's a bit much for young children. The pre-show area is almost a work of art but, unless you can get here early, save this for late in the day. TTTT.

**Kongfrontation**: Universal's engineers have really gone to town on this attraction, a full-scale encounter with the giant ape on a replica of the Roosevelt Island tram. The startlingly real special effects (King Kong even has banana breath!) and clever spiel of your tram driver all add up to a breathtaking experience that will convince you that you have met King Kong and lived to tell the tale. It's only a five-minute ride and queues regularly top an hour, so going early is the best plan of campaign. TTTT.

**The Blues Brothers**: fans of the film will not want to miss this live show as Jake and Elwood Blues (well, pretty good doubles, anyway) put on a stormin' performance on New York's Delancey Street four or five times a day. They cruise up in their Bluesmobile and go through a selection of the film's hits before heading off into the sunset, stopping only to sign a few autographs. Terrific entertainment, not to be missed. AAAA.

**Islands of Adventure Preview Center**: Next to Kongfrontation, here's your chance to see what Universal have in store in their new theme park. All five Islands are explained in eye-catching detail and there is a fascinating overview of the whole Universal Studios Escape development – all $2.6 billion of it! AAA.

For your dining convenience (or so it says here), you have the choice of two contrasting restaurants. **Finnegan's Bar and Grill** offers the likes of shepherd's pie, fish and chips, corned beef and cabbage along with more traditional New York fare like prime rib, burgers,

fries and beer as well as live Irish-tinged entertainment and Happy Hour from 5–7pm (half-price beer and wine). **Louie's Italian Restaurant** has counter-service pizza and pasta, Italian ice cream and the delicious tiramisu (the Italian version of trifle only jazzier). For shops you have the choice of Safari Outfitters Ltd (and the chance to have your picture taken in the grip of King Kong!), The Aftermath for Twister souvenirs, Bull's Gym for athletic apparel and collectibles and Second Hand Rose, a thrift shop featuring old collectibles, antiques and clothing. New York also boasts a particularly noisy, and therefore kid-friendly, amusement arcade presented by Sega.

## San Francisco/Amity

Crossing Canal Street brings you all the way across America to **San Francisco/Amity** and two of the biggest queues in the park.

**Earthquake – The Big One**: this three-part adventure has them lining up from first thing in the morning until almost last thing at night. Go behind the scenes first of all to two special stage sets where, with audience help, some of the special effects of the blockbuster film, starring Charlton Heston, are explained in detail. Then you enter the Bay Area Rapid Transit underground and arrive in the middle of a full-scale earthquake that will shake you to your boots. Tremble as the walls and ceilings collapse, trains collide, cars fall in on you and fire erupts all around, followed by a seeming tidal wave of water. It's not for the faint-hearted (or small children), while those who have bad backs or necks, or are pregnant, are advised not to ride. TTTT.

**Jaws**: the technological wizardry alone will leave you gasping on this attraction, where queues of more than an hour are commonplace. The man-made lagoon holds five million gallons of water; nearly 2,000 miles of wire run throughout the seven-acre site, which required 10,000 cubic yards of concrete and 7,500 tons of steel; and the 32-foot monster shark attacks with a thrust equal to a Boeing 727 jet engine! Yes, this is no ordinary ride (at more than $45m to build, it couldn't be) and its six-minute duration will seem a lot longer as your hapless tour boat guide tries to steer you through an ever more spectacular series of stunts, explosions and watery menace from the Great White. Yes, of course it's only a model, but I defy you not to be impressed – and just a little terrified – by this fabulous ride. TTTTT.

**Beetlejuice's Graveyard Revue**: Disney-MGM Studios has Beauty and the Beast and the Little Mermaid, Universal goes for Dracula, Frankenstein, the Wolfman, the Phantom of the Opera and Frankenstein's Bride in this 18-minute musical extravaganza. It eschews completely the twee prettiness of Disney's attractions yet still comes up with a fun family show, with versions of hits like Wild Thing and Great Balls Of Fire all in a spectacular stage setting, especially in the evening. AAAA.

**The Wild, Wild, Wild West Stunt Show**: corny gags, fistfights, explosions, high-level falls and dramatic shootouts all add up to 15 minutes of rootin', tootin' Wild West adventure, Universal Studios style. Hilarious finale and some very loud bangs (not good for small children) are accompanied by large crowds, but the auditorium seats almost 2,000 so there is usually no serious queuing here (provided you arrive 15 minutes early). AAAA.

San Francisco also has the best choice of eating establishments in the park, with **Lombard's Landing** the pick of the bunch (reservations accepted). Great seafood, pasta and sandwiches are accompanied by a good view out over the main lagoon, and there is a separate pastry shop for desserts and coffee. **Richter's Burger Co** offers a few interesting burger variations, while the **Midway Grill** serves smoked sausages and Italian sausage hoagies. For a quick snack, **Chez Alcatraz** has shrimp cocktails, clam chowder and speciality hot sandwiches, **Boardwalk Snacks** does corn dogs, chicken fingers, candy floss and frozen yoghurt and there is a Haagen Dazs ice cream counter.

For shopping, try Quint's Nautical Treasures for seaside souvenirs and Shaiken's Souvenirs for more up-market mementoes. The added attraction of this area is a boardwalk of fairground games (which will cost you an extra few dollars to take part), including a Guess Your Weight stall which usually attracts a good crowd for the fun patter of the person in charge.

## Expo Center

Crossing the footbridge from Amity brings you into **Expo Center** and Universal's other five-star thrill attraction.

**Back To The Future ... The Ride**: simulators just do not come more realistic than this journey through space and time in Dr Emmit Brown's time-travelling De Lorean. The queues are immense, but a lot of the queuing time is taken up by some attention-grabbing pre-ride information on the many TV screens above your head. Once you reach the front of the queue, there is still more information to digest and clever surroundings to convince you of the scientific nature of it all. Then it's into your time-travelling car and off in hot pursuit of baddie Biff, who has stolen another time-car. The huge, wraparound screen and violent movements of your vehicle bring

6

the realism of the ride to a peak, and it all adds up to a huge experience, well worth the wait. Restrictions, 3ft 4in. TTTTT.

**Animal Actors Stage**: prepare to be amazed now by the feats of acting giants like Lassie, Mr Ed, Beethoven and Babe as they put on their own show to upstage all those pesky humans. It's a big theatre, too, and there is never much of a wait, so roll up and see those dogs put their

Excitement at the Terminator 2 experience

6

**Terminator 2 3-D**

trainers through the hoops! This is also a good one to avoid the afternoon crowds. AAAA.

**Fievel's Playland**: strictly for kids but also a big hit with parents for taking them off their hands for a good half hour or so, this playground based on the miniaturised world of the cartoon mouse offers youngsters the chance to bounce under a 1,000-gallon hat, talk to a 20-foot Tiger the Cat, climb a 30-foot spider's web and shoot the rapids (a 200-foot water slide) in Fievel's sardine can. TTTT (young 'uns only!).

**A Day In The Park With Barney**: Again, this is strictly for the younger set (ages two to five). The purple dinosaur from the hugely popular kids' TV show is brought to Super-Dee-Duper life on stage in a 65,000-square foot arena that

features a pre-show before the main event, which lasts about 15 minutes, plus an interactive post-show area. The show and its jokes are guaranteed to make mum and dad cringe, but the youngsters seem to love it and they are the best judges in this instance. PS: Check out the state-of-the-art restrooms! AAA.

**ET Adventure**: this is as glorious as scenic rides come, with a picturesque queuing area made up like the pine woods from the film and then a spectacular leap on the trademark flying bicycles to save ET's home planet. Steven Spielberg (Universal's creative consultant) has added some extra special effects and characters, and the whole experience is a huge hit with young to teenage kids and their parents. Queues here occasionally touch two hours at peak periods, so be aware that you need to do this one either early or late. AAAAA.

For food here there is only one choice – the **Hard Rock Café** (until the larger version opens next to CityWalk). This guitar-shaped restaurant of the internationally famous chain is right next door to Expo Center (past Fievel's Playland and the picture opportunity Bates Motel house), and you need to get a hand stamp to exit the park as it is not part of Universal Studios itself. Hard Rock devotees will make an immediate pilgrimage here, and if you fancy a loud, raucous, rock 'n' roll dining experience, surrounded by the world's largest collection of rock memorabilia, then make sure you get to lunch or dinner EARLY as the queues take some believing. Otherwise, you have the choice of the **International Food Bazaar** (a food court-style indoor diner) offering Greek, Italian, Chinese, German and American dishes in air-conditioned comfort, or **Animal Crackers**, which offers hot dogs, chicken fingers, smoked sausage hoagies and frozen yoghurt. Shop at Back To The Future Gifts, Universal's Cartoon Store, the Barney Store or ET's Toy Closet and Photo Spot.

## Hollywood

Finally, your circular tour of Universal brings you back towards the main entrance via **Hollywood** (where else?). Visit **AT & T At The Movies** for a number of hands-on exhibits taking you through the history and future of film-making. Another unusual attraction is the **Gory, Gruesome and Grotesque Horror Make-Up Show** (not recommended for under 13s) which demonstrates some of the often highly amusing ways in which films have attempted to terrorise us. It's a 20-minute show, queues are rarely long and the secrets of the special

effects are well worth learning. AAA.

**Terminator 2: 3-D Battle Across Time:** another first-of-its-kind attraction, this is quite hard to describe accurately. Part film, part show, part experience but all action, it cost a staggering $60 million to produce and is guaranteed to leave its audience stunned and awed. The 'Wow!' factor really works overtime here as you go through a 10-minute pre-show to represent a trip into the workshops of the Cyberdyne Systems, from the *Terminator* films, and then into a 700-seater auditorium for a 'presentation' on the company's latest robot creations. Needless to say, nothing runs according to plan and the audience is subjected to a mind-boggling array of (loud) special effects, including indoor pyrotechnics, real actors interacting with the screen and the audience, and a climactic 3-D film finale that takes the original film sequence a step further. The original cast, including Arnold Schwarzenegger and director James Cameron, all collaborated on the new 12-minute film footage (which, at $24 million, is the most expensive frame-for-frame film ever made) and the overall effect of this technological marvel is simply dazzling. Needless to say, you need to arrive early or expect queues well in excess of an hour all day. Not recommended for under 13s. TTTTT.

The last attraction (or first, depending on which way you go round the park) is **Lucy: A Tribute**, which will mean little to all but devoted fans of the late Lucille Ball and her 60s TV comedy *The Lucy Show*. Classic shows, home movies, costumes and scripts are all paraded for close viewing, but youngsters will find it rather tedious. AA.

If you haven't eaten by now there is a choice of two contrasting but highly enjoyable eateries, **Mel's Drive-In**, a re-creation from the film *American Graffiti*, serving all manner of burgers, hot dogs and milkshakes to the accompaniment of the Hollywood Hi Tones a cappella quartet who sing 50s tunes several times a day outside, and **Café La Bamba**, a counter-service Mexican diner offering tacos, burgers, barbecue chicken and steak, with margaritas and beer (Happy Hour from 3–6pm). There is also **Schwab's Pharmacy** for old-fashioned milkshakes, sundaes and ice cream cones. Shop for hats in the Brown Derby, for Terminator gifts and clothing in Cyber Image, for movie memorabilia (especially Lucille Ball) at Silver Screen Collectibles and for some of the smartest but most expensive clothing, hats and sunglasses at Studio Styles.

## Photo opportunities

In addition to all the set-piece action, watch out for photo and autograph opportunities with cartoon characters like Scooby Doo, Fred Flintstone, Woody Woodpecker and Yogi Bear, and filmstar lookalikes of Charlie Chaplin, W.C. Fields, Marilyn Monroe and Groucho Marx. Don't be surprised, either, if part of the park is suddenly closed off for filming – these are working film studios.

If you would like to enjoy a character breakfast with some of your favourite cartoon stars, call 407 354 6339 in advance to make a reservation or go first thing to the Guest Relations office (on the right through the main gates). Adults cost $15.50, kids $10. It is staged in different locations and is not always available, so it is advisable to call in advance.

Finally, and this is a big finally, don't leave before the Studios' nightly *tour de force*, the **Dynamite Nights Stunt Spectacular** on the main lagoon, 15 minutes before the park closes. Here you'll see some top film stunt men put through their paces on speed boats and jet-skis as a Miami Vice-type drugs bust swings into operation and the bad guys try to shoot it out with some eye-popping results. Half the lagoon seems to get blown up right in front of you, and what they can't do with these high-speed boats isn't worth mentioning. But be warned: the best vantage points around the lagoon get taken up to an HOUR before. The designated splash zones are well marked for good reason, believe me you can get SERIOUSLY wet! Don't miss it. TTTT.

In addition, the Studios feature some brilliant extra entertainment for Mardi Gras (in March) and Hallowe'en, when their Horror Nights (which takes place from early Oct–Nov 1) add a wonderfully blood-thirsty touch, as well as New Year's Eve and the 4th of July, when the park gets into full party mode. There is an extra charge, however, for the attractions of Mardi Gras and Hallowe'en.

# Islands of Adventure Preview

When Orlando's newest theme park opens its gates, it promises to be a stunning experience, from the 40 or so rides, which will feature a whole series of new technological wizardries, to the themed shopping and restaurants (real green eggs and ham in Seuss Landing and Dragon Scale Ale in the Lost Continent) through to the fabulous architecture and landscaping. The five Islands (six with Port of Entry) spread over 110 acres all offer at least one five-star thrill ride, a family attraction and a kids' amusement area, plus some of neatest ideas (dinosaurs that blink, breathe and flinch when touched, for example), adding up to 'total immersion entertainment'.

Here is a full outline of Universal's plans for The Theme Park For The New Millenium.

## Port of Entry

This wildly embellished and hugely ornamental (in architectural terms) entrance plaza offers a taste of things to come in its outlandish theming, from the dazzling proportions of the towering lighthouse to the elaborate shops, restaurants and guest services that are its main components. You can also set out from here on the **Island-Hopper Cruises** over the central lagoon or simply head off on foot.

## Seuss Landing

With not a straight line in sight the characters of Theodor 'Dr Seuss' Geisel come to vibrant life on this 10-acre island. Main attractions

The Cat in the Hat

'couches' through 18 different show scenes, 130 special effects and 30 animatronic characters, **One Fish, Two Fish, Red Fish, Blue Fish**, a fairly gentle circular whirl around a myriad of water spouts and streams (with 'squirt posts' dousing riders who don't steer their fish wisely), the **Caro-Seuss-El**, an original carousel ride featuring interactive animation, and **Sylvester McMonkey McBean's Very Unusual Driving Machines**, an elevated indoor/outdoor ride throughout Seuss Landing with passengers able to bump the car ahead to set off special

Dueling Dragons roller coaster

sound effects. **If I Ran The Zoo** is a three-part interactive playland for kids. Eating outlets include the **Green Eggs And Ham Café** and the **Circus McGurkus Café Stoo-pendous**.

## The Lost Continent

A forbidding, medieval forest inhabited by fiery dragons and mythical gods, exotic traders and legendary adventurers, the three main attractions here should all be humdingers. **Poseidon's Fury: Escape From The Lost City** is a multi-media show that pits a 'captive' audience in the midst of a battle between Poseidon and Zeus, with 350,000 gallons of water, 200 flame effects and exploding fireballs. **Dueling Dragons** is a must for roller-coaster fans, a cutting-edge technology twin coaster that sees the two tracks entwine, untwist and hurtle towards each other at a combined 115mph. **The Eighth Voyage of Sinbad** is a spectacular stunt show, with the mythical hero setting sail in search of riches and finding danger all the way. Dining options include the top-of-the-range **Mythos Restaurant**, an offshore grotto inside a 'dormant' volcano full of special effects, and the **Enchanted Oak Tavern**, with guest appearances by the wizard Merlin.

## Jurassic Park

Living, breathing dinosaurs, lush, tropical scenery and a strong dash of excitement and danger characterise this re-creation of the famous book and film. The **Jurassic Park River Adventure** is the stand-out attraction, a phenomenal interactive ride into the prehistoric world, with riders hunted by a predatory Tyrannosaurus Rex and hurtling down an 85-foot plunge, the longest, fastest, steepest water descent built

**Dr Doom's Fearfall**

date. The **Pteranodon Flyers** will give guests a bird's eye view of the park as they soar above the magnificent tropical landscape, while the **Triceratops Encounter** is the first 'living' dinosaur experience, incorporating state-of-the-art mechanics and robotics. The **Discovery Center** is more 'edu-tainment', a research laboratory of history and technology, with a seemingly real Raptor being hatched in one of the demonstration areas, and **Camp Jurassic** is more fun for kids, a mountainous jungle adventure playground. **Thunder Falls Terrace** is the premier eatery, giving diners the chance to see riders on the harrowing plunge down the River Adventure while trying rotisserie chicken and rib specialities. Kids will also want to check out the **Dinostore** here.

## Toon Lagoon

Cartoons come to hilarious 3-D life on this island where characters as diverse as Dudley Do-Right (from Rocky and Bullwinkle) and Blondie (star of newspaper strip cartoons in the 1950s) live side by side. While some will be slightly obscure to the British audience (Beetle Bailey,

6

Krazy Kat, Pogo and Family Circus), others will be well known (Popeye and Hagar the Horrible), and kids should have a rip-roaring time with them all. Many of the attractions will also see everyone get pretty wet. **Dudley Do-Right's Ripsaw Falls** is the feature attraction, with guests assisting the hapless Mountie on a wild log flume ride that culminates in a drop through an exploding dynamite shack and 15ft BELOW the surface of the water, another innovative venture. Then there are **Popeye & Bluto's Bilge-Rat Barges**, a white water raft ride through Octopus Grotto with guests aboard Popeye's Boat firing water cannons at you, the **Theater of the Islands** amphitheatre and **Me Ship, The Olive**, a three-storey young 'uns adventure playland with dozens of activities for all ages. **Comic Strip Lane** is where all the characters spring to life out of five decades of newspaper pages, along with four imaginative shops and eateries like **Blondie's Deli: Home of the Dagwood**. Mort Walker, creator of Beetle Bailey, said: 'It's a great thrill to see these characters evolve to another dimension. I feel like a proud parent after giving birth. For so many years they have existed only in my mind and on paper. To see them 'alive' and walking around is amazing.' Once again, Universal's relentless search for the 'something different' factor looks like paying off in spades.

## Marvel Super Hero Island

The final stop on the tour is possibly the most dramatic, with the 200ft edifice of Dr Doom's Fearfall and the glowing green Hulk Coaster marking it out as the home of some serious thrills (and perhaps a few heart attacks!). With more comic book experiences coming to life, guests are promised a dazzling array of unprecedented technology. **The Adventures of Spider-Man** should be the biggie, a mind-boggling combination of 3-D action, moving ride vehicles, live elements and special effects. A cross between Back to the Future and Terminator 2 3-D in Universal Studios, riders are plunged into a battle between Spider-Man and the forces of evil, led by Doctor Octopus with his Doomsday Anti-Gravity Gun, with the action taking place all around them and featuring a 400ft sensory drop. I can't wait! **The Incredible Hulk Coaster** is another techno-logical marvel as it blasts riders from 0–40mph in TWO SECONDS, experiencing a complete inversion (and weightlessness) 100ft up, before zapping them through six more roll-overs and two subterranean enclosures. Get your screaming tonsils ready! **Dr Doom's Fearfall** is the one that scares me most just writing about it – two 200-ft steel towers where guests sit on the outside, feet dangling, to be fired to the top and then plummet back down as Dr Doom drains the fear from them. Chilling. Other attractions here include two arcades, four more shops and six cafés or snack bars including the **Captain America Diner** and **Fantastic Four Café**, and more super-hero encounters.

As if all that were not enough, there will be live entertainment, strolling characters and special events, as well as the odd surprise or two which I am sure Universal have up their sleeve. In contrast to Disney, who took a softly-softly, almost secretive approach to previewing Animal Kingdom, Universal have been refreshingly open and revealing. Mark Woodbury, the Steven Spielberg of the theme park world, is the creative genius behind the Islands of Adventure, and he told me: 'We wanted it to be different in every way, something people had never seen before and an experience that has never been possible before.'

It is a mouthwatering prospect …

# SeaWorld Adventure Park

**Just five years ago SeaWorld was the ideal place in which to become gently acquainted with the idea of running yourself ragged in the cause of enjoyment in central Florida. It was quiet, low-key and happy to live in the Second Division of the entertainment world. Not any more.**

A dramatic and highly successful development programme by corporate owners the Anheuser-Busch Company has given SeaWorld the big-park treatment with a dramatic new 12-acre entrance plaza and rebranding as an Adventure Park, and it is now one of the most refreshing and vibrant of them all, demanding a full day's attention.

Happily, the queues and crowds here have yet to reach the monster proportions of elsewhere, so this is a park where you can still proceed at a relatively leisurely pace, see what you want to see without too much shoulder-jostling and yet feel you have been superbly entertained (even if meal-times do get crowded in the various restaurants around the park).

SeaWorld is also still a good starting point if this is your first visit to Orlando as it will give you the hang of negotiating the vast areas, navigating by the various maps and learning to plan your visit around the different showtimes which all the parks offer. There is also a strong educational and environmental message to much of what you see, so much so that I defy you not to become emotionally involved with the Manatees: The Last Generation? exhibit, which features a number of letters from similarly concerned British visitors on its exit rampway. To underline the educational points, there are three hour-long behind-the-scenes tours you can take (book up as soon as you enter) which provide a greater insight into SeaWorld's marine conservation, rescue and research programme, as well as their entertainment resources. You can take the one-hour **Polar Expedition,** which provides a close-up of the penguin and polar bear environments, **To The Rescue**, which showcases the park's animal rescue and rehabilitation programme, or the **Sharks!** tour for a backstage view of Terrors of the Deep. You have to pay an extra $5 ($4 for children) for these tours, but they are well worth it and, if you take one of them early on, they will increase your appreciation of the rest of the park.

A new and exciting extra option is the Dolphin Interaction Program, which gives guests the chance to don a wetsuit and wade in to meet the park's bottlenose dolphins under the supervision of experienced trainers. It costs a whopping $148/person, but it books up fast and you need to call 407 370 1385 for reservations.

## Location

SeaWorld is located off Central Florida parkway, between I4 (exit 27A going [north] east or 28 heading [south] west) and International Drive, and the parking fee is $5. It is still a good idea to arrive a bit before the officially-scheduled opening time so you're in good position to book one of the back-stage tours at a time convenient to you or scamper off to one of the few attractions that does attract crowds, like **Wild Arctic** and the new **Journey to Atlantis**.

The park covers in excess of 200 acres, with 10 shows (11 with the nightly Polynesian Luau dinner show which costs an extra $29.63, £20.09 for kids eight to 12 and $10.55 for

1 MANATEES: THE LAST GENERATION?
2 JOURNEY TO ATLANTIS
3 PENGUIN ENCOUNTER
4 PACIFIC POINT PRESERVE
5 SEA LION & OTTER STADIUM
6 TERRORS OF THE DEEP
7 NAUTILUS THEATER
8 CLYDESDALE HAMLET
9 ANHEUSER-BUSCH HOSPITALITY CENTER
10 SHAMU'S HAPPY HARBOR
11 WILD ARCTIC
12 BAYSIDE STADIUM
13 HAWAIIAN RHYTHMS
14 SEAWORLD THEATER
15 TROPICAL REEF
16 WHALE & DOLPHIN STADIUM
17 SHAMU STADIUM
18 INFORMATION
19 KEY WEST AT SEAWORLD
20 TURTLE POINT
21 STINGRAY LAGOON
22 TIDE POOL
23 DOLPHIN NURSERY
24 DOLPHIN COVE

SEA
WORLD

**The Dolphin Interaction Program**

three to sevens, and for which you don't necessarily have to visit the rest of the park), 10 large-scale continuous viewing attractions and nine smaller ones, plus relaxing gardens, a kids' play area and a particularly smart range of shops (which is a noticeable feature of the Anheuser-Busch parks). Their hire pushchairs (strollers) are also the most amusing – shaped like baby dolphins so you push them along by the tail! Be warned, though, the size of the park will take you by surprise and requires a lot of to-ing and fro-ing to catch the various shows, which can be wearing. Keep a close grip on your map and entertainment schedule and try to establish your own programme that gives you regular time-outs to sit and enjoy some of the quieter spots. For something different, you can also sign up for the free Anheuser-Busch **Beer School** at the Hospitality Center for a glimpse into beer-making (and tasting!). Here's how the attractions line up.

**Wild Arctic:** this interactive ride-and-view experience provides a realistic environment which is both educational and thrilling. It consists of two elements, an exciting (simulator) jet helicopter journey into the Arctic wilderness which arrives at a cleverly recreated research base, Base Station Wild Arctic, where the 'passengers' are disgorged into a frozen wonderland to meet some denizens of

the North, like real polar bears, Beluga whales and walruses. The imaginative detail includes a replica sunken galleon and other nautical touches, as well as some genuine scientific research. Not to be missed (but not just after a Shamu show when the hordes descend en masse). TTTT plus AAAAA.

> BRIT TIP: The weather may occasionally mean some of the outdoor entertainment is cancelled, but don't let it stop you enjoying yourself. Buy one of the cheap, plastic ponchos that will appear for sale in the shops at the first sign of rain.

**6**

## Killer whales

**Shamu Stadium**: SeaWorld has long since outgrown its tag as just the place to see killer whales, but the Shamu show is still one of its most amazing experiences. See the killer whales and their trainers pull off some spectacular stunts, as well as explaining all about these majestic creatures. There are two distinct shows, the more humorous Shamu Adventure during the day (lasting 25 minutes) and the louder Shamu Rocks America at night (20 minutes).

**Wild Arctic**

## SeaWorld Adventure Park at-a-glance

| | |
|---|---|
| **Location** | 7007 Sea World Drive, off Central Florida Parkway (Junctions 27A and 28 off I4) |
| **Size** | More than 200 acres, incorporating 20 shows |
| **Hours** | 9am–7pm off peak; 9am–10pm high season (Easter, Summer holidays, Thanksgiving, Christmas) |
| **Admission** | Under 3-free, 3–9, $34 (1-day ticket), $52 (2-day ticket), $82.95 (7-day Flex Ticket), $107.95 (10-day Flex Ticket); adult (10+) $42, $62, $99.95, $129.95 |
| **Parking** | $5 |
| **Lockers** | Yes, by main entrance; 4 × 25c |
| **Pushchairs/ Wheelchairs** | $5 (from Information Centre, to left of main entrance) $5 and $25 (same location) |
| **Top Attractions** | Shamu Stadium, Terrors Of The Deep, Journey to Atlantis, Penguin Encounter, Wild Arctic |
| **Don't Miss** | Red, Bright and Blue Fireworks; Manatees: The Last Generation?; Behind-the-Scenes Tours |
| **Hidden Costs** | **Meals** Burger, chips and coke $6.08 |
| | **Kids' meal** $2.99 |
| | **T-shirts** $14.95–$20.95 |
| | **Souvenirs** $0.99–$295 |
| | **Sundries** Caricature Drawings $8–$20 |

Both are worth seeing, and are easily the most popular events in Sea World, so do make an effort to arrive early. Also, be warned: the first 14 rows of the stadium will get VERY wet. When a killer whale leaps into the air in front of you, it displaces a LOT of water on landing! AAAAA

**Sea Lion & Otter Stadium**: this is home to the new show featuring Clyde and Seamore Take Treasure Island, the resident sea lions who, with their pals the otter and walrus (plus a couple of humans to be the fall-guys!), put on a hilarious 25-minute performance of watery stunts and gags. Arrive early for some first-class audience mickey-taking from the resident (human) bellhop. AAAA.

## Marine research

**Key West Dolphin Fest:** more breathtaking marine mammal stunts and tricks in a funky beach theme, with the accent once again on informing and educating the audience in a gentle manner on the current state of research into dolphins and false killer whales and the dangers they face. The show is 20 minutes long and is rarely over-subscribed, but once again the first few rows face a soaking. AAAA.

**Bayside Stadium**: the new Intensity Games opened in 1998 with an explosion of high energy action in water stunts and gymnastics featuring water-skiing, wakeboarders, jet skis and more. AAAA.

**SeaWorld Theater**: this air-conditioned venue is a little haven when it's hot during the main part of the day. Pets on Stage is the new show here, a 20-minute giggle featuring the talents of a menagerie of dogs, cats, birds, rats, pot-bellied pigs and others, the majority of which were rescued from animal shelters. AAA.

**Nautilus Theater**: this is home to another featured show, with the most recent being the South American acrobats, dancers, music and special effects of Cirque de la Mer. AAA.

**Hawaiian Rhythms**: an amusing song and dance pastiche of Polynesian culture on SeaWorld's beach stage, lasting 25 minutes but with little shade from the fierce sun in summer. Beware the audience member chosen to go on stage – it's an embarrassing experience! AAA.

**Clydesdale Hamlet**: these massive stables are home to the Anheuser-Busch trademark Clydesdale dray horses. They make great photo opportunities when fully harnessed for one of their regular

> BRIT TIP: For all the main shows, make sure you arrive 20 minutes early during peak periods to grab one of the better seats and avoid the last-minute rush.

tours of the park, and there is a life-size statue outside on which to sit the kids to take their picture. AA.

**Anheuser-Busch Hospitality Center**: adjoining Clydesdale Hamlet, this offers the chance to sample the company's most famous product, beer (in fact, the world's No 1 bottled beer, Budweiser, and its cousins). Sadly, it's only one sample per over-21 visitor, but it still makes a nice gesture, and you can take your free sample and sit on a pleasant outdoor terrace which makes for a

relaxing break from all the usual theme park hustle and bustle. AAA. It is also home to the Beer School, while **The Deli** restaurant here is an attractive proposition, serving fresh-carved turkey and beef, German sausage, sauerkraut, fresh-baked breads and delicious desserts.

## Endangered

**Manatees: The Last Generation?**: here is an exhibit that will really tug at your heart-strings as the tragic plight of this endangered species of Florida's waterways is illustrated. Watch these lazy-looking creatures (half walrus, half hippo?) lounge around their man-made lagoon from above, then walk down the ramp to the special circular theatre where a five-minute film with amazing 3-D effects will reveal the full dangers facing the harmless manatee. Then pass into the underwater viewing section, with hands-on TV screens offering more information about them. It's a magnificently-staged exhibit and a few tears at the animals' uncertain future are not unknown. It is also right behind the Key West Dolphin Fest, so DON'T go just after one of the shows there. AAAAA.

**Pacific Point Preserve**: another SeaWorld first, this carefully recreated rocky coast habitat shows the park's seals and sea lions at their most natural. A hidden wave-making machine adds the perfect touch of reality, while park attendants are on hand at regular intervals to provide informative talks on the animals. You can also buy small packs of smelt from two stalls to throw to the ever-

> BRIT TIP: Touching the rays and dolphins is an experience at SeaWorld that you won't easily forget.

**Simulator ride Wild Arctic**

hungry sea beasts. AAAA.

**Shamu's Happy Harbour**: three acres of brilliantly designed adventure playground await youngsters of all ages here, with all things climbable or crawlable. Activities include a four-storey net climb, two tented 'ball rooms' to wade through, and a giant 'trampoline' tent. It does get busy in mid-afternoon, but the kids seem to love it at any time. TTTTT.

**The Key West Dolphin Fest**

## Sharks and morays

**Terrors Of The Deep**: the world's largest collection of dangerous sea creatures can be found here, brought vividly and dramatically to life by the walk-through tubes that surround you with prowling sharks, barracudas and moray eels. It's an eerie

**The touch pool at Stingray Lagoon**

experience (and perhaps too intense for small children), but brilliantly presented and, again, highly informative. Queues do build up here at peak times, though. AAAAA or TTTTT. Take your pick!

**Tropical Reef**: after the dramas and amusements elsewhere, this may seem a little tame, but stick with it. Literally thousands of colourful fish inhabit the centrepiece 160,000-gallon tropical reef, while 17 smaller tanks show off other intriguing species. AAA.

**Penguin Encounter**: always a hit with all the family (and hence one of the more crowded exhibits at peak periods) are the eternally comical

**Journey to Atlantis**

penguins in this brilliantly presented (if decidedly chilly) showpiece. You have the choice of going close and using the moving walkway along the whole of the display or standing back and watching from a non-moving position, while both positions afford views of how the 17 different species are so breathtaking under water. Feeding time is the most popular time for visitors, so arrive early if you want a prime position, while there is also a special question-and-answer session at 1pm every day – the winner gets to pet a penguin. AAAA.

**Key West at SeaWorld** is not so much a one-off attraction as a collection of existing exhibits added to a four-acre extension and grouped under the clever Key West theme. **Stingray Lagoon**, where you can feed and touch fully grown rays, has been enlarged to 40,000 gallons to include a nursery for newborn rays, while the park's rescued and rehabilitated sea turtles have been brought out from behind the scenes into a new exhibit, **Turtle Point**, which helps to explain the dangers to these saltwater reptiles. The centrepiece exhibit, the 2.1-acre **Dolphin Cove**, is a more spectacular, naturalistic development of the old Dolphin Community Pool, and offers visitors the chance to get right up close and feed this friendly community of Atlantic bottlenose dolphins. There is an underwater viewing area to the 700,000-gallon lagoon, which also features waves, a sandy beach and a recreated coral reef. The Community Pool is now the doubly cute **Dolphin Nursery** for new mums and their calves. The whole area is designed in the tropical, seaside flavour of America's southernmost city, Key West, with beach huts, lifeguard chairs, dune buggies, themed shops and other eclectic lookalike elements, right down to the tastes of the Keys with conch and pineapple fritters, but it also underlines the environmental message of conservation through a series of interactive graphics and video displays adjacent to the animal habitats, and children of all ages will find it a fun, educational experience. The shops are above average, too, with the Coconut Bay Trader among the smartest in the park, while there are evening 'street parties' in the best Key West tradition. AAAA.

**Shamu: Close-Up**: this recent exhibit can be found at the opposite side of Shamu Stadium, affording a much closer and more natural look at the killer whales while at their leisure. Attendants are on hand to answer all your questions. AAA.

**Journey to Atlantis**: new in 1998, the massive 10-storey edifice marks out this 'water-coaster', one of only two such rides in the world (the other is in Japan), which gives SeaWorld its first genuine five-star

thrill appeal. The combination of extra elements here ultimately makes it unique, with a series of illusionary special effects giving way to a high-speed water ride that becomes a runaway roller-coaster. An amusing TV show preamble about the 'discovery' of Atlantis opens the way to your eight-passenger Greek fishing boat, which sets off gently through the lost city. The evil spirit Allura takes over and riders plunge into a dash through Atlantis, dodging gushing fountains and water cannons, with hundreds of dazzling holographic and laser-generated illusions, before the heart-stopping 60-foot drop, which is merely the entry to the roller-coaster finale back in the candle-filled catacombs. An amazing creation. Once again, be prepared to get *seriously* wet (like, soaked) in the course of the ride, which is great in the heat of the summer but not so clever first thing in the morning in winter. TTTTT. Riders exit into the **Sea Aquarium Gallery**, a combination gift shop and 25,000-gallon aquarium full of sharks, stingrays and tropical fish (don't forget to look up!).

## SeaWorld at Night

Every night at SeaWorld is the Fourth of July, with a park-wide party of the **Rockin' Nights**. Live entertainment, music and the party atmosphere are boosted by two main events, **Shamu Rocks America**, with a series of dazzling theatrical effects in Shamu Stadium, and the **Red, Bright and Blue Spectacular**. The latter is a pyrotechnic extravaganza in front of the Bayside Stadium that brings the day's entertainment to a close. Fireworks and lasers erupt all over the lagoon – more than 2,000 explosions in all – and guests are left in no doubt this is a tribut to America the Brave. A touch OTT for foreigners but great fun nonetheless. AAAA.

In addition to all the main set-pieces there are several smaller ones which can be equally rewarding for their more personal touch. The **Flamingo, Pelican** and **Spoonbill Exhibits** offer, amongst other things, the answer to the eternal question 'Dad, why has that pink duck got only one leg?'. The **Tide Pool** is another hands-on experience with starfish and sea anemones, and, for an extra $2.50, you can ascend the **Sky Tower** for a lofty overview of the park (and the lower portion of International Drive). Watch out, too, for the best photo opportunity of the day as a big, cuddly Shamu greets kids just inside the main entrance. For the kids who can't do without a daily video game fix, there is a **Midway Games Area** of amusements and fun challenges just left of Shamu's Happy Harbour.

There are also 10 different places to eat, with the **Buccaneer Smokehouse** (barbecued, mesquite-grilled chicken, ribs and beef), **The Deli** (mentioned, above, in the Anheuser-Busch Hospitality Center), **Bimini Bay Café** (for a relaxing, full-service lunch or dinner) and **Mango Joe's Café** (delicious grilled fajitas, speciality salads and sandwiches) the best of the bunch. As in the other main parks, try to eat before midday or after 1.30pm for a crowd-free lunch, and before 5.30pm if you want a leisurely dinner.

Your wallet will also be in severe peril in any of the 30 shops and photo-opportunity kiosks. Make sure you visit at least **Shamu's Emporium** (for a full range of cuddly Shamu toys and souvenirs), **Manatee Cove** (more cuddlies), **Friends Of The Wild** (dedicated to animal lovers everywhere) and **The Label Stable** for Anheuser-Busch gifts and merchandise (some of it very smart). Your purchases can be forwarded to Package Pickup in Shamu's Emporium for you to collect on your way out, provided you leave at least an hour for this service to work.

6

# Busch Gardens

Question: when is a zoo not a zoo? Answer: when it is also a theme park like 335-acre Busch Gardens in nearby Tampa.

Busch Gardens, the second big Anheuser-Busch park in the area, started life as a mini-menagerie for the wildlife collection of the brewery-owning Busch family. In 1959, they opened a small hospitality centre next to the brewery and things have kind of mushroomed ever since. Now, it is a major, multi-faceted family attraction, the biggest on Florida's west coast and little more than an hour from Orlando, fully justifying its place in the Magnificent Seven (or Great Eight when Islands of Adventure opens).

It is rated among the top four zoos in America, with more than 2,700 animals representing 340 species of mammals, birds, reptiles, amphibians and spiders. But that's just the start. It boasts a safari-like section of Africa spread over 65 acres of grassy veldt, with a special monorail

**Silverback gorilla in the Myombe Ape Reserve**

viewing attraction. Interspersed among the animals are 28 bona fide theme park rides, including the mind-numbing roller-coasters Kumba and Montu, which guarantee a new experience for coaster addicts, and yet another in the series of simulator rides, the amusing and novel Akbar's Adventure Tours. There are shows, comedians, musicians, strolling players and a family show extravaganza in the impressive Moroccan Palace Theater, Hollywood Live On Ice.

The overall theme is Africa, hence the park is subdivided into areas like Nairobi and The Congo, and the dining and shopping opportunities are the equal of any of the other big theme parks. It doesn't quite have the pizazz of an Epcot® or Universal, and the staff are a bit more laid back (not quite so many 'Have a nice days' or eager-to-please smiles), while the attention to detail is not as overwhelming as the other five. In a way, it is like the big brother of the Chessington World of Adventures in Surrey, although admittedly on a much grander scale (and in a better climate). But it has guaranteed, five-star family appeal, especially with its selection of rides just for kids and it is a big hit with the British market in particular.

**Congo River Rapids**

1 **CONGO**
2 CONGO RIVER RAPIDS
3 KUMBA
4 THE PYTHON
5 **TIMBUKTU**
6 DOLPHIN THEATER
7 THE SCORPION
8 FESTHAUS
9 **STANLEYVILLE**
10 TANGANYIKA TIDAL WAVE
11 STANLEY FALLS
12 STANLEYVILLE THEATER
13 **LAND OF THE DRAGONS**
14 **BIRD GARDENS**
15 KOALA DISPLAY
16 HOSPITALITY HOUSE/BEER SCHOOL
17 LORY LANDING
18 **MOROCCO**
19 MOROCCAN PALACE THEATER
20 **MYOMBE RESERVE**
21 **CROWN COLONY**
22 SKYRIDE AND MONORAIL STATION
23 CROWN COLONY RESTAURANT &
   HOSPITALITY CENTER
24 CLYDESDALE HAMLET
25 **EGYPT**
26 AKBAR'S ADVENTURE TOURS
27 TUT'S TOMB
28 MONTU
29 **SERENGETI PLAIN**
30 EDGE OF AFRICA

BUSCH
GARDENS

6

## Busch Gardens at-a-glance

| | |
|---|---|
| **Location** | Busch Boulevard, Tampa; 75-90 minutes drive from Orlando |
| **Size** | 335 acres in 11 themed areas |
| **Hours** | 9.30am–6pm off peak; 9am–9pm high season (Easter, Summer holidays, Thanksgiving, Christmas) |
| **Admission** | Under 3-free; 3–9, $31.95 (1-day ticket), $107.95 (10-day Flex Ticket, inc. Universal Studios, SeaWorld and Wet 'n' Wild); adults (10+) $37.95 and $129.95 |
| **Parking** | $5 |
| **Lockers** | Yes; in Morocco, Congo, Egypt and Stanleyville; 2 × 25c |
| **Pushchairs/ Wheelchairs** | $6 and $11 (Stroller and Wheelchair Rental in Morocco) $6 and $30 (same location) |
| **Top Attractions** | Kumba, Congo River Rapids, Edge of Africa, Tanganyika Tidal Wave, Myombe Reserve, Montu |
| **Don't Miss** | Hollywood Live On Ice, Elephant Wash, Mystic Sheikhs band |
| **Hidden Costs** | **Meals** Burger, chips and coke $6.28. Three-course meal $17.90 (Crown Colony House) |
| | **Kids' meal**  $2.99 |
| | **T-shirts**  $17.90–$19.99 |
| | **Souvenirs**  $1.49–$300 |
| | **Sundries**  Old-time photo booth $19.50 |

## Location

Busch Gardens is the hardest place to locate on the sketchy local maps and the signposting is not as sharp as it could be, but, from Orlando, the directions are pretty simple. Head (south) west on I4 for almost an hour (it is 55 miles from I4's junction with Highway 192) until you hit the intersecting motorway I75. Take I75 north for three-and-a-half-miles until you see the exit for Fowler Avenue (Highway 582). Continue west on Fowler Avenue for another three-and-half-miles, and, just past the University of South Florida on your right, turn LEFT into McKinley Drive. A mile down McKinley Drive and Busch Gardens' car park entrance will be on your left, where it is $5 to park.

You may think you have left the crowds behind in Orlando, but, unfortunately, in high season you'd be wrong, although outside peak periods it can be a queue-free zone. It is still advisable to be here in time for the 9am opening, if only to be first in line to ride the dazzling roller-coasters Kumba and Montu, which are easily the most popular attractions and draw queues of up to an hour during the main holiday periods. The Congo River Rapids, Stanley Falls log flume ride and Tanganyika Tidal Wave (all opportunities to get very wet!) are also prime rides, as is Akbar's Adventure Tours and the other two roller-coasters, Python and Scorpion. The queues take longer to build up here, so for the first hour or so you can enjoy a relatively crowd-free experience, even in high season.

Busch Gardens is divided into 11 main sections, with the major rides all furthest away from the main entrance, so the best tactic at opening time is to dash straight through to The Congo at the far side for Kumba, the Congo River Rapids and Python, with nearby Stanleyville offering the chance to do the other two water rides early on. The latter is always advisable as it gives you the maximum amount of time to dry out! Alternatively, turn to your right through the gates and head for Egypt, Akbar's and Montu. Here is the full 335-acre layout.

## Morocco

Coming through the main gates brings you first into **Morocco**, home of all the main guest services and a lot of the best shops. Epcot's Moroccan pavilion sets the scene rather better, but the architecture is still impressive and this version won't overtax your wallet quite as much as Disney does. For a quick meal try the **Zagora Café**, especially at breakfast when the marching, dancing, eight-piece brass band called the **Mystic Sheikhs** swing into action to entertain the early morning crowds. Alternatively, the **Boujad Bakery** will serve you coffee and pastries, including Mexican churros, which are like long, thin doughnuts. Watch out, too, for the strolling **Men Of Note**, a four-piece a cappella group, and the costumed

characters like TJ the Tiger and Hilda Hippo. The **Sultan's Tent** gives you your first animal encounter in the form of a resident snake charmer, while turning the corner brings you face to face with the alligator pen. Morocco is also home to two of the biggest shows in Busch Gardens. The **Marrakesh Theater** offers various variety shows that change from time to time (American Jukebox was featured in 1998; check the daily Entertainment Guide for full details), while the **Moroccan Palace Theater** houses the award-winning show Hollywood Live On Ice. Even if the thought of an ice show doesn't immediately appeal to you, think again, because this is a surprising and highly entertaining 30-minute spectacular that consists of a tribute to musicals, horror films, silent movies and James Bond performed by an all-star ice-dance cast in dazzling costumes and lavish settings (it's also air-conditioned, which is a great relief in summer). AAAA.

## Crown Colony

**Crown Colony** sits in the bottom right-hand corner of Busch Gardens and has five distinct components. Here, you can take the **Monorail ride** (AAAA) around the 80-acre Serengeti Plain (see below) or the **Skyride** cablecar (AAA) on a one-way trip to The Congo. The station for both is in the same building, with various lemurs, monkeys and birds staring out of their cages at these strange humans all in long lines. Who's watching who, you wonder. The **Clydesdale Hamlet** is also here, but if you've seen the massive dray horses and their stables at SeaWorld, the set-up is identical.

**Akbar's Adventure Tours** (actually part of Egypt's attractions but located in Crown Colony because it replaced the Questor ride

6

**The Mystic Sheiks**

in 1998) is another in the array of simulator rides, though this relies as much on fun as thrills. The TV pre-show leads its audience into the world of down-at-heel Akbar (brilliantly played by comedian Martin Short) and his home-made (and untried) excursion machine. It explores, in unconventional fashion, the secrets and treasures of ancient Egypt, but don't expect a smooth ride – a mysterious force assumes control in the forbidden tomb and the journey takes a high-speed turn for the unexpected! It is not recommended for anyone who suffers back or neck problems or expectant mothers, while the height restriction is 3ft 6in. TTTT.

The **Crown Colony Restaurant and Hospitality Center** is a large Victorian-styled building overlooking the Serengeti Plain and affording either counter-service salads, sandwiches or pizzas (downstairs) or a full-service restaurant upstairs with magnificent views of the animals roaming the Plain. For a memorable lunch, book here early in the day or, better still, come back for dinner in the early evening and see the animals come down to the water hole.

## Serengeti

The **Serengeti Plain** itself is home to buffalo, antelope, zebra, giraffe, camels, lions, baboons, hippos, rhinos and many exotic birds, and can be viewed either fairly close-up on the Monorail or at a more relaxed distance for part of the journey on the Busch Gardens **Trans-Veldt Railroad**, a full-size, open-car steam train that chugs slowly from its main station in Nairobi to Egypt and all the way round to Congo, Stanleyville and back (AAA). You get a different view of the Plain from both forms of transport, so make a point of doing both during your day. Queues for the Monorail build up steadily through the main part of the day from late morning onwards.

**The Serengeti Safari**

## Edge of Africa

Busch Gardens' newest area, which opened in 1997, is the largest animal expansion in the park's history, a 15-acre 'safari' experience that guarantees a close-up encounter that is almost as good as the real thing. The walk-through attraction puts you in an authentic setting of natural

**Hippos at the Edge of Africa animal attraction**

BRIT TIP: Edge of Africa offers some wonderful photo opportunities, but, in the hot months, come here early in the day as many animals seek refuge from the heat later in the day.

wilds and native villages (right down to the imported plants and even the smells), from which you can view giraffes, lions, baboons, meerkats, crocodiles, hyenas, vultures and even get an underwater view of a specially designed hippopotamus habitat. Look out for the abandoned jeep – you can sit in the front cab while lions lounge in the back! Wandering 'safari guides' and naturalists offer informal talks, and the attention to detail is wonderful. AAAAA.

## Nairobi

**Nairobi** is home to the awesome **Myombe Reserve**, one of the largest and most realistic habitats for the threatened highland gorillas and chimpanzees of central Africa. This three-acre walk-through has a superb tropical setting where the temperature is kept artificially high and convincing with the aid of lush forest landscaping and hidden water mist sprays. Take your time, especially as there are good, seated vantage points, and be patient to catch these magnificent creatures going about their daily routine. It is also highly informative, with attendants usually on hand to answer any questions. AAAAA.

At **JR's Gorilla Hut** you can buy your own cuddly baby gorilla, while you can get a snack or soft drink at the **Myombe Outpost**. This is also the place to see the Gardens' Asian elephants (check the advertised times for the **Elephant Wash**, which is always worth watching) and the **Nairobi Animal Nursery**, which houses all manner of rehabilitating and hand-reared creatures that can be seen close-up. Continuing round the Nursery brings you to the oddly out of place **Showjumping Hall of Fame**, the **Reptile House** and the inevitable

6

Petting Zoo, for kids to stroke goats, sheep and baby deer. **The Curiosity Caverns**, just to the left of the Nursery, are easy to miss but don't if you want to catch a glimpse of various nocturnal and rarely seen creatures in a clever, cave-like setting.

## Timbuktu

Passing through Nairobi brings you into the more ride-dominated area of the park, starting with **Timbuktu**. Here in a North African desert setting you will find many of the elements of a traditional fun fair, with a couple of brain-scrambling rides and two top-class shows.

Scorpion, a 50mph rollercoaster, features a 62-foot drop and a full 360-degree loop that is guaranteed to dial D for dizzy for a while afterwards. The ride lasts just 120 seconds, but it seems longer! The queues build up here from late morning to mid-afternoon, and you have to be at least 3ft 6in tall to board. TTTT. **The Phoenix** is a positively evil invention, sitting its passengers in a gigantic, boat-shaped swing that eventually performs a full 360-degree rotation in dramatic, slow-motion style. Don't eat just before this one! TTTT. **Sandstorm** is a fairly routine whirligig contraption that spins and levitates at fairly high speed (hold on to your stomach). TTT. The **Crazy Camel** is an odd sort of ride resembling a giant sombrero that spins and tilts its riders into a state of dizziness. TT. Then there are a series of scaled-down **Kiddie Rides** that always seem popular with the under-10s (and give mum and dad a break for a few minutes as well). The **Carousel Caravan** offers the chance to ride a genuine Mary Poppins-type carousel, while there is also the inevitable **Electronic Arcade** and a **Games Area** of side shows and stalls

that require a few extra dollars to play. The **Festhaus** is a combined German Bierfest and entertainment hall, offering a mixture of German and Italian food. It's a jolly, rather raucous establishment, with the International Celebration show featuring singers, dancers and musicians four or five times a day. The final element of Timbuktu is the **Dolphin Theater**, complete with its aluminium sculpture outside that is a homage to the value of recycling. The Dolphins Of The Deep show borrows heavily from SeaWorld's dolphin offering, but still comes up with some terrific leaps, stunts and tricks. AAAA.

## Congo

You're really into serious ride territory as you come into **The Congo**, with the unmistakable giant turquoise structure of **Kumba**. First of all it's the largest and fastest roller-coaster in the south-east United States and, at 60mph, it features three unique elements: a diving loop which plunges the riders a full 110 feet; a camelback, with a full 360-degree spiral that induces a feeling of weightlessness for three seconds; and a 108-foot vertical loop, the world's largest. For good measure, it dives underground at one point! It looks terrifying close up, but it is absolutely exhilarating, even for non-coaster fans. The height restriction here is an ungenerous 4ft 6in. TTTTT. The **Congo River Rapids** look pretty tame after that, but don't be fooled. These giant rubber tyres will bounce you down some of the most convincing rapids outside of the Rockies, and you will end up with a fair soaking for good measure. TTTT. The **Ubanga-Banga Bumper Cars** are just that, typical fairground dodgems (TT), and you won't miss anything by passing them by for the more daring **Python**, the third of Busch Gardens' roller-coasters, with this one featuring a double spiral corkscrew at 50mph from a drop of some 70 feet. Height restriction here is 4ft, and the whole ride lasts just 70 seconds, but it's a blast. TTTT. Nearby, the **Monstrous Mamba** is almost a carbon copy of Timbuktu's Sandstorm, but just with a different name and paint job, while there are more **Kiddie Rides** to stop the smaller visitors feeling left out. The **Vivi Storehouse Restaurant** offers a typical mix of burgers, sandwiches and roast beef fare, while there are three gift shops, including the Tiger's Den.

## Stanleyville

You pass over **Claw Island**, home of the park's spectacular rare white Bengal tigers, to get to **Stanleyville**, which all rather merges into one area from the Congo. Here there are more watery rides, with the popular **Stanley Falls** log flume ride (almost identical to the ones at Chessington, Thorpe Park and Alton Towers), which guarantees a good soaking at the final drop (TTT) and the distinctly cleverer **Tanganyika Tidal Wave**, which takes you on a scenic ride along 'uncharted' African waters before tipping you down a two-stage drop which really does set you down with tidal wave force. TTTT.

> BRIT TIP: Don't stand on the bridge into the neighbouring **Orchid Canyon** unless you want to catch the full weight of the Tidal Wave!

**Stanleyville Theater** is a good place to relax and put your feet up for a while as you are entertained by a number of circus-style acts in the World Talent Showcase. For a hearty, if somewhat messy, meal, visit the **Stanleyville Smokehouse** – their woodsmoked ribs platter is a real lip-smacking delight. As you leave Stanleyville behind, say hello to the warthogs and orang-utans (who are rarely active during the heat of the day) in the large pens either side of the Train Station.

## Land of the Dragons

Parents will want to know about this large, wonderfully clever area of activities, entertainment, rides and attractions purely for the young 'uns. It features a three-storey tree house complete with towers and maze-like stairways, a rope climb, ball crawl and outdoor Dragon's Tale Theater, which portrays the story of Dumphrey the Dragon and Sir Bumbly the Knight. It is all good, knockabout, well-supervised stuff, and some of the kiddie rides are superbly inventive, as well as offering plenty of opportunity to get wet. TTTTT (youngsters only – but mums and dads can watch!).

## Bird Gardens

Your anti-clockwise route now brings you to the final and most peaceful area, the **Bird Gardens**. Here it is possible to unwind from the usual theme park hurly-burly. The exhibits and shows are all family-orientated, too, with the World of Birds presented in the **Bird Show Theater** and the **Hospitality House Stage** offering ragtime jazz at regular intervals. A recent addition is **Lory Landing**, a desert island-themed walk-through bird encounter featuring lorikeets, hornbills, parrots and more, with the chance to become a human perch and feed the friendly lorikeets (and have your ear nibbled!). A cup of

6

nectar costs $1, but is a great investment for a memorable photo. Take a slow walk round to appreciate the lush, tropical foliage, and special displays such as the walk-through **Aviary**, the **Birds of the Pacific, Flamingo Island, Eagle Canyon** and the emus. The highlight of the Bird Gardens, confusingly enough, is the **Koala Display**, in the south-west corner, where these natives of Australia happily sit and seemingly do nothing all day while drawing large crowds for doing so. A free taste of

**Myombe Reserve**

to be the park's centrepiece, has been pulled down as it was too small and inefficient, and there are 17 acres waiting redevelopment here. Current suggestions include a new roller-coaster or animal attraction (see below).

## Egypt

The final area of Busch Gardens is tucked away through the Crown Colony, so it is best visited either first thing or late in the day. **Egypt** is eight acres of carefully-recreated pharaoh country, dominated by the trademark new roller-coaster **Montu**, named after an ancient Egyptian warrior-god. It is a truly breathtaking creation, the world's tallest and longest inverted coaster, covering nearly 4,000 feet of track at speeds topping 60mph and peaking with a G-force of 3.85! Like Kumba,

**Tanganyika Tidal Wave**

Anheuser-Busch products is on offer in **Hospitality House**, and you can go a step further here by enrolling for **Beer School**, a 30-minute session into the age-old process of beer-making. It offers a fascinating glimpse into the brewery world, and is excellently explained, with the bonus of some tasting included! You also get a Brewery Master certificate. AAA. The old brewery, which used

**Kiami and Adele in the koala habitat**

The breathtaking Montu roller-coaster

6

Serengeti Safari

it looks terrifying, but in reality it is an absolute five-star thrill as it leaves your legs dangling and swoops and plunges (underground at two points) for almost three minutes of brain-scrambling fun. Height restriction is 4ft 6in. TTTTT.

You can travel back in time on a tour of **Tut's Tomb**, as it was discovered by archaeologist Howard Carter, with clever lighting, audio and even aroma effects. AAA. There is also a neat **Sand Pit** that invites youngsters to undertake their own excavations (and there are even some little 'treasures' to be found!), while the shopping here takes on a high-quality air with its hand-blown glass items, elaborate sculptures and authentic cartouche paintings.

You should finally return to Morocco for a spot of shopping there in the area's tempting bazaars. Middle Eastern brass, pottery and carpets will all try to tempt you into opening your wallet yet again, while there is also a full range of Anheuser-Busch products and gift ideas if you haven't already succumbed to the array of gift shops and cuddly-toy emporiums around the rest of the park.

## And ...

In addition to all the aforementioned activities, you can enhance your visit to Busch Gardens by taking the **Serengeti Safari** tour, an excursion aboard flat-bed trucks to meet the Plain's giraffes, zebras, ostriches and rhinos close up and learn more about the park's environmental efforts. You book up at the entrance to Edge of Africa for an extra $20, and places soon fill up.

For a full family day out, you can combine Busch Gardens with next-door water park **Adventure Island** (on McKinley Drive) which is particularly welcome when it hots up (provided you plaster on the sun tan cream). The 25 acres of watery fun, in a Key West theme, offer a full range of slides and rides, like the 76ft freefall plunge of the Tampa Typhoon and the spiralling Calypso Coaster, kids' playground, cafes, gift shops, arcades and volleyball, plus the wonderful Splash Attack adventure, a water activity maze culminating in a 1,000-gallon bucket dump on the unwary! Adventure Island is open from mid-February to late October (weekends only Sept–Oct) from 10am–5pm (later in high season) and a combined ticket with Busch Gardens costs $45.19 for adults and $38.77 for 3–9s.

STOP PRESS: Speculation over a new attraction was confirmed with news of a roller-coaster addition for June 1999. **Gwazi** will be Florida's first duelling wooden coaster, based on an African lion legend. It will feature two 7,000ft tracks up to 90ft high that will leave the station at the same time and head towards each other six times at combined duelling speeds of 100mph. Cool or what! Height restriction will be 3ft 6in, rating TTTTT (expected).

And that's it. The Magnificent Seven (or Eight) theme parks in all their glory and detail. And if that doesn't reveal the full importance of planning a strategy for your Orlando visit, then I don't know what will. Especially as we're now about to plunge into an even wider-ranging area of attractions, activities, sports and recreation that will demand just as big a portion of your holiday as the main theme parks themselves ...

# 7 The Other Attractions

*(or, One Giant Leap for Tourist Kind)*

If you think you have seen everything Orlando has to offer by simply sticking to the theme parks, in the words of the song, 'You ain't seen nothin' yet'. It would be relatively easy to add the Kennedy Space Center to the parks in Chapter 6 because, although it's not strictly a theme park, it is adding new attractions all the time and is fast becoming a full day's excursion from Orlando to the east or 'space' coast.

Then there are Cypress Gardens and Silver Springs to give you a taste of the more natural things Florida has to offer, the Kissimmee attraction Splendid China for a completely different park experience, the mind-boggling Gatorland, with its multitude of alligators, crocs and gator shows (and great value, too), Disney's wildlife sanctuary Discovery Island and the one-off family centres like Mystery Fun House, WonderWorks, the Orlando Science Center and Ripley's Believe It Or Not.

For more individual attractions, you have the unique aviation experience of Fantasy of Flight, the outstanding haunted houses of Skull Kingdom, Terror on Church Street and the Haunted Mansion plus the area's magnificent array of water fun parks, with three in Walt Disney World, one on International Drive and one in Kissimmee.

Chapter 8 then introduces a range of alternatives that help you Get Off the Beaten Track and discover some of the real Sunshine State, while there are also the options for an

evening out in Orlando by Night. The choice, as they say, is yours, but it is an immense selection. Let's start here with One Giant Leap for Mankind.

## Kennedy Space Center

The real beauty of visiting the home of America's space programme is that it doesn't necessarily cost you any money. Parking and many of the films and exhibits are completely free, and you can spend several hours wandering around the complex and adjoining **Rocket Garden**, learning all about the past, present and future of space exploration. You can inspect a full-size, replica **Space Shuttle**, see real moonrock and spacecraft, take in the **Satellites and You** show which uses some great audio-visual effects to reveal how satellites affect our lives, visit the **Spaceport Theater** for two alternating films, 'The Boy from Mars' and 'Apollo 13: Houston We Have A Problem', check out the on-going **Mission to Mars**, get to grips with a whole range of hands-on educational exhibits and have your picture taken with a fully-suited Spaceman! You should also stop by the **Astronauts Memorial**, a stark, sombre but very moving tribute to the men and women who have died in the course of the space programme.

### Tours

For most people, that just whets the appetite and you can then choose from several paid-for attractions that

The spectacular Apollo/Saturn V rocket centre at the Kennedy Space Center

include a tour of the Space Center and three special film presentations in the giant IMAX cinemas. Owners Delaware North Parks Services have lavished a fortune on upgrading the Center and, for my money, it's an

Space Shuttle Launch

unmissable experience for all but pre-school children. In many ways, it knocks the artificiality of Disney and Co into a cocked hat. The air-conditioned coach tour, fully narrated throughout, makes three important stops in addition to driving around much of the working areas of the Space Center, including the truly massive Vehicle Assembly Building. The first stop is the new $7m **LC39 Observation Gantry**, just one mile from shuttle launch pad 39A, a combination four-storey observation deck and exhibition centre. The exhibits consist of a 10-minute film on the preparation of a shuttle for launch, models and videos of a launch countdown and touch-screen information on the shuttle programme. Next is the awesome **Apollo/Saturn V Center**, one of the area's truly great exhibits, where you can easily spend 90 minutes. It highlights the Apollo programme and first moon landing with two deeply impressive theatrical

## KEY TO ORLANDO – MINOR ATTRACTIONS

A = WINTER PARK
B = AQUATIC WONDERS TOURS
C = BOGGY CREEK AIRBOAT RIDES
D = PORT CANAVERAL
E = HAUNTED MANSION
F = WARBIRD AIR MUSEUM
G = GREEN MEADOWS PETTING FARM
H = SANFORD/RIVERSHIP ROMANCE
I = WONDERWORKS
J = POINCIANA GOLF AND RACQUET RESORT
K = METROWEST COUNTRY CLUB
L = MARRIOTT'S ORLANDO WORLD CENTER
M = LAKE CANE TENNIS CENTER
N = ORANGE LAKE COUNTRY CLUB
O = SANLANDO PARK
P = FLORIDA FUN-TRAIN
Q = DAVE'S SKI SCHOOL
R = KATIE'S WEKIVA RIVER LANDING

S = GRAND CYPRESS EQUESTRIAN CENTER
T = HORSE WORLD RIDING STABLES
U = PIRATES DINNERSHOW
V = ORLANDO ARENA
W = CITRUS BOWL STADIUM
X = OSCEOLA COUNTY STADIUM
Y = CENTRAL FLORIDA ZOO
Z = SEMINOLE GREYHOUND PARK
A1 = MELBOURNE GREYHOUND PARK
B1 = ARABIAN NIGHTS
C1 = KARTWORLD
D1 = ORLANDO SCIENCE CENTER
E1 = CAPONE'S
F1 = MARK II DINNER THEATER
G1 = MEDIEVAL TIMES
H1 = KING HENRY'S FEAST
I1 = WILD BILL'S
J1 = SKULL KINGDOM

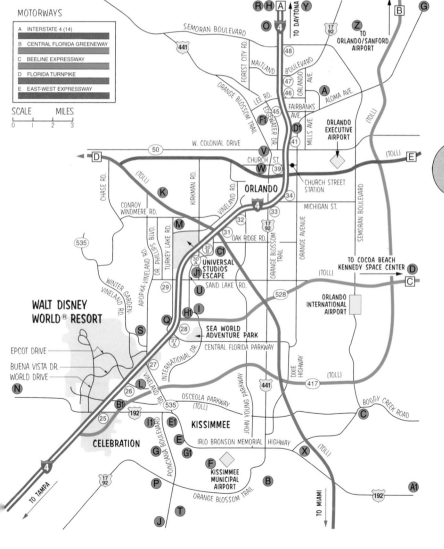

MOTORWAYS

A = INTERSTATE 4 (14)
B = CENTRAL FLORIDA GREENEWAY
C = BEELINE EXPRESSWAY
D = FLORIDA TURNPIKE
E = EAST-WEST EXPRESSWAY

SCALE MILES
0  1  2  3

presentations on the risks and triumphs, with an actual 363-foot Saturn V rocket and a hands-on gallery that brings the past, present and future of space exploration into sharp focus. It is also quite a humbling experience. Third stop is the new $4m **International Space Station Center**, another interactive attraction featuring the construction of this current project, with incredibly detailed mock-ups of the modules and a fascinating viewing gallery showing the workings of the Center. The tour costs $14 for adults and $10 for 3–11s, and you can spend as much time as you like at each stop as the coaches depart every 10 minutes or so. You should allow a good 3–4 hours to do the tour justice though.

Equally impressive are the IMAX cinemas – 55-foot screens which give the impression of sitting on top of the action. The 37-minute film **The Dream Is Alive** puts you inside a space shuttle mission, the new 40-minute **Mission To Mir** depicts American–Russian co-operation, and the 3-D **L5: First City In Space** is a breathtaking slice of science fiction based on science fact. Films cost $7.50 for adults and $6.50 for 3–11s. You can get a Crew Pass for the coach tour and one IMAX film for $19 and $15.

BRIT TIP: If you plan to do any of the tours or see one of the IMAX films, head straight for the **Ticket Pavilion**, in the centre of the complex, when you arrive. The ticket staff can prepare your schedule according to what you want to see, marrying up the tours with the film times.

The Space Center boasts an excellent Space Shop, three restaurants, four snack counters and a play area for the little ones. Even the Apollo/Saturn V Center has its own café where you can sit and marvel at it all.

To get to the Kennedy Space Center, take the Beeline Expressway out of Orlando (Highway 528, and it's a toll road, remember) for about 45 minutes then bear left on the SR 407 (DON'T follow the signs to Cape Canaveral or Cocoa Beach at this point) and turn right at the T-junction on to SR 405. The Space Center's Visitor Center is located six miles along SR 405 on the right-hand side. Opening hours are 9am to dusk every day except Christmas Day, and the Center gets busiest around lunchtime. The first tours and IMAX presentations start at 9.30am, and the final tour of the day is two hours before dark. **Total attraction rating: AAAAA.**

The greatest attraction of all, however, is an actual shuttle launch, of which there are six or seven a year. You can call 407 867 4636 for dates and information, while free car passes to a Launch Viewing area some six miles from the launch pad are available by writing three months in advance to NASA Visitor Services, Mail Code: PA-Pass, Kennedy Space Center, Florida 32899. There are also 1,500 $10 Launch Viewing Opportunity tickets for a bus trip to a site just a mile from the launch pad (or $15 for an LVO ticket, IMAX film and mission briefing). These go on sale on a first-come basis five days before launch and must be purchased in person from the Ticket Pavilion. Alternatively, prime viewing sites are along Highway 1 in Titusville and Highway A1A through Cape Canaveral and Cocoa Beach. To be on hand for a shuttle launch is an awe-inspiring experience.

## US Astronaut Hall of Fame

While the Kennedy Space Center tells you primarily about the machinery of putting men in space, the neighbouring Astronaut Hall of Fame (on SR 405, just before the main entrance to the Space Center) gives you the full low-down on the people involved. This museum to the space programmes houses some fascinating memorabilia, interactive exhibits and engaging explanations of the people behind the spacesuits. Prepare to be amazed at how incredibly small the cockpits of the early manned spaceflights were and amused by personal touches like Buzz Aldrin's High School report!

A recent reorganisation and expansion has created a more chronologically coherent approach divided into six main sections. **The Entry Experience** introduces the visions of space flight, with an eight minute video of the astronauts as modern explorers, and leads into **Race To The Moon**, the stories of the Mercury, Gemini and Apollo missions and their people. **The New Frontier** opens the way for Skylab

> BRIT TIP: Every Friday is Space Camp graduation day, so avoid the Hall of Fame then unless you want to be surrounded by dozens of highly enthusiastic 'space cadets' and their parents.

and Shuttle missions, adjacent to the **Astronaut Hall of Fame**, the museum's heart and soul. **Space Explorers Today and Tomorrow** includes the audio-visual experience aboard the replica Shuttle To Tomorrow and a glimpse of the Space Camp for kids, before introducing the hands-on **Astronaut Adventure** with its working models, G-force and flight simulators (a cabin that does six 360° rolls!), space-walk 'chairs', moon exploration, interactive computers and Mars Mission experience. Active minds will be more than rewarded.

Admission is $13.95 for adults and $9.95 for kids (6–12), with opening hours from 9am–6pm (9–7pm in summer), seven days a week. **Total attraction rating: AAAA**. If you enjoyed the Kennedy Space Center, try to spend a couple of hours here.

There is also the usual gift shop, with refreshments provided by the Cosmic Café. The residential **Space Camp** may be of interest to you if you have children of 10–14 who would like to train to be junior astronauts for five days. It's not a cheap programme – $675 – but it is a magnificent educational recreation for kids, and the Camp is happy to take visitors from the UK. You have to book up about two months in advance of your visit, but then just bring your youngsters along on Sunday afternoon and they are taken off your hands until Friday morning (now is that an attractive proposition for harassed parents?). They are arranged into groups and go through activities like flight and space-walk simulators, simulated space missions, studying rocket propulsion, space technology and other scientific experiments. If your youngster is mad keen on being an astronaut, sign him or her up for Space Camp! For more details, phone 407 269 6100.

## Cypress Gardens

Turning from the futuristic to the more natural, Cypress Gardens offers more than 200 acres of immaculate botanical gardens, spectacular flower festivals, world famous water-ski shows and plenty of good ol' southern hospitality. It was, in fact, the first 'theme park' in Florida, pre-dating Walt Disney World by some 35 years, and it has gradually expanded in recent years to remain a pleasant alternative to the usual park experience.

It is about a 45-minute drive from Kissimmee, down I4, turning off at Exit 23 and south on to Highway 27 and then right on SR 540 six miles past Haines City. Cypress Gardens is about five miles along SR 540, on the left-hand side.

After the major tourist hustle of Orlando, the Gardens are an island of peace and tranquillity. Plan on spending the best part of a day here, too, as there is plenty to keep everyone amused. Start with a boat tour round the canals of the **Botanical Gardens**, then stroll round the gardens themselves, taking note of the immense **Banyan Tree** (unlike the Magic Kingdom's Swiss Family Treehouse, this one is real!), the photogenic **Southern Belles** in their colourful period outfits and the beautiful **Gazebo**, which hosts more than 300 weddings

**The beautiful Gazebo**

a year. Visit the Oriental and French gardens, then retrace your steps and take in the spectacular new **Ski Xtreme Show**, which features world-class skiers and world-famous

**The Spring Flower Festival**

routines (odd fact: Cypress Gardens' ski show is the world's longest-running single attraction, operating every day since 1942). There is also a new behind-the-scenes tour and skiing adventure programme for $75 per person. Have your picture taken in front of the scenic **Mediterranean Waterfall**, then marvel at the delights of the centrepiece garden attraction; the **Spring Flower Festival** runs from March to May, the **Victorian Garden Party** all year long, the **Mum Festival** (featuring more than 2.5 million Chrysanthemum blooms) in November and the **Poinsettia Festival** from the end of November to early January. For my money, the elaborate Victorian Garden Party, featuring clever topiary 'statues', is the highlight of four hugely imaginative programmes.

Continuing through the park brings you to the **Plantation Gardens**, which offers the practical side of gardening with tips on 'how to grow' herbs, vegetables, roses and other flowers. Also here is the **Wings Of Wonder** exhibit, a huge butterfly house where more than 1,000 butterflies hatch from glass cabinets and flutter around in tropical splendour. Stop off for afternoon tea at the beautifully restored **Magnolia Mansion** and listen to live music on the terrace. **The Island in the Sky** will then lift you up 15 storeys on its circular revolving platform for a grandstand view of the park. Model railway fans are also well catered for with the **Historical Florida Garden Railway**, 5,000 ft of lovingly re-created landscape, and the indoor 20-train **Cypress Junction**, while next door is **Carousel Cove**, a selection of games, rides and other activities to keep the youngsters amused for a while. There are four

A member of Cypress Gardens' Ski Xtreme team

show arenas, offering contrasting live entertainment all day. The **Crossroads Arena** stages the Russian Variete Internationale circus acts. **The Palace** houses the spectacular Hot Nouveau Ice show (in great air-conditioned comfort), the **Gardens Theater** features botanical seminars, and **Nature's Arena** offers the Reptiles and Raptors show. New features are a mini zoo (including the inevitable gators) called **Nature's Way, Nature's Boardwalk**, which provides a superb natural setting down to the edge of the lake to

discover animal habitats like wallaby and fallow deer, and the **Birdwalk Aviary**, a walk-through encounter with lorikeets that eat out of your hand. Another new feature is an hour-long eco-tour cruise of the local lakes for an extra $6 (5 and under free).

There are 14 shops and gift stores to tempt you into buying yet more souvenirs, from the children-friendly **Butterfly Shop**, to **Sweet Creations** (home-made fudge and real citrus juice, marmalades and jellies). The **Village Fare** food court offers a good choice of eating, from freshly-carved roast beef to pizza and salads, while the **Cypress Deli** serves up barbecue-smoked chicken and ribs, and the **Crossroads Restaurant** is full-service dining in air-conditioned comfort. Again, there's no shortage of choice, quality is consistently high and value for money is good.

Cypress Gardens is open from 9.30am to 5.30pm, with extended hours during the festivals, including until 9pm for the spectacular **Spring Lights** (Feb–April) and **Glitter, Glisten and Glow** (late Nov–Feb), which both feature laser shows, millions of lights and the 110ft Tree of Life. Admission is $29.95 for adults, $24.50 for Seniors (55+) and $19.50 for children six to 12 (although kids up to 17 were being admitted FREE in 1998, and probably in 1999 as well). Parking is free. **Total attraction rating: AAAA**.

**7**

Silver Springs glass-bottomed boat

## Silver Springs

Continuing the theme of more natural attractions, we have Silver Springs, just under two hours' drive to the north of Orlando. This 350-acre nature park (don't worry, you won't have to walk round all of it) surrounds the headwaters of the crystal-clear Silver River. Glass-bottomed boats take you for a close-up view of the artesian springs (the largest in the world) that bubble up here, along with plenty of marine wildlife. Expect close encounters with alligators, turtles, racoons and plenty of waterfowl, while the park also contains a collection of more exotic animals, like bears, giraffes, camels and zebras that can be viewed from either land or water. Three animal shows, a five-acre tropical wildlife exhibit, the world's largest bear exhibit, a new kids' playground and a white alligator exhibit complete the rest of the attractions. Once again, you will feel you have left the crowds far behind. To ruin a few more illusions of the film industry, this was the setting for the famous 1930s and 40s films of the Tarzan series starring Johnny Weissmuller. This was where they staged all the spectacular scenes of Tarzan's great swimming exploits, including his regular wrestling battles with alligators, and once you have absorbed the amazing tropical nature of the undergrowth, you will understand why they decided to save on the cost of shipping the film crew all the way to Africa.

Silver Springs is located on SR 40 just through the town of Ocala, 72 miles to the north of Orlando. Take the Florida Turnpike north (it's a toll road, remember) until it turns into I75 and 28 miles further north you turn off and head east on SR 40. Another 10 miles brings you to Silver Springs, just past the Wild Waters water park on your right.

Silver Springs' main attraction is its **Glass-Bottomed Boats**, 20-minute rides which go down well with all the family and gives a first-class view of the seven different springs and a host of marine life. Similarly, the **Lost River Voyage** is another 20-minute boat trip down one of the unspoilt stretches of the Silver River including a visit to the park's animal hospital where the local park ranger introduces you to all his current charges. The third boat trip on offer, the **Jungle Cruise**, is effectively a water safari along the Fort King Waterway, where animals from six continents are arranged in natural settings along the riverbanks. As an alternative to messing about on the river, the **Jeep Safari** is a 15-minute ride in the back of an open trailer through a natural forest habitat home to more animals from other corners of the world, such as marmosets, tapirs, antelope and vultures. Then there are the three **Cypress Island Animal Shows**, each one lasting 15 minutes and featuring an entertaining – and occasionally hair-raising – look at the worlds of reptiles, household pets and creepy crawlies. The hair-raising occurs only if you are the unlucky victim chosen to display a large tarantula, giant cockroach or scorpion. As you exit the animal shows take 15 minutes to wander the **Board Walk** and see the largest American crocodile in captivity, the 16-foot, 2,000lb Sobek, as well as a collection of alligators, turtles and Galapagos tortoises. **The Osceola Gardens** provide a peaceful haven to sit and watch the world go by for a while, and the only odd note is struck by the somewhat out-of-place **A Touch of Garlits Museum**, which houses vintage American cars and racing cars. Two recent additions are the **World of Bears**, a two-acre spread devoted to bears of all kinds (the largest of its type in the world), from grizzly to spectacled and black bears, and the **Kids Ahoy!** playland, with its centrepiece riverboat featuring slides, rides, an air bounce, ball crawl, 3-D net maze, carousel, bumper boats and other games. **Doolittle's Petting Zoo**, with its deer and goats, is another draw for the young 'uns. The brand new **Big Gator Lagoon** showcases more than two dozen alligators in a natural cypress swamp, while the **Panther Prowl** offers a unique look at the endangered Florida panther and the Western cougar. The usual collection of shops and eateries are fairly ordinary here, in contrast to the slick appeal of Orlando's parks, although **The Deli** offers some pleasant sandwich alternatives for lunch. In all, you would probably want to spend a good half day here, with the possibility of a few hours in the neighbouring nine-acre water park of **Wild Waters** which offers slides like the new Twister, a pair of 60ft-high flumes, the free-fall Thunderbolt, the twin-tunnelled Tornado, the 220-foot long Silver

---

BRIT TIP: Silver Springs and Wild Waters both get busiest at the weekend. Otherwise, you shouldn't encounter many queues here.

---

Bullet and the helter-skelter Osceola's Revenge, as well as a 400-foot tube ride on the turbo-charged Hurricane, a huge Wave Pool, an area of junior slides 'n' fun called Cool Kids Cove and a nine-hole mini-golf course.

Parking is $3 and admission fees are $29.95 for adults and $20.95 for children (three to 10 years). A joint ticket (Silver Springs and Wild Waters) is $31.95 and $22.95. Open 9am–5.30pm all year round. **Attraction rating: AAAA.**

## Splendid China

New in 1994 and still expanding and modifying its various displays and exhibits, Splendid China is unique to central Florida and a completely different type of attraction. Here, you won't find rides and other flights of fancy, but you will be taken on a fascinating journey through one of the biggest and most mysterious and breathtaking countries of the world.

This elaborate 76-acre park offers a range of intricate, miniaturised features like the Great Wall of China, the Forbidden City and the Stone Forest, some fascinating full-size exhibits, thrilling acrobats and martial arts experts, and, naturally enough, some great food. Recent additions include five-person golf cart tours around the park and an enlarged playground for young children. Realistically, it will not hold the attention of small kids for long, and in high summer there is little escape from the relentless heat, but where it scores impressively as an attraction is in its amazing eye for detail, its total air of authenticity (genuine Chinese craftsmen were brought in to hand-build every miniature) and its peaceful atmosphere – quite an achievement in the tourist bustle of Orlando!

Splendid China is located at the western end of the main tourist drag of Highway 192, three miles west of its junction with I4 and opposite the big Key W Kool Restaurant. Three to four hours is the minimum time requirement here, and you can easily spend half a day taking in all the different shows and one of the excellent restaurants. Here's how its 10,000-mile journey through 5,000 years of history works. The four elements of the park are essentially:

**1) The Exhibits.** More than 60 painstakingly recreated scale models of China's greatest buildings, statues and landmarks. **The Great Wall** is one of the most striking, at half a

7

mile long and up to five-and-a-half feet high. It is constructed of more than six million tiny bricks, all faithfully put into place by hand. Other highlights include Beijing's **Imperial Palace** and the **Forbidden City**, the 26-storey **Grand Buddha of Leshan** (reduced to a 'mere' 36 feet tall), and the **Mausoleum of Genghis Khan**. The stairs by the side of the **Mausoleum of Dr Sun Yat Sen** afford a wonderful high-rise overview of the park, while the famous **TerraCotta Warriors** exhibit offers a chance to get in the air-conditioned cool for a minute or two. Splendid China is fully three-quarters the size of The Magic Kingdom®, so it demands a fair amount of leg work to appreciate fully all the exhibits (noting how the specially imported Chinese grass is manicured around the smallest figures!), and it is not the time to discard your walking shoes (although you can get a five-person guided tour by electric cart for $48. A guided walking tour is $5.35 extra per person).

**Snow Tiger Adventure**

**2) The Shows.** There are eight centres for the performing arts which showcase the talents of some of China's top musicians, artists, acrobats and martial arts exponents. The **Temple of Light Theater** is the main centre, featuring national song and dance exhibitions of around 30 minutes a time and the **Magical Snow Tiger Adventure**, a fascinating animal show that starts with reptiles and spiders and works up to panthers, lions and tigers, all with a strong environmental message. Have your picture taken with a snow tiger, up close and personal! **Harmony Hall** features films about China and the creation of Splendid China and its sister park near Hong Kong, which is a good starting point for any visit. Outside, the **Chinatown Show Area** is home to various musical and martial arts specialities, while the **Pagoda Gardens** also stage acrobatic shows. The **Panda Playground**, where the kids can get rid of some excess energy, doubles up as the venue for some more daring acrobats, and the **Imperial Bells Theater** and the **Wind and Rain Court** hold other traditional acts, like the daring knife-climbing ceremony. The new **Golden Peacock Theater** presents a special $1\frac{1}{2}$-hour evening spectacular, the Mysterious Kingdom of the Orient, which showcases the talents of 70 dancers, acrobats and jugglers in magnificent costumes. You need to get your entry ticket validated if you leave early and want to return for this show, or you can pay the $16 for the show on its own (at 6pm, not on Mondays).

**3) The Restaurants.** The park sets great store by the quality of its food, whether it be in its sumptuous five-star restaurant or its cafeteria-style buffet. The jewel in the crown is the elegant **Hong Kong Seafood Restaurant** for full-service, gourmet cuisine, while more budget-priced is

**The spectacular Mysteries of the Orient show at Splendid China**

the **Seven Flavors**, a cafeteria-style diner offering American food as well as Chinese dishes. The **Pagoda Garden**, in the furthest corner of the park, is a straightforward American deli-style establishment offering burgers and sandwiches while the **Wind and Rain Court Restaurant** has the greatest range of Chinese dishes outside the Hong Kong. **The Great Wall Terrace** serves a mixture of authentic Chinese and traditional Western meals.

4) **The Shops.** Unlike all the other theme parks, Splendid China's shopping opportunities are all located in the Chinatown front area of the park which is open to the general public without park admission. The 11 gift shops are also one up on their counterparts by stocking a more up-market and distinctive range of goods, from Bonsai trees to furniture, jewellery to T-shirts, silk and satin clothing to children's toys, and antique curios to contemporary artefacts. In many instances you can also watch the local craftsmen and women at work producing the various wares.

The mixture of Chinese and Floridian staff adds to the friendly atmosphere that the park generates, but ultimately it is a difficult concept to describe so the best advice is to see it for yourself. Adult admission is $28.88, children (five to 12) are $18.18 while children four and under are free. Opening hours are 9.30am to 6 or 7pm seven days a week. **Attraction rating: AAAA.**

**Gatorland's imposing entrance**

# Gatorland

For another taste of the 'real' Florida this is as authentic as it gets when it comes to the wildlife, and consequently it is hugely popular with children of all ages. When the wildlife consists of several thousand menacing alligators and crocodiles in various natural habitats and three fascinating shows, you know you're in for a different experience. 'The Alligator Capital of the World' was founded in 1949 and is one of the few family-owned attractions left in Florida, hence it possesses a home-spun charm which few of its big-money competitors can match.

> BRIT TIP: If you have an evening flight home, Gatorland is a handy place to visit on your final day. Conveniently located, it is the ideal place to soak up a couple of 'spare' hours.

Start by taking the **Gatorland Express Railroad** around the park to get an idea of its 50-acre expanse. Wander around the natural Florida countryside beauty of the 2,000ft **Swamp Walk**, as well as the **Alligator Breeding Marsh Walkway**, with its three-storey-high observation tower, and get a close-up view of these great reptiles who seem to hang around the 2,000-foot walkway in the hope someone might 'drop in' for lunch. Breeding pens, baby alligator nurseries and rearing ponds are also situated throughout the park to give you an idea of the full growth cycle of the Florida alligator and enhance the overall feeling that it is the visitor who is behind bars and not the animals themselves. Kids now have their own section of the park in **Alligator Alley**, a stretch that encompasses

Allie's Barnyard petting zoo, the Very Merry Aviary, for the chance to meet and feed friendly lorikeets, the new deer park and python exhibits, Gator Grunt's Nursery and Lilly's Pad, an imaginative water playground guaranteed to get them good and wet! However, the alligators are the main attraction and it is the two gator shows which really draw the crowds (although you will never find yourself on the end of a queue here). The 800-seat **Wrestling Stadium** sets the scene for some real Cracker-style alligator feats (a Cracker is the local term for a Florida cowboy) as Gatorland's resident 'wranglers' catch themselves a seven- to eight-foot gator and proceed to point out the animal's various survival features, with the aid of some stunts that will have you seriously questioning your cowboy's sanity. The **Gator Jumparoo** is another eye-opening spectacle as some of the park's biggest creatures use their tails to 'jump' out of the water and be hand-fed tasty morsels such as whole chickens! You can also take in the **Snakes of Florida** show which demonstrates that these reptiles, although dangerous, are not slimy and nasty after all, but are, in fact, dry-skinned and shy (and that Florida is home to more venomous varieties than you would imagine).

Newly-opened in late summer 1998 was the fearsome **Jungle Crocs of the World** exhibit and show, with some of the deadliest animals from places like Egypt, Australia and Cuba. Authentic lairs, well-versed guides, themed gifts and food all add up to a brilliant extension to the park. Obviously, face-to-face encounters with these living dinosaurs is not everyone's cup of tea, but it's an experience you're unlikely to repeat anywhere else. In addition to the attractions, you can also dine on smoked alligator ribs and deep-fried gator nuggets at **Pearl's Smokehouse,** with excellent kids' meals at $3.99. The park is also home to hundreds of nesting herons and egrets, providing a fascinating close-up view of the nests from March–August.

Gatorland scores in its great value for money for three–four hours entertainment, with adult tickets at $13.95, children 10–12 $8.94 and 3–9s free with each paying adult, while there is also an extremely worthwhile combination ticket with nearby Boggy Creek Airboats available exclusively through TicketShop USA (tel 0181 600 7000) at £19 for adults and £5 for 3–12s. .Gatorland is located on the South Orange Blossom Trail, two miles south of its junction with the Central Florida Greeneway and three miles north of Highway 192. Opening hours are 9am to dusk daily. **Attraction rating: AAAA.**

## Disney's Discovery Island Park at Walt Disney World® Resort

Still with the nature zoo theme, Discovery Island Park is a rather more refined look at some tropical wildlife, with two animal shows and more than 130 species of animals and 250 of plants. This is a real island in Bay Lake and one of Walt Disney World's harder-to-find spots. You won't find it signposted on any of the main routes into the vacation kingdom, but aim for Disney's Fort Wilderness Resort and you will find the (free) parking area for Disney's Discovery Island and Disney's River Country at Gateway Depot. Leave your car there and catch one of Walt Disney World's free shuttle buses to Disney's Fort Wilderness Campground, from where you walk the last 100 yards to the Discovery Island Jetty (if you are staying in the Walt Disney World hotels around the Magic Kingdom® Park, there are also regular boats to the island). You

can stop off by the bus-stop to let the children play with the animals of the Fort's **petting farm**, or even visit the stables and take a **trail ride** around the 800 wooded acres on horseback (book at Pioneer Hall or, in advance, on 407 824 2621). Compared to the extravagant nature of Walt Disney World's theme parks, this attraction is almost spartan, but

> BRIT TIP: Disney's Discovery Island is the perfect combination with Disney's River Country water park for a day's fun. Start off at the Island, then cool down in splashing fashion.

there are still plenty of clever touches that mark it out as a cut above your average zoological park. It will take you about an hour to walk around the 11-acre sanctuary on the extensive boardwalks and paths which ring the island. Around the circuit you will find the **Alligator Swamp, Tortoise Beach, Flamingo Lagoon, Pelican Bay, Primate Point** and the **African** and **South American Aviaries** where exotic reptiles, mammals and birds thrive in this tropical haven. Kids will also enjoy **Discovery Island HQ**, where there is an animal hospital and nursery, while the two shows are both family orientated and will add the best part of an hour to your visit. **Feathered Friends** features a range of birds, including parrots and birds of prey, and **Reptile Relations** is another chance to meet Florida's number one scaly exhibit, the alligator, and his friends.

Admission is $11.95 for adults and $6.50 for kids aged three–nine (under threes free). Discovery Island admission is included free for the duration of an All-in-One Hopper Pass. Opening hours are 10am to dusk every day. **Attraction rating: AAA**.

## The Disney Institute

The newest, most elaborate (and hard to describe) resort area

© Disney

**Chef Mark Dowling at the Disney Institute's Culinary Program**

attraction in Walt Disney World® Resort is the Disney Institute, a 90-acre vacation centre, offering the chance of a more educational leisure programme for older children and adults. Basically, it is a residential course that gives you the chance to take part in such diverse activities as healthy cooking, gardening and TV production and rock-climbing. The **Basic Plan** packages all include accommodation in one of the resort's well-appointed bungalows or town houses (but no meals), a full day's leisure programme each day and baggage gratuities. Prices start at $529 per person for a three-night stay in one of the bungalows, up to $1,664 for a week's stay in a two-bedroomed town house, which sleeps up to six. Obviously that isn't cheap, but the choice of facilities, the quality of the programmes and the enthusiasm and dedication of the Institute instructors and staff make for an utterly memorable experience. Golf and tennis lessons, green fees and spa treatments are extra, but

then there is a **Deluxe Plan** which includes all your meals at the Institute's lovely Seasons Dining Room (for an extra $51 per day) and a **World Choice Plan** which adds breakfast at the Institute, lunch and dinner at a choice of WDW restaurants, unlimited admission to ALL the other attractions during your stay and use of bicycles and other non-motorised recreation at any Walt Disney World resort (for an extra $76 a day).

There are more than 20 individual programmes divided into several main interest areas. These are: *Television and Film*, in which guests are guided through techniques of communication, entertainment and photography; *Sports and Fitness*, which include sports clinics and tennis; *Culinary Arts*, where state-of-the-art kitchens (with no washing up!) with individual work stations offer programmes in preparation and appreciation of the world's great cuisines; *Behind the Scenes*, involving Disney story-telling and adventure, plus what makes the Magic Kingdom® Park tick; *Gardening and the Great Outdoors* is a must for any green-fingered naturalist who wants to learn more about their own garden, landscaping, topiary creations or Florida's countryside (including canoe adventures); and the always-popular *Animation and Story Arts*, for the full techniques of animation. Instructor-to-guest ratios are never more than 1:15 (and usually less), while the extra facilities include an outdoor amphitheatre, a state-of-the-art cinema and

> BRIT TIP: Significantly, it is now possible to buy a one-day pass to the Institute's programmes to sample their style for a relatively modest $99.

performance centre, a closed-circuit TV and radio station, a 38,000-square foot sports centre with a full-service spa (for massage, hydrotherapy, aromatherapy, facials and beauty treatment), four clay tennis courts, an 18-hole championship-quality golf course, six swimming pools and a separate supervised youth centre, Camp Disney, with a series of unique and educational programmes for 7–15-year-olds. The resort is fully accessible for guests with disabilities. All in all, it is a magnificent creation for those who want a bit more, both mentally and physically, from their holiday and it is well worth investigating just for a visit if you are nearby. Package deals are hard to find as the Institute has been a difficult sell for the tour operators, but you can call 407 827 4800 for more information and reservations.

© Disney

**Rock climbing at the Sports and Fitness Program at the Disney Institute**

## Mystery Fun House

This three-part adventure playground is primarily for kids and will happily occupy Junior for up to three hours. The three elements are the Mystery Fun House itself, the new Jurassic Putt Golf Park, and Starbase Omega, an elaborate laser battle game that mum and dad get as much of a kick out of as the kids.

Start with the **Mystery Fun House** and work your way through the mirror maze into the Egyptian Tomb. Another 14 chambers of surprises await you, including a fire-breathing dragon in the Topsy-Turvy Tilt Room, the mysteries of the Forbidden Temple, the dangers of the Chamber of Horrors (why do kids seem to revel in the gruesome

BRIT TIP: The Mystery Fun House is ideal for kids of all ages – unless they are really afraid of the dark.

7

delights of death and torture?), and concluding in the Grand Ballroom with its circus theme. Next, take in the high-tech **Starbase Omega**. You'll be fully kitted out with electronic power-vest and laser blaster, briefed for your 'mission' (usually a battle with all the visitors divided into two teams) and then unleashed on the combat zone via the Millennium 333 transporter. The unique 'alien environment', space mist and rousing music add to the fun and this 21st-century version of cops and robbers is guaranteed to bring out the kid in everyone. The **Mini-Golf** set-up offers a few variations on the standard crazy golf courses with which Orlando is overstocked. The Jurassic Putt theme means you have to test your skill against a number of dinosaur obstacles, including an 18-foot Brachiosaurus and a dangerous Velociraptor. If all that is not enough to keep your youngsters entertained the Mystery Fun House also has one of Orlando's largest video games arcades, an ice cream parlour, several gift shops, a shooting gallery, an 'old-tyme' photo booth, and a restaurant that features the periodic Wiz-Bang Revue. The Mystery Fun House also offers a number of birthday party packages from $10.50 per person ($11.75 with pizza or hot dogs); for details call 407 351 3356.

BRIT TIP: On a (rare) wet day, the Mystery Fun House can be a boon to parents with active kids to keep amused for a morning or afternoon. There is no entry fee just to play the video games.

Visits can be made on the special Fun House Trolley along the main tourist length of International Drive and is free if you ride all the way to the Fun House. Otherwise you can pay $2 for the round trip back to your hotel.

The Mystery Fun House is located on Major Boulevard, just off Kirkman Road as you approach Universal Studios. It is open 365 days a year from 10am to 9pm (10pm at peak periods) and a combination ticket for all three features costs $19.85. Individually, it is $10.95 for the Mystery Fun House, $9.95 for Starbase Omega, and $4.95 for the Jurassic Putt Mini-Golf. **Attraction rating: TTT.**

## Ripley's Believe It Or Not

You can't miss this particular attraction, next door to the Mercado Shopping Centre on International Drive, as its extraordinary tilted appearance makes it seem as though it was designed by an architect with an aversion to the horizontal. However, once inside you will soon find yourself back on the level and for an hour or two you can wander through this museum dedicated to the weird and wonderful.

Robert L. Ripley was an eccentric and energetic explorer and collector who, for 40 years, travelled the world in his bid to assemble a collection of the greatest oddities known to man. The Orlando branch of this now worldwide museum chain features 8,900 square feet of displays that include authentic artefacts, video presentations, illusions, interactive exhibits and music. The elaborate re-creation of an Egyptian tomb showcases an Egyptian mummy and three rare mummified animals, while the collection of miniatures includes the world's smallest violin and a single grain of rice handpainted with a tropical sunset. Larger-scale exhibits

BRIT TIP: Like the Mystery Fun House, Ripley's is a handy retreat to know about on the occasional rainy days.

include a portion of the Berlin Wall, a two-thirds scale 1907 Rolls Royce built entirely out of matchsticks and a version of the 'Mona Lisa' textured completely from toast!

Admission is $10.95 for adults and $7.95 for children aged four to 12 and it is open from 9am to 11pm daily. **Attraction rating: AAA.**

## Haunted Holidays

The walk-through haunted house idea has become big business in Orlando and, when we say big, we mean large. Take **Skull Kingdom**, which was new in 1997, for example. Not content with a house, here is a full-blown *castle* on International Drive (opposite Wet 'n' Wild) dedicated to frights, horrors and grisly goings on at every turn. The setting and lavishness of the Kingdom of the Skull Lord marks it out as way above average, and the combination of elaborate light and sound effects, robotics and the scream-inducingly brilliant live actors (who are kept suitably creepy by two full-time make-up artists) makes for a hair-raising experience. Needless to say, the shock tactics

> BRIT TIP: Friday and Saturday evenings are peak periods for Skull Kingdom, with queues of up to 30 minutes. The experience is also toned down a touch during the day for families.

are state of the art, with the best elements of horror films and haunted houses well maintained over the two-storey spread of mazes, caverns and other demonic challenges (watch out for the real monster spit!). There is also the inevitable Haunted Gift Shop and Ghoulish Arcade Games at the end of your 20- to 30-minute (depending on how much you 'enjoy' the experience!) Skull Kingdom immersion. It is open from noon until 'the graveyard closes' (i.e. midnight) every day, with admission $9.95, and its gets a glowing recommendation from *Fright Times*, the official publication for the industry of haunted attractions – yes there *is* such a publication. Go with a

few friends, or have a drink or three first! TTTTT. The owners also have plans for a mini-golf course (36 Holes of Horror) and Orlando's first haunted night club, Creatures of the Night.

Similarly, the new **Haunted Mansion** on Highway 192 in Kissimmee (by Marker 13) operates a shudderingly realistic world of vampires, open crypts, skeletons and unexpected attacks from live and animated spooks. Take a trip to alien space, visit the Mad Doctor and tumble into a black hole. All these terrors await – and more, plus one of the world's finest collections of horror and Hallowe'en antiques in the haunted museum halfway round. Again, the scale is suitably impressive, and the gift shop at the end is one of the biggest. Proprietor Tom Godard says: 'We hope everyone finds that special item they need. If we don't have what they want … we'll dig it up for them!' The Haunted Mansion is open every day from noon–midnight, with admission $9 for adults and $6 for under 12s. TTTT.

Completing the trio of all things horrific, **Terror on Church Street** was Orlando's original fright site back in 1991 and, with its downtown setting (on the junction of Church Street and Orange Avenue) is still the most popular. Here lurks another world of dark, winding passageways, hi-tech special effects, live actors and spine tingling soundtracks. There are 25 individual chilling chambers, including the new Garden of the Immortal, Black Vortex and Mannequin Mayhem, wherein some 40 monsters lurk in

> BRIT TIP: If this appeals to you, go before 9pm as the queues build up quite horrendously from then on.

7

**Skull Kingdom**

fog-shrouded splendour, and even the smells are panic-inducing. As with the others, visitors move through in small groups (woe betide the leader and tail-end Charlie!) at their own fear-ridden pace. Terror on Church Street is open every night from 7pm–midnight (Sunday to Thursday) and 7pm–1am (Friday and Saturday), admission $12 for adults and $10 for 17s and under. TTTTT.

WARNING: All three are most definitely not suitable for children – unless you want them to have nightmares for months afterwards!

The other recent I-Drive attraction is the simulator thrill ride, **Movie Rider**, of which there is also one on Highway 192 in Kissimmee. Together, these two mini-cinemas offer a double feature of two five-minute films which propel the 36 guest 'riders' in each cinema through eye-popping adventures like the Jurassic Park-themed Dino Island, the space thriller Alpha One Cowboy and The Rattler, the world's tallest, fastest and longest wooden roller-coaster. The great benefit is not having to queue for the ride as you do in the theme parks, although the admission price of $8.95 is a bit steep for barely 10 minutes' fun. However, the rides are fast, loud and quite violent (people with back injuries, heart problems, motion sickness or in pregnancy should

definitely NOT ride) and the height restriction requires riders to be at least 42in tall. Both Movie Riders are open seven days a week, from 10am to midnight (10am–10pm in Kissimmee). Call 1-800 998 4418 for more information locally.

## Fantasy Of Flight

Another recent addition to central Florida is this $30million aviation museum attraction which is an absolute must even for anyone not usually interested in the history of flight or the glamour of the Golden Age of flying. Just 25 minutes down I4 towards Tampa (take Junction 21, Polk City, go north on SR 559 for half a mile then turn left into the main entrance), Fantasy of Flight is a three-part adventure featuring the world's largest private collection of vintage aircraft, a series of expertly recreated 'immersion experiences' into memorable moments in aviation history (like a World War II bomber mission with a real Flying Fortress!), and eight incredibly realistic fighter simulators that take you through a WWII aerial battle. You get a pre-flight 'briefing' on how to handle your simulator (a Vought Corsair),

**Fantasy of Flight**

**Step back in time at Fantasy of Flight**

diner and original gift shop, and there is strong British appeal with the war depictions and many of the exhibits, like the last air-worthy Sunderland Flying Boat. Admission is $18.95 for adults, $16.95 for Seniors (60+) and $9.95 for kids (5–12, under fives free). It is open from 9am–8pm in peak holiday periods and 9am-5pm at other times. Their newest offering is the Great Balloon Experience, a 20-minute flight in a tethered, 25-passenger balloon offering a grandstand view of much of central Florida. The entrance price allows you to ride as often as you like all day. Other recent additions include the world's last flying B-26 Marauder in the collection of 30-plus historic aircraft. You can also take an Ultralight flight lesson over Fantasy of Flight for 15 minutes for $25. Fantasy of Flight is the brainchild of American entrepreneur and aviation whizz Kermit Weeks and I have yet to encounter an attraction put together with more genuine love and care. In fact, it is as much a work of art as a tourist attraction, and the masses have yet to discover it, too. For more information call 941 984-3500. **Attraction rating: AAAA.**

and then climb in to the totally enclosed cockpit to do battle with the Japanese Air Force over the Pacific. It's difficult, absorbing, fun and totally addictive. The whole experience is crafted in 1930s Art Deco style, including a full-service

7

**The upside-down world of WonderWorks**

## Orlando Science Center

Because this is Orlando, there is no such thing as a simple museum or science centre. Everything has to be all-singing, all-dancing just to compete. Hence, the new **Orlando Science Center** is more than a mere museum and far more fun than the average science centre. Here, you get a series of hands-on experiences and habitats that entertain as well as inform, and school-age children will get a lot from it (not to mention mum and dad). The Science Center has seven main components, plus an inviting café and a night sky observatory. **Natureworks** creates a number of typical Florida habitats, **Science City** introduces fun ways to understand and use physical science and maths (including some mind-bending puzzles) and the **Cosmic Tourist** offers a trip round our solar system with an amusing travel theme. The **Darden Adventure Theater** takes up more 'science is fun' topics with the Einstein Players, and **Bodyzone** offers some fascinating medical insights into the human body. For those a bit too young for the educational element, **Kids Town** has plenty of junior-sized fun and games for under eights while **TechWorks** completes the main tour, a three-part adventure into light, imaginary landscapes and showbiz science. You'll be amazed at how much you learn in the course of having fun. In addition, the Center has two separate programmes based in the **Dr Phillips CineDome**, a 310-seat cinema that practically surrounds its audience with large-format films, digital planetarium shows (a virtual tour of the universe, anyone?) and 3-D laser shows. The underwater presentation The Living Sea is so life-like you end up holding your breath! The CineDome also boasts a 28,000-watt digital sound system that helps make the experience unforgettable. The Science Center is located on East Princeton Street in downtown Orlando, just off exit 43 of I4, is open 9am–5pm Mon–Thur, 9am–9pm Fri & Sat and noon–5pm Sun, and costs $8 for adults and $6.50 for three to 11s ($12 and $9.50 if you take in a film or planetarium show). It is closed on Thanksgiving Day in November and Christmas Day. **Attraction rating: AAA½.**

## WonderWorks

International Drive's newest attraction is the unmistakable 'interactive entertainment centre' of **WonderWorks**, a three-storey chamber of real family fun with a host of novel elements. Unmistakable? You bet – how many buildings do you know that are *upside down*. That's right, all of the 82ft tall edifice is constructed from the roof up! The basic premise (working on the theory that every attraction has to have a story behind it) is that WonderWorks is a secret research facility into unexplained phenomena that got uprooted by a tornado experiment and dumped in topsy-turvy fashion in the heart of this busy tourist district (Yeah, right!). Well you've got to give them full marks for imagination, and the interior attractions are almost as entertaining as the exterior façade. You enter through an 'inversion tunnel' that orientates you the same way round as the building (look out of the window if you don't believe me) and there are then four chambers of entertaining and mildly

> BRIT TIP: The CineDome film and laser show can operate until midnight on Friday and Saturday for a show independent of the Science Center.

Resort
Wilderness Lodge
Contemporary Resort
( Disney's All Star Resort
( Disney's World Resort
( cheaper

Interstate 4   more up-
market hotels

P. 46 Central Reservation
P. 58. Park Plaza Hotel

Michael    34 - 34
Nichola    28 - 32.

David    CD
  Yes — Tales from
              Telegraphic Ocean

# Gastrocote LIQUID

DELIVERS RELIEF FROM REFLUX DYSPEPSIA

BRIT TIP: WonderWorks is perfectly situated, next door to The Pointe, to allow for a full family diverson. Mum and Dad can happily dump the kids for a couple of hours' fun in WonderWorks while they enjoy a drink at Lulu's Bait Shack, The Pointe's outstanding bar.

educational hands-on experiences that demand several hours to explore fully. Without ever actually using the words 'science' or 'museum', WonderWorks steers you through the **Mystery Lab** (experience earthquakes and hurricanes and see famous disasters on a bank of interactive computer monitors), **Physical Challenge Lab** (virtual basketball, table tennis, hang-gliding and even horse-racing, baseball test, health and lifestyle quizzes and the wonderfully creepy Shocker Chair, a high voltage simulation that gives you the feeling of 2,000 jolts rather than volts – it's *weird*!), **Illusions Lab** (with the Bridge of Fire static electricity generator, a computer ageing process and 'elastic surgery', hall of mirrors and bubble table), plus the **WonderWorks Emporium** gift shop, souvenirs and pizza parlour. A new **laser-tag** game centre is due to be set up in the near future which will add to the centre's appeal (plus a couple of dollars to the entrance fee). At the time of writing it was $12.95 for adults, $9.95 for seniors (55+) and $9.95 for kids 4–12, and opening hours are 10am–10pm daily. AAA and TTT.

## The Water Parks

If anyone has been down the slides and flumes at the local leisure centre, they will have an inkling of what Orlando's five big water parks are all about. Predictably, Walt Disney World® Resort weighs in with three of the most elaborate ones, but the independently run Wet 'n' Wild and Water Mania are equally adept at providing hours of watery fun with slides and wave pools in an amazing variety of styles that owe a lot to the imagination of the theme park ride creators.

All five parks require at least half a day of splashing, sliding and riding to get full value from their rather high admission charges, but, if you prefer to get your kicks in watery rather than land-borne fashion, these are definitely for you and you will want to try at least a couple of them. Lockers are provided for valuables and you can hire towels.

BRIT TIP: Ladies, down some of the whizziest slides it is advisable to wear a one-piece swimsuit rather than a bikini. Your modesty could be at stake here!

## Disney's Typhoon Lagoon Water Park

Until Disney's Blizzard Beach Water Park opened in '95, Disney's Typhoon Lagoon was the biggest and finest example of Florida's water parks. In high season, it is also the busiest, so be prepared to run into more queues and congestion in all the main areas. The 56 acres of Disney's Typhoon Lagoon Water Park are spread out around the two-and-a-half-acre lagoon that is fringed with palm trees and white

**Disney's Typhoon Lagoon Water Park**

> BRIT TIP: While these parks are a great way of cooling down, it is easy to forget this is also the best way to pick up a five-star case of sunburn. So don't forget high factor (at least 15), waterproof suntan lotion.

sand beaches. If it wasn't for the high-season crowds, you could easily convince yourself you had been washed up on some tropical island paradise. With the exception of Disney's Blizzard Beach Water Park, Typhoon Lagoon goes in for the most extravagant landscaping and introduces some unique and clever details. The walk up Mount Mayday, for instance, provides a terrific overview of the park as well as adding scenic touches like rope bridges and tropical flowers. Sun loungers, chairs, picnic tables and even a few hammocks are provided to add to the comfort and convenience of areas like Getaway Glen.

The park is overlooked by the 90-foot **Mount Mayday**, atop which is perched the luckless *Miss Tilly*, a shrimp boat that legend has it landed here during the typhoon that gave the park its name. Watch for the water fountains that shoot from *Miss Tilly*'s funnel at regular intervals, accompanied by the ship's hooter, which signal the outbreak of another round of four-foot high waves in the lagoon itself (where you can hire innertubes to bob around on or just try body-surfing). Circling the lagoon is **Castaway Creek**, a three-foot deep lazy flowing river that offers the chance to float happily along on the rubber tyres that are provided for just this purpose (although around midday you may

find yourself shoulder-to-shoulder with hundreds of people who all have the same idea).

The series of slides and rides are all clustered around Mount Mayday and vary from the breathtaking **Humunga Kowabunga**, which drops you 214 feet at up to 30mph down some of the steepest inclines in waterdom (make sure your swimming costume is SECURELY fastened for this one!), to the children's area **Ketchakiddee Creek**, which offers a selection of slides and fun pools for all youngsters under four feet tall. In between, you have the three **Storm Slides**, another body slide-type which twists and turns through caves, tunnels and waterfalls, **Mayday Falls**, a 460-foot innertube ride down a series of twisting, turning drops, **Keelhaul Falls**, an alternative tube ride that takes

**Fun at Disney's Blizzard Beach Water Park**

slightly longer, and **Gang Plank Falls**, a group or family ride whose tubes take up to four people down the 300 feet of mock rapids. The hugely imaginative **Shark Reef** offers the chance to snorkel around this upturned wreck and coral reef among 4,000 tropical fish and a number of real, but quite harmless, nurse sharks. Like all the areas, this

> BRIT TIP: If the main changing rooms are busy (as they will be throughout the morning during peak periods), go instead to one of the restrooms where changing facilities are also provided.

one is carefully supervised, and those who aren't quite brave enough to dive in amongst the marine wildlife can still get a close up through the underwater port holes of the sunken ship (Shark Reef is closed to swimmers during the coldest of the winter months). There are height and health restrictions on Humunga Kowabunga (no bad backs, necks, or pregnant women), while the queues for this slide, plus the Storm Slides and Shark Reef can touch an arduous hour at times which can take a lot of the fun out of the experience (an hour's wait for a 20-second slide? Not for me, thanks). Getting out of the sun can also be slightly problematic as the provision of shaded areas is not overwhelming, but a quick plunge into Castaway Creek usually solves any overheating problems. Disney's Typhoon Lagoon Water Park does have the most picturesque areas to soak up the sun.

For snacks and meals, **Lowtide Lou's** and **Let's Go Slurpin'** both offer snacks and drinks while **Typhoon Tilly's** and **Leaning Palms** both serve a mixture of burgers, sandwiches, salads and ice cream. It is essential to avoid main meal times here if you want to eat in relative comfort. You do, however, have the option of bringing your own picnic along here (unlike all the other theme parks) as there are several scenic areas laid out for you (but no alcohol or glass containers are allowed). You CAN'T bring your own snorkels, innertubes and rafts into the park, but snorkles are provided at Shark Reef and you need to hire innertubes only for the Lagoon. If you have forgotten any vital item like a sunhat or bucket and spade for the kids, or even your swimsuit, they are all available (along with the usual range of gifts and souvenirs) at **Singapore Sal's**.

To avoid the worst of the summer crowds (when the park's 7,200

> BRIT TIP: As the busiest of the water parks, Disney's Typhoon Lagoon can hit capacity quite early in the day in the summer. Call 407 824 4321 in advance to avoid being shut out.

capacity is frequently reached), Monday morning is about the best time to visit (steer clear of the weekends at all costs), while on other week days arrive either 30 minutes before opening time or in mid-afternoon when some people decide to call it a day to dodge the daily rainstorm. Early evening is pleasant as the park lights up.

Opening hours are 9am to dusk every day, with admission $24.95 for adults and $19.50 for kids three to nine (under threes free). It is free, of course, with an All-in-One Hopper Pass. **Attraction rating: AAAAA or TTTT** (depending on which slides you enjoy!).

## Disney's River Country Water Park

At just a quarter of the size of Disney's Typhoon Lagoon, you might think this is a good, out-of-the-way spot that most people overlook. But you'd be wrong. It may be smaller, but the same number of folk seem to try to cram in here. As it is not unknown for the gates to close by late morning because capacity has been reached, it is a good idea to arrive early or after 4pm (when admission prices are also reduced).

However, just because it is the country cousin to Disney's Typhoon Lagoon and Blizzard Beach in terms of size doesn't mean Disney's River Country is any less well organized or lacking in charm. In fact, its theme as an old-fashioned swimming hole gives it a rustic, backwoods America flavour straight out of *Huckleberry Finn*.

The heart of the park is **Bay Cove**, a roped-off section of Bay Lake which offers the chance to climb on ropes, tyre swings, a barrel bridge and boom swing and ride the

BRIT TIP: Disney's River Country Water Park is not the best of the water parks in the winter. Despite the heated pool, Bay Lake can be pretty cold and the park often closes for a month for refurbishment. Call 407 824 4321 to check opening times.

cable, all finishing with an emphatic splash into the lake. **Whoop-N-Holler Hollow** contains the two main thrill opportunities, a pair of similar bodyslide flumes that end with a seven-foot drop into the

heated swimming pool. **White Water Rapids** is a somewhat more sedate trip via innertube down a series of chutes and pools that gives you rather more chance to admire the scenery, while young children are also exceptionally well catered for with their own area, **Bay Cove**, which contains several small slides, pools and a separate stretch of beach. Just to do each of the main activities will take you about half the time that Disney's Typhoon Lagoon does, but there is a more relaxing, rural feel to Disney's River Country that encourages you to stick around for a while longer. And, if you get bored with splashing in the water, you can always take a boat ride or walk around on the **Nature Trail**, a 1,000-yard boardwalk through a pretty, well-shaded cypress grove.

**Pop's Place** serves the usual array of fast food (and a Kid's Picnic Basket at $3.59) while the **Waterin' Hole** offers snacks and drinks. There is no gift shop here, however.

To find Disney's River Country Water Park, follow the rather frustratingly convoluted directions for Discovery Island Park and bear left just before the boat jetty. Admission is $16.95 for adults and $13.50 for 3–9s, while it is free with an All-in-One Hopper, and is open 10am–dusk. **Attraction rating: AAA or TTT**.

## Disney's Blizzard Beach Water Park

Ever imagined a skiing resort in the middle of Florida? You haven't? Well, Disney have, and this is the result. Disney's Blizzard Beach Water Park aims to put the rest of the parks in the shade for size as well as extravagant settings, with the whole park arranged as if it were in the Rocky Mountains rather than the sub-tropics. That means snow-effect scenery, Christmas trees and water slides cunningly converted to look like skiing pistes and toboggan runs. It delivers a real feast for water lovers and Disney admirers in general, and the basic premise of snow-surfin' USA is an unarguable five-star knockout. Feature items are **Mount Gushmore**, a 90-foot mountain down which all the main slides run (including the world's tallest free-fall speed slide, the terrifying 120-foot-long **Summit Plummet**, which rockets you down a simulated ski jump at up to 60mph!), **Tike's Peak**, a kiddie-sized version of the park with scaled-down slides and a mock snow-beach, **Ski-Patrol Training Camp**, a series of slides and challenges for pre-teens, **Melt-Away Bay**, a one-acre pool fed by 'melting snow' waterfalls, and **Cross Country Creek**, a lazy-flowing river around the whole park which also carries floating guests through a bone-chilling 'ice cave' (watch out for the mini-waterfalls of ice-cold water!). A clever ski chair-lift operates to the top of Mount Gushmore, providing a magnificent view of the whole park and the surrounding areas of Walt Disney World® Resort. Don't miss the outstanding rides – **Teamboat Springs**, a wild, family innertube adventure, **Runoff Rapids**, a one-person tube plunge, and the **Snow**

Wet 'n' Wild

Wet 'n' Wild

**Stormers**, a daring head-first 'toboggan' run. **Toboggan Racers** give you the chance to speed down the 'slopes' against seven other head-first dare-devils. All four go to new heights of water park imagination and provide good-sized thrills without overdoing the scare factor (yes, I know, I'm a total coward). A recent addition is the **Double Dipper**, two side-by-side slides which send you down 215-ft long tubes in a race that is timed on a big clock which you can see at the bottom, and which gives you a real jolt halfway down! For those not quite up to Summit Plummet lunacy, the wonderfully-named **Slush Gusher** is a slightly less terrifying speed slide. There is also a 'village' area including the **Beach Haus** shop and **Lottawatta Lodge** restaurant, offering diners a grandstand view of Mount Gushmore and Melt-Away Bay beach. Predictably, the crowds are suitably massive, so avoid the weekends and from mid-morning onwards on Wednesdays to Fridays.

Disney's Blizzard Beach Water Park is located just north of the All

**Wipe Out at Water Mania**

Star Resorts off Buena Vista Drive, and charges are $24.95 per adult and $19.50 per child (3–9, and again free for all for the duration of an All-in-One Hopper) with opening times from 9am to early evening. **Attraction rating: AAAAA or TTTTT.**

## Wet 'n' Wild

If Walt Disney World scores highest marks for its scenic content, the area's original water park back in 1977, Wet 'n' Wild (also known as the Scream Factory) goes full-tilt for thrills and spills of the highest quality. If you really want to test the material of your swimsuit to the limit, this is the place to do it!

Wet 'n' Wild is repeatedly one of the best-attended water parks in the country, and its location in the heart of International Drive makes it a major tourist draw. Consequently, you will once again encounter some serious crowds here, although the 12 slides and rides, **Lazy River** attraction, an elaborate kids' park

BRIT TIP: The Children's Playground was built especially for those under 48 inches, right down to kid-sized beach chairs and tables, and the only junior wave pool in the world.

(with mini versions of many of the slides), **Surf Lagoon** and restaurant and picnic areas all manage to absorb a lot of punters before the queues start to develop. Waits of more than half an hour at peak times are rare. Its popularity with locals means it is busiest at weekends, with July the month that attracts most crowds.

You are almost spoilt for choice of main rides, from the highly popular group innertube rides of **The Surge** and **Bubba Tub**, through the more demanding rides of **Raging Rapids** to the high-thrill factor of the **Black Hole** (like the Magic Kingdom's Space Mountain, but in water!), **Blue Niagara** (also an enclosed body-slide) and **Mach 5** to the ultimate terror of **Der Stuka** and the **Bomb Bay**. These latter are definitely not for the faint-hearted. 'I was convinced I was going to die!' was the mild observation of one battle-hardened water park veteran. Basically they are two 76-foot-high bodyslides with a drop as near vertical as makes no difference.

**7**

**Cruisin' Creek at Water Mania**

Der Stuka is the straightforward slide version, while the Bomb Bay adds the extra terror of being hoisted into place and then allowed to free-fall on to the top of the slide. And they call it fun?! Suffice it to say, your author has not put himself at risk on these particular contraptions, and has absolutely no intention of doing so! For some reason only 15–25 per cent of the park's visitors pluck up the courage to try it. Can't think why. There are height restrictions (minimum 4ft required) on the Bomb Bay, Der Stuka, Blue Niagara and Wild One, while older kids get their own chance for thrills on the huge, inflatable **Bubble Up**, which bounces them into 3ft of water.

Recent additions are the thrilling toboggan-like **Fuji Flyer**, which takes four passengers in eight-foot-long, in-line tubes which whoosh down more than 450 feet of banked curves and speed-enhancing straights, and the bungee-like **Hydra Fighter**, a two-person swing equipped with a fire-type hose that sends the contraption into mad gyrations as you increase the water pressure!

The neighbouring lake is also part of the fun (although not in winter when its temperature drops below that of merely chilly), adding the opportunities to try the cable-operated **Knee Ski** and ride the **Wild One** (large innertubes tied behind a speedboat). Alternatively, take a breather in the slow-flowing **Lazy River** or abandon the water altogether for one of several shaded picnic areas. Staying cool out of the water is rather harder, however, especially at peak times when the best spots are quickly snapped up. For food, **Bubba's Bar-B-Q** serves chicken, ribs, fries and drinks, the **Beach Club Snack Bar** features burgers, hot dogs, chicken and sandwiches and there are another seven snack bars offering similar fast-food fare, including a pizza bar and a kiddies' counter (for the likes of peanut butter sandwiches, hot dogs and chips). For the energetic, there is also beach volleyball and the chance to ride the **Robo Surfer** at selected times, a watery version of the mechanical bucking bronco. All-day lockers, shower facilities, tube and towel rentals are all well provided, but if you bring your own floating equipment is has to be checked by one of the many lifeguards on duty. Picnics can also be brought in, provided you don't include alcohol or glass containers.

Wet 'n' Wild is located half a mile north of International Drive's junction with Sand Lake Road and is open year-round from 9am in peak periods (10am at other times) until variously 5, 6, 7, 9 or 11pm. The extended hours from late June to late August, known as Summer Nights programme, offer particularly good value as admission is half price after 5pm and you still have six hours of watery fun ahead of you. There is also live music, dancing, karaoke and competitions, including the interactive challenges of the rock-climbing walls and the catapult-orientated Water Wars, plus the bungee trampoline and dunk tank, in a real fun, party atmosphere. Admission is $25.95 for adults, $20.95 for 3–9s and free for under 3s, while Wet 'n' Wild is included in both the 7- and 10-Day Flex Tickets with Universal Studios, SeaWorld and Busch Gardens. Tube rentals are $4, towels $2 and lockers $4. Parking is $3. **Rating: AAA or TTTTT!**

## Water Mania

If Wet 'n' Wild attracts the serious water-thrill seekers, Kissimmee's version Water Mania is more family-orientated and laid back, with the crowds highest at weekends when the locals flock in and lowest early in the week. That's not to say Water Mania doesn't have its share of scary slides (or Wet 'n' Wild doesn't cater for families), it's just their emphasis is slightly different and those

> BRIT TIP: Kids are again extremely well catered for, and Water Mania can even host birthday parties in Mr Kool's Party Land. Call 407 396 2626 for details.

looking to avoid the crowds often end up here. Where Water Mania scores a minor victory over its rivals is in the provision of three acres of wooded picnic area that makes a welcome change from the concrete expanses and from the feverish splashing activities. You are again welcome to bring your own picnic (although no glass bottles or mugs).

Eight different slides, including a patented non-stop surfing challenge called **Wipe-Out**, the usual **Cruisin' Creek**, a 720,000-gallon **Wave Pool** (waves every 15 minutes, up to four feet high) and two separate kids' areas provide the main attractions, and there is again enough here to keep you occupied for at least half a day. Top of the list for those daring enough to throw themselves down things like Der Stuka is **The Screamer**, an aptly-named 72-foot-high free-fall speed slide, and **The Abyss**, 380 feet of enclosed-tube darkness. **The**

**Anaconda** and **Banana Peel** both feature family-sized innertubes down long, twisting, turning slides, while the **Double Berzerker** offers two different ways to be whooshed along and spat out into a foaming pool.

**The Rain Forest** is designed for two to 10 year olds, with a 5,000-square foot pool ranging from three inches to two feet deep and featuring mini-slides, fountains, water guns, and a giant pirate ship. **The Squirt Pond** and **Barnacle Bob's Bumper Boats** offer more pint-sized fun, while there is also the **Aqua Express** train ride and **Electric Arcade** for the young 'uns. However, the stand-out feature, for both trying and watching, is the **Wipe-Out**, one of only two such attractions in the world. The challenge is to grab a body surfboard and try to ride the continuous wave, risking going over the edge into another pool if you stray too wide, or being sent flying backwards if you lose your balance. A real blast!

In addition to the cooling picnic areas, there are also several snack bars, a mini-golf course, volleyball and basketball courts and a large shop.

Water Mania is located on Highway 192, just a mile east of the I4 intersection and is open variously from 9.30am (June to early September), 10am (March to the beginning of June and September and October) and 11am (November to February) until 5, 6 or 7pm (8pm at weekends in peak season). Admission is $24.95 for adults and $18.95 for kids three–12. Parking is $3. **Attraction rating: AAA or TTTT**.

Okay, that sums up the main big-scale attractions on offer, but many people are now looking for the 'something different' factor, so let's explore some alternatives to the mass-market experience …

# Off the Beaten Track

## *(or, When you're All Theme Parked Out)*

**A**fter several days in the midst of the hectic tourist whirl of mainstream Orlando, you may find yourself in need of a day or two's rest from the non-stop theme park activities; a holiday from your holiday. If that is the case, this Chapter is for you.

Hopefully, you will already have noted the relatively tranquil offerings of Cypress Gardens and Silver Springs, but, to get away from it all more completely and to enhance your view of central Florida still further, the following are guaranteed to take you well off the beaten tourist track. The Chapter is divided into two parts, the first dealing with a **Taste of the Real Florida**, and introducing the areas of Winter Park, Seminole County, nature boat rides and eco-tours, and journeys by airboat, balloon, ship, train and plane; part two edges back into mainstream territory with **Orlando by Night** and the full range of options open to you here, including the big entertainment centres of Disney's Pleasure Island, Universal's CityWalk, Church Street Station and The Pointe, the many dinner shows, plus the full range of bars, discos and night clubs.

## Winter Park

This elegant northern suburb of Orlando is one of its best-kept tourist secrets as it is little more than 20 minutes' drive from the hurly-burly of areas like International Drive and yet a million miles from the relentless commercialism. It offers several renowned museums and art galleries, some top-quality shopping, 17 restaurants (including the top-of-the-range **Park Plaza Gardens**), several pleasant walking tours, a delightful 50-minute boat-ride around several of the area's lakes and, above all, a chance to *slow down!*

The central area is **Park Avenue**, a classy street of fine shops, boutiques, two museums and a wonderfully shaded park. At one end of the avenue is **Rollins College**, a small but highly respected arts education centre which also houses the **Cornell Fine Arts Museum** (open daily, except Monday, admission free) and **Annie Russell Theater**. The museum features regular art exhibitions and lectures, as well as having its own collection. **The Morse Museum of American Art** is a must for admirers of American art pottery, American and European glass, furniture and other decorative arts of the late 19th and early 20th centuries, including one of the world's foremost collections of works by Louis Comfort Tiffany (open 9.30am–4pm Tue–Sat, and 1–4pm Sun, admission $3 for adults, $1 for children). The **Albin Polasek Museum and Sculpture Gardens** are also worth a look for culture buffs and the serene, tranquil setting devoted to this Czech-American artist. Open 10am–4pm Wednesday to Sunday, there is no admission charge and it is also a superb setting for weddings. The **Scenic Boat Tour** is located at the east end of Morse Avenue, and offers a charming, narrated tour of the 'Venice of America', travelling 12 miles around the lakes and canals for a fascinating glimpse of some of the most beautiful private houses, boat houses and lakeside gardens (properties in the area start at $750,000 and top $3million in several instances!). The tours run every day from 10am to 4pm and cost $6 for adults and $3 for children two to 11, and it is one of the most relaxing hours you will spend in Orlando.

The shops are also a cut or two above anything you will encounter elsewhere, and while you may find the prices equally distinctive, just browsing is an enjoyable experience with the charm of the area highlighted by the friendliness of everyone hereabouts. Regular pavement craft fairs and art festivals (especially the Spring Art Festival in March/April, which is a big part of the local social scene) also add splashes of colour to an already inviting scenario. In addition to the Park Plaza Gardens, which specialises in continental cuisine (see Chapter 9 on Eating Out), you can dine on French, Italian, Thai and Vietnamese offerings.

An additional high point of a visit to Winter Park is the **Kraft Azalea Garden** on Alabama Drive (off Palmer Avenue at the north end of Park Avenue), 11 acres of shaded lakeside walk-ways, gardens and hundreds of magnificent azaleas. The main focal point, the mock Grecian temple, is a particularly beautiful setting for the many weddings that are held here.

Winter Park is located off exit 45 of I4, Fairbanks Avenue. Turn right on to Fairbanks and head east for two miles until it intersects with Park Avenue and turn left; public parking is well indicated.

## Aquatic Wonders Boat Tours

To go further into the real world of Florida nature and its wildlife, **Aquatic Wonders Tours** operates a delightful break from the theme park business on Lake Tohopekaliga in Kissimmee. Operated by Captain Ray Robida and limited to a maximum of six people per trip, the choice of seven 2- to 5-hour cruises offers a series of gentle adventures

> **BRIT TIP:** Amazingly, the waterways feeding Lake Toho stretch all the way to Miami in the south. Captain Ray is a mine of fascinating geographical and historical information.

that are both entertaining and educational as well as relaxing. Every cruise is a little different depending on the local conditions and Capt Ray's individual style, which is wonderfully laid back yet still informative. His local knowledge of the waterways and wildlife is outstanding and children will get a lot out of it if they have enquiring minds.

The 3–4 hour **Aquatic Wonders** cruise studies the complex of local

**Airboat rides**

lakes and rivers, water ecology and the fish, insects and other animals of the area ($35 for adults, $26.95 for children 12 and under). The **Eagle Watch Tour** is an ornithologist's delight as it goes out for two hours to look at the nesting bald eagles on the lake, rare ospreys and many other species of birds ($18.95 and $12.95). The rather romantic **Sunset Sounds** is another two-hour trip aboard the 'Eagle Ray' to enjoy the sights and sounds of dusk over the lake as the birds come home to roost ($18.95 and $12.95). **Starlight Wonders** is a two-hour tour for a spot of star-gazing, gentle music and Native American stories surrounding the origins of the constellations ($18.95 and $12.95, or combine it with Sunset Sounds for $31.95 and $23.95). **Rivers In Time** is a two-hour journey back in time to the days of the river boat and the Seminole Indian War, a fascinating live history lesson with all the sights and sounds of the lake for good measure. The **Gator Watch Tour** is a two-hour night-time journey to view some of the locals hunting, nesting and just hanging out (and there are plenty of them out there!) as well as sounds of the lake at night (again, both are $18.95 and $12.95). **Family Fishing Adventures** offers four to five hours of fishing fun with all bait and tackle (but not fishing licence) provided, especially for beginners (from $135–$175 per person depending on the number involved). There are also games and videos for the kids in case their attention wanders! All tours have non-alcoholic drinks and snacks provided, and Capt Ray is fully licensed by the US Coast Guard, unlike some boat operators in the area, so you are guaranteed a high level of safety as well as entertainment. The Eagle Ray departs daily from Big Toho Marina at the west end of Lakeshore Boulevard off Ruby Avenue in downtown Kissimmee. Call 407 846 2814 for more details and to make reservations for these tours, which are proving increasingly popular.

## Airboat Rides

Staying with the watery theme, Florida also offers the thrill of airboat rides on many of its lakes, rivers and marshes. An airboat is a totally different experience to any boat ride you will have taken as it is more like flying at ground level. It is as much a thrill as a scenic adventure, but it also has the advantage of exploring areas otherwise inaccessible to boats.

> BRIT TIP: Best time to do the daily ride is first thing on a weekday morning when the local wildlife is not hiding from the weekend boaters.

Airboats simply skim over and through the marshes, to give you an alternative, close-up and very personal view. Travelling at up to 50mph also means it can be loud (hence you will be provided with headphones) and sunglasses are also a good idea to keep stray flies out of your eyes. It is NOT the trip for you if you are spooked by crickets, dragonflies and similar creepy crawlies that occasionally land inside the boat!

There are several operations offering airboat rides in the area, from you-drive boats that do barely 5mph to much bigger rides, but for safety and quality the *Brit's Guide* tip goes to **Boggy Creek Airboat Rides** at two locations in Kissimmee, especially as they now offer a discounted ticket with Gatorland so anyone purchasing the ride at Boggy Creek saves $4.50 on adult admission to Gatorland and

BRIT TIP: Watch out for discount coupons in all the freely distributed tourist literature offering up to $3 off airboat rides.

takes a child in free. Boggy Creek's airboats can be found on Lake Toho at Southport Park (all the way down Poinciana Boulevard, off Highway 192 between Markers 10 and 11, and across into Southport Drive) or on East Lake Toho (their main site). For the latter, you can either take Exit 17 of the Central Florida Greeneway (417) and go south on Boggy Creek Road, then right into East Lake Fish Camp, or, from Highway 192, go north on Simpson Road, which becomes Boggy Creek Road, turn right at the Boggy Creek T-junction, then right into East Lake Fish Camp.

The Fish Camp is itself a little gem, offering a variety of boating and angling opportunities (call 407 348 2040 for details) as well as the wonderfully authentic rural Florida charm of the **restaurant and gift shop** (open 8am–9pm every day). If you are heading for a morning airboat ride, consider arriving early for one of their magnificent (huge!) all-day breakfasts, while the more adventurous will want to try the local delicacies – catfish, frogs' legs and gator tail.

Boggy Creek's half-hour ride

BRIT TIP: Want to sample the Florida Everglades but don't fancy the three-hour trip south? Boggy Creek Airboats are the perfect substitute, and at a fraction of the cost.

features two of the most modern airboats in Florida, skimming over the local wetlands for a close-up view of the majestic cypress trees and wildlife that can include eagles, ospreys, snakes and turtles as well as the inevitable alligators.

You do not need to book in advance, just turn up and go (from 9am–5.30pm seven days a week), and rides cost $16 for adults and $8 for children 8 and under. They also do a one-hour Night Tour for a thrilling and fascinating alternative view of the local gators – their eyes glow red in the dark – but you do need to book on 407 344 9550.

## Everglades and The Keys

Day trips are increasingly being offered from Orlando south to the Everglades, Miami and the Florida Keys, and, if you are prepared to put up with a long day out (up to 16 hours) you can see a lot of the State this way. However, they are not well-suited to children, with long periods on a coach, while the half-hour airboat ride once you get to the Everglades is a pretty brief highlight in all that time.

The one operator I have seen so far that seems to make light of those drawbacks is **Island Tours**, both for the quality of the elements of their trip, which also takes in beautiful Naples and Marco Island on the south-west coast, and the sheer value for money they offer. Their one-day getaway (offered four times a week) is only $89 for adults and $69 for children 4–12, and they use only top-quality motor-coaches and airboats, include an alligator and snake-handling show in your Everglades adventure, throw in a two-hour sightseeing cruise from Naples and full use of the facilities at the five-star Marriott Marco Beach Resort. Just about every detail is anticipated, while Island Tours also offer a tempting two-day trip to

8

Miami and Key Largo, which includes a boat tour round Miami's waterways, admission to the magnificent John Pennekamp State Park, with a glass-bottom boat cruise, and overnight accommodation at the superb Westin Key Largo Resort. The two-day trip costs $189 for adults and $159 for children, but no under-4s please. Be aware you will make an *early* start! Call 1-800 435 6855 for more details and reservations.

## Balloon trips

Florida is one of the most popular areas for ballooning and, if you are up early enough in the morning, you will quite often see three or four balloons floating over the Orlando countryside.

The experience is a majestic one. If Orlando represents the holiday of

> BRIT TIP: Ladies please note dresses are NOT advisable for climbing in and out of the balloon's basket and stout, sensible shoes are a must for everyone.

a lifetime, then a balloon flight is the ride of a lifetime. Believe me, Disney has nothing to touch this one! The utterly smooth way in which you lift off into the early morning sky is breathtaking in itself, but the peace and quiet of the ride, not to mention the stunning views from 2,000 feet above ground, are quite awesome. It is not a cheap experience, however, but it is equally appealing to couples and families, although small children can be a little scared by the unusual nature of it all. Needless to say, it is not recommended for anyone who suffers vertigo or a fear of heights. It is a very personalised ride, as four people make for a full trip. Some

baskets can take up to nine, but you need to be on good terms with each other!

There are numerous outfits offering balloon flights in the Orlando area, and you should be advised that several have earned themselves a bad reputation for lacking full safety requirements or showing scant regard for the areas where they take off and land. Hence, if you are considering a balloon flight, it is important to ensure your trip is with a reputable operation.

**Orange Blossom Balloons**, the premier company in central Florida, with more than 15 years' unblemished experience, fit that description admirably, especially as they are a British-owned and run operation. You meet at the Travelodge Hotel on Disney's Hotel Plaza Boulevard at 6am (the best winds for flying are always first thing in the morning) and then transfer to the take-off site, where you help the crew set up and inflate one of their three balloons. Owner-operator Richard Ornstein and his team are a real hoot, and you are soon up, up and away in awe-inspiring style, floating serenely up to 2,000ft or

**Up, up and away ...**

sinking down to skim the surface of one of the many lakes (disturbing the occasional gator or deer). After about an hour you come back to earth for a traditional champagne landing ceremony and return to the Travelodge for a full breakfast and your special balloonist's certificate. The full experience lasts some four hours and the cost is $169 per adult (inclusive of tax) and $85 for 10–16s (under 10s go free with their parents). Call 407 239 7677 for reservations as they are usually popular (especially for Brits).

## Warbird Air Museum

Vintage aeroplane and nostalgia buffs will want to make a note of this offbeat museum adjacent to Kissimmee Airport, which builds and restores old World War II fighters and bombers. Kids who enjoyed building Airfix kits will especially enjoy the one-hour tour of the facilities, which basically represent a couple of large hangars with aircraft in various stages of restoration and repair. It is one of the most amazing programmes of its kind you will find, with the exhibits ranging from a fully-restored B-25 Mitchell bomber and a P-51 Mustang to scraps of fuselages and engines that will gradually be incorporated into the latest rebuilding project. It's a place where you see, smell and touch the history of the old 1940s newsreels. The tour guides have a detailed working knowledge of everything they show you. You could be forgiven for thinking you have walked into a scrapyard on your way in, but the main hangars reveal the full scale of the operation, with the wholesale restoration of a B-17 Flying Fortress being their pride and joy. In fact, owner Tom Reilly insists: 'All those clean, tidy sterile museums you have seen in the past, well, this isn't one of them. We have oil on the floor we refer to as *bomber blood* and if you are lucky, you might get some on you to take home as a souvenir.' The site detail includes a charming little gift shop that houses some more museum pieces, uniforms and memorabilia from World War II. It is open seven days a week from 9am to 6pm (9–5pm on Sundays), and there is always some reconstruction work under way. Charges are $8 for adults and $6 for over 60s and under 12s (under sixes free). The museum can be found just off Highway 192, half a mile down Hoagland Boulevard on the left. They also offer biplane rides, call 407 933 1942 for details.

## Green Meadows Petting Farm

From one extreme to another, here is guaranteed fun for kids of two up to about 11, and their parents (and don't forget your cameras). It's the ultimate hands-on experience as, on your two-hour guided tour, you get the chance to milk a cow, pet a pig, cuddle a chick (or duckling), feed goats and sheep, meet buffalo, chickens, peacocks and donkeys and learn what makes an animal farm tick. There are pony rides for the young 'uns and tractor-drawn hay rides for all, plus Kandu the Magician and the Green Meadows Express steam train for a scenic ride through the farm. The shaded acres, free-roaming animals and peaceful aspect all make for another pleasant change of pace, especially as Green Meadows is barely five minutes from the tourist hurly-burly of Highway 192 (south on Poinciana Boulevard). It is open from 9.30am–5.30pm daily (last admission at 4pm) and costs $15 per person (under 2s free), and you should allow 3–4 hours for your visit. Kids of the requisite age absolutely adore it.

8

## Florida Fun-train

When is a train not a train? When it is the '200-mile amusement park' of the one-off Florida Fun-train, a rollicking, multi-coloured creation that runs between Kissimmee and Hollywood, near Miami, in south Florida and Kissimmee and Tampa to the west. A combination of transport and entertainment (transertainment, entertainsport?), the Fun-Train is a rather bizarre concept designed for the family market, with carriages of fun for the kids and more adult-orientated diversions in the shape of a South Seas-style Tiki Bar, dance floor and live music, a 50s Diner, Wine Bar and Pub. All the carriages offer something different, from glass-domed observation cars where you can watch Florida roll by or enjoy a table-service meal, to The Junction, packed with video games, virtual reality adventures and even a space shuttle play area, and up to the new CyberLink, a 68-seat 'cinema' offering the latest in virtual reality screens and sound. Clowns and other entertainers are on board to keep everyone amused, and some of the cars even feature two-tiered lounges with quiet corners for a drink or chat. The Hollywood trip requires an overnight stay, however, which means it takes up almost two days of your holiday and, while there is nothing wrong with Hollywood itself, it is not how I would choose to spend my vacation time in Florida, although it is definitely a different way to travel (and, if they start packaging a Miami stay with it, it may have much greater appeal). Of more interest is the Tampa trip, which can easily be done in a day, and offers the chance to visit another lively city. One-way fares start at $69.95 for adults, $49.95 for children 12 and under (2 and under free), and the schedules vary, so call 407 518 0224 for the latest information and reservations. At the time of writing, the boarding area was in the Kissimmee suburb of Poinciana, down Poinciana Boulevard, right on to Highway 17-92 (the Orange Blossom Trail) and left into Avenue A two blocks later. Bizarre it might be, fun it most definitely is, especially for train-lovers. All the on-board games, food and drinks do cost extra, though.

## Disney and cruising

Taking a cruise is fast becoming a regular option with your Orlando stay and, with the advent of Disney Cruise Line in 1998, you will see a lot of publicity for these competitively-priced two-, three- and four-day sailings out of fast-developing Port Canaveral.

Although they are cruise newcomers, **Disney** have set their stall out with some of the most breathtaking hardware in the form of their first two ships, the 85,000-ton *Disney Magic* (in 1998) and *Disney Wonder* (1999). Classic design, plus the usual Disney imagineering, has produced these two vessels, which are big even by modern standards and incorporate special features for kids, teenagers AND couples without children. Both ships boast an amazing destination experience in their own right, with four restaurants, a 1,040-seat theatre, cinema, night-club complex, sports club and a full health spa, while they will also visit the Bahamas and Disney's truly stunning private island. It is not a cheap option and a three- or four-day cruise can be purchased only as a week's package with a Walt Disney World® Resort stay, but, if the idea appeals to you, check out tour operators Bridge Travel, Virgin, British Airways Holidays, First Choice and Transolar for Disney cruise packages (or, for more advice, buy my book, *A Brit's Guide to Cruise Planning*).

The first cruise sailed on July 30 and the initial impressions were quite amazing. The impact of the four-restaurant set-up (where you dine in a different one each night, including the amazing Animator's Palate which comes to life all around you), the fabulous entertainment 'district', the vast array of kids' facilities (including Buzz Lightyear's Cyberspace Command Post), the magnificently appointed beaches of their Castaway Cay island and the sheer ocean-going quality throughout fair knocked your socks off. The one shame is that you can spend a maximum of only four days enjoying this state-of-the-art experience.

Alternatives out of Port Canaveral include **Cape Canaveral Cruise Line** (two-day trips to the Bahamas from $129 per person, call 407 783 4052), **Premier Cruise Line** (three- and four-day cruises, call 407 783 5061 for prices and details), **Carnival** (the 'fun ships', offering three- and four-day Bahamas cruises, call 1-800 327 9501) and **Royal Caribbean International** (also three- and four-day trips, call 1-800 327 6700).

For a smaller and more low-key approach, the **Rivership Romance**, daily out of downtown Sanford, is highly recommended, especially for their lunch cruises on the wildlife-rich St John's River. Their old-fashioned steamer can take up to 200 in comfort and adds a fine meal, live entertainment and a river commentary, as well as providing a relaxing alternative to the usual tourist scenario. You choose between the 3-hour lunch cruise (Wed, Sat and Sun, 11am–2pm) at $35 a head, the 4-hour cruise (Mon, Tue, Thur and Fri, 11am–3pm) at $45 or an evening dinner dance voyage (Fri and Sat, 7.30–11pm) at $50. They are also planning regular, two-day trips to beautiful St Augustine near Jacksonville, and for reservations and information call

1-800 423 7401. The Rivership Romance can be found off exit 51 of I4, east into Sanford and then left on to Palmetto Avenue.

## Seminole County

Having arrived in the historic town of Sanford, the heart of Seminole County, it is worth pointing out the possible diversions of a day out in this area that will get you well off the beaten track. The **Central Florida Zoological Park** is a private, non-profit-making organisation that puts a pleasant, natural accent on the zoo theme, set in 109 wooded acres of unspoilt Florida countryside and with boardwalks and trails around all the attractions. These include more than 100 species of animals, weekend feeding demonstrations, educational programmes, a picnic area, pony rides and a butterfly garden. It's good value, too, at $7 for adults and $3 for kids three to 12, and the park (off exit 52 of I4) is open every day (except Thanksgiving Day and Christmas Day) from 9am–5pm.

**St John's River Cruises** are another natural attraction, exploring the back-waters of the river on fully-narrated two-hour tours, meeting alligators and other Florida wildlife, including many of its bird species and, in season (November to April), the endangered manatee. The two-hour tour goes out daily (except Monday) from 11am, with sunset cruises from April to October, and costs $12 for adults and $6 for under-12s. There is also a full-day cruise (8am–5pm), which includes a stop at scenic Blue Springs State Park, for $45. Always call for reservations on 407 330 1612, and cruises leave from Sanford Boat Works, at the end of Celery Avenue, east out of Sanford town centre. Don't miss their Gator Landing restaurant for a taste of real Florida to go along with the sights. Look out also for the new **Naturally Florida Eco-Passport**, which provides pre-paid access to attractions like these. Call 904 532 1352 for prices and details.

**Sanford** itself is a designated historic centre, full of brick-paved streets and antique shops. It is very much small-town America, having lost the growth battle with Orlando many years ago, but it makes a peaceful diversion. It also offers the **Rose Cottage Tea Room**, one of the prettiest restaurants you will find in Florida, which serves a mouth-watering array of soups, sandwiches, salads and quiches, as well as fabulous fruit teas. This little treasure of the culinary world (open 11am–3pm daily) can be found on Park Avenue, 13 blocks out of Sanford town centre, call 407 323 9448 for reservations (which are usually required).

## Beach escapes

When the temperatures start to soar, the lure of Florida's many white sand beaches becomes strong, and there are some excellent choices little more than an hour's drive away. Be warned first, though, that Orlando natives all get the same idea at the weekend, so unless you head out EARLY (i.e. before 9am) and come back late (i.e. after 8pm) you are likely to encounter some serious traffic. The choice is actually quite simple for a change. If you head EAST, you have **Cocoa Beach**, at about 40 miles the closest to Orlando (straight along the Beeline Expressway, then south on Highway A1A) and a great mix of wide sands, gently-sloping beaches and moderate but fun surfing waves. As it's the Atlantic, the sea can be pretty chilly from November to March, but Cocoa Beach is rapidly developing into a major coastal resort, so the facilities are excellent. While in Cocoa Beach, be sure to visit **Ron**

**St Petersburg Beach**

**Jon's Surf Shop**, a mind-boggling pink and purple emporium of warehouse proportions open 24 hours a day, stocking every kind of beach paraphernalia imaginable. From here north to **Daytona Beach** you have almost 100 miles of beautiful beaches that have been developed to a lesser extent, while Daytona itself (home to some great annual motor-sport) is one of the most famous beaches in the world. To reach Daytona Beach direct from Orlando, it is about 90 minutes' drive along I4 east, pick up I95 north then Highway 92 east, which turns into International Speedway Boulevard and leads to the beaches.

To the WEST you have the **Gulf Coast**, which is a good 90 minutes' drive down I4 and through Tampa on I275 south to **St Petersburg Beach** (105 miles) or **Clearwater Beach** (110 miles) or two hours-plus down I4 and then I75 to **Bradenton** (130 miles), **Sarasota** (140 miles) and **Venice** (160 miles). The beaches are less 'hip', that is, more relaxed and refined, and the sea a touch warmer and much calmer, so it is better for families with small children. You will find it easier to get away from the crowds here, too. **Naples** is another hour further south on I75 but is currently rated one of the most welcoming beach destinations in Florida.

## Sport

In addition to virtually every form of entertainment known to man, central Florida is also one of the world's biggest sporting playgrounds, with a huge range of opportunities either to watch or play your favourite sport.

## Golf

Without doubt, the number one activity is **Golf**, with almost 150 courses within an hour's drive of Orlando. The weather, of course, makes it such a popular pastime, but some spectacular courses add to the attraction, and there are numerous holiday packages geared entirely towards keen golfers of all abilities. With an 18-hole round, including green fees, cart hire and taxes, from as little as $40 on some courses (and the average around $60), it is an attractive proposition and a very different one from those used to British courses. If you go in for 36-hole days, it is possible in most cases to save up to $30 by replaying the same course. Sculptured landscapes, manicured fairways and abundant

use of spectacular water features and white sand traps make for some memorable golfing. January to May is the busiest golf 'season', but many courses are busy year-round. Check also when you book about each club's dress code, as there are differences from course to course.

Inevitably, **Disney** have been quick to attract the golf fanatic, with five championship-quality courses, including the 7,000-yard Palm, rated one of Golf Digest's top 25. Fees vary from $90–$120 for Disney resort guests and $100–$130 for visitors, with half-price reductions after 3pm. Call 407 939 4653 for tee-times.

Other quality courses open to the public include the **Grand Cypress**, next door to Walt Disney World® Resort (tel 407 239 1904, rates from $100–$140), **Metro West Country Club**, on South Hiawassee Road off Conroy-Windermere to the north of Universal Studios (tel 407 299 1099, $75) and **Marriott's Orlando World Center** (tel 407 238 8660, $60–$110). Alternatively, **Tee Times USA** (tel 1-800 374 8633) offer a unique advice and reservation service, while **Stand-by Golf** will get you discounted prices and guaranteed times at many of the major courses (tel 813 899 2665 for details).

## Fishing

**Fishing** also attracts a lot of specialist holiday-makers, although not very many, it has to be said, from Britain. The abundance of lakes and rivers makes for plentiful sport of the angling variety, with bass the prime catch. A seven-day licence will cost you $16.50 (available from all tackle shops, fishing camps, sports stores and Wal-Mart and K-Mart supermarkets), and there are dozens of boats for hire on the St John's River, Lake Toho in Kissimmee, Lake Kissimmee and both coasts for

**Golfing in Orlando**

8

some serious sea fishing. Expect to pay $160–$195 for half a day and $200–$295 for a full day trip bass fishing. For the most complete angling service in central Florida try **Cutting Loose Expeditions**, a highly experienced, personalised operator who can organise fresh or sea-water expeditions and arrange hotel pick-up if necessary. All your bait and licence requirements are included. The service is run by A. Neville Cutting, one of America's greatest fishing adventurers, and he maintains high standards with his guides and other staff. Rates start at $200 for a half day's bass fishing, but other trips, including offshore for marlin, can be arranged. Phone 407 629 4700 or write to Cutting Loose Expeditions, PO Box 447, Winter Park, Florida 32790–0447.

## Water sports

Florida is also, of course, mad keen on **Water sports** of all persuasions. Consequently, on any area of water bigger than your average pond don't be surprised to find the locals water-skiing, jet-skiing, knee-boarding, canoeing, paddling, wind-surfing, boating or otherwise indulging in watery pursuits. Walt Disney World® Resort offers all manner of boats, from catamarans to pedaloes, on the main **Bay Lake**, as well as the smaller lakes of **Seven Seas Lagoon, Club Lake** and **Lake Buena Vista**. There are several operators on the lakes around Orlando and Kissimmee, too, but some of them leave much to be desired, safety-wise. **Dave's Ski School** on Lake Bryan at Lake Buena Vista (right next to the Holiday Inn Sunspree Resort) get the official *Brit's Guide* recommendation for their safety-conscious approach and their virtual guarantee to get beginners up and water-skiing. You can also rent jet-skis and wave-runners, take tube

BRIT TIP: Don't be tempted by the several offers of U-Drive airboats – they are puny and unreliable. Instead, try East Lake Fish Camp's boating possibilities on East Lake Toho in Kissimmee. Call 407 348 2040.

rides or go on one of the organised beach parties. Many of the main tour operators also endorse this ski school and for rates and other details, call 407 239 6939. For a more gentle experience and a close-up of the local wildlife try **Katie's Wekiva River Landing**. Here you can try up to a full day's canoeing on some of the most scenic waters of central Florida (take I4 [north] east to exit 51 and Highway 46 west for almost five miles, and Wekiva Park Drive is on your right). It's fairly leisurely, but does have its faster-flowing sections, and you can take time-outs for a picnic or to go fishing. The entire portion of the Wekiva River here has been designated a protected Scenic and Wild area, while the neighbouring forest with its hiking trails is an official aquatic preserve, which gives you an idea of the territory. Thick cypress forest, clear, spring-fed waters, abundant water and wildlife, it's all here for nature-lovers. Katie's offers four different canoe trips, from a leisurely two-hour, six-mile paddle to a 19-mile overnight camping trip, all with a pick-up service at the end or transport up-river to start with. Prices range from $13 to $26 (children three to 11 half-price), and the trips are suitable for beginners and more experienced canoeists alike. Katie's also offers camping, boating and fishing. For more details call 407 628 1482.

# Mini-golf

Not exactly a sport, but definitely for tourist consumption are the many and quite extravagant opportunities for **Mini-golf** around Orlando. Not only are they quite picturesque, some of them offer prizes for particularly tricky shots. They are a big hit with kids and good fun for all the family (if you have the legs left for 18 holes after a day at the theme park!). Several other attractions and parks offer mini-golf as an extra, but for the best, try out the self-contained centres, of which there are six main ones.

Predictably, Disney have seen the growth in the popularity of this type of attraction and come up with two terrific varieties of their own. **Disney's Fantasia Gardens Miniature Golf**, next to The Swan hotel just off Buena Vista Drive, is a two-course challenge over 36 of the most varied holes of mini-golf you will find. Hippos dance, fountains leap and broomsticks march on the 18-hole crazy golf-themed **Fantasia Gardens** – yes, its style is taken from the Disney animated classic *Fantasia*, and that means lots of cartoon fun along the way as the park's imagineers challenge you with a riot of visual gags as well as some diabolically difficult mini-golf. Watch out for 'Toccata and Fugue in D Minor' where good shots are rewarded with musical tones, and 'The Nutcracker Suite', where obstacles include dancing mushrooms! **Fantasia Fairways** is a cunning putting course on undulating astroturf, complete with fairways, rough, water hazards and bunkers which will test even the best golfers. The 18 holes range in length from 40 to 75 feet, and it can take well in excess of an hour to play a full round. It costs $9 (adult) and $7.50 (child) for Fantasia Gardens, and $9 and $8 for Fantasia Fairways, and they are open from 10am to midnight every day. **Pirate's Cove** has a twin-course set-up at Lake Buena Vista (by the Crossroads shopping plaza) and International Drive (just south of the Mercado Centre), with mountain caves, waterfalls and rope bridges to test your skill and please the eye. **River Adventure Golf** (on Highway 192, almost opposite Medieval Times) offers a Mississippi River adventure

> BRIT TIP: International Drive picks up a lot of bonus points for having so much extra of this kind of tourist development so handily situated.

with rolling rapids, waterfalls and an authentic water wheel. **Bonanza Miniature Golf and Gifts** (next door to the Magic Mining Co restaurant on the western side of Highway 192) has another imaginative – and tricky – 36 holes set in a gold-mine theme with the backdrop of huge waterfalls. **Pirate's Island** (further along Highway 192 to the east) is another spectacular 36-hole spread, while arguably the most impressive of the lot is the **Congo River Golf and Exploration Co**, which has courses on Highway 192, International Drive and Highway 436 in Altamonte Springs. They could almost be Disney-inspired, they are so artificially scenic. The Kissimmee location also has paddle boats to try, while International Drive has the option of go-karts, and all three have games and video arcades. Charges are $6–$8 per round, but look out for coupons which all have a couple of dollars off each one. They open from 9am to 10pm or 11pm daily. **Million Dollar Mulligan** is also worthy of mention here, although it

8

is neither mini-golf nor the real McCoy. Instead, Million Dollar Mulligan, just off Highway 192 on Florida Plaza Boulevard (next to Old Town – look for the giant golf ball), is a nine-hole, floodlit pitch-and-putt course, plus driving and target range, that looks spectacular at night with its lake and fountains lit up. The pitch-and-putt is $11 ($7 for kids), a practice bucket for the range $4, while there is also a natural grass putting course ($5 and $3), all open from 9am–midnight.

## Go-karting

On a similar footing, there are a number of **Go-kart** tracks around the main tourist areas that will also seek to side-track you for an hour or two. The biggest is **Fun 'n' Wheels** (on International Drive at Sand Lake Road, and on West Vine Street, Kissimmee), which is open daily from 9am to either 7pm or 11pm (depending on the season). You buy tickets at $1.25 each (or 30 for $30) and then have the choice of four kart tracks, mini-golf, bumper boats and cars, waterslides, a big wheel, a kiddie play area, games arcade and snack bars. You really do need plenty of energy to tackle this (not surprisingly, it's a big hit with kids), and the almost non-stop roar of the karts can get a bit tedious. **Kartworld** (at the top of International Drive and on Highway 192) has some of the largest tracks in the world, up to a mile long, as well as

**Fun 'n' Wheels go-karting**

large games arcades. The newest attraction of this kind is **Fun Spot** on Del Verde Way just off International Drive and Kirkman Road, with four different tracks, including the four-corkscrew Quad Helix, a giant ferris wheel, bumper cars and boats, a Junior Spot of rides for young 'uns and a two-storey games arcade, as well as a food court.

## Horse riding

If **Horse riding** takes your fancy (or your children's), you will certainly want to know that Orlando is home to one of the foremost equestrian centres in America, if not the world. It is the **Grand Cypress Equestrian Center**, part of the 1,500-acre Grand Cypress Resort, and all its rides and facilities are open to non-residents. This stunningly well-equipped equine haven offers a dazzling array of opportunities for the horse enthusiast of all abilities. A full range of clinics, lessons and other instructional programmes are available, from half-hour kids' sessions to all-summer academies, plus a variety of trail rides. The centre's facilities include a floodlit covered arena, a dressage ring, a floodlit outdoor jumping ring, an exercise track, turnout paddocks, tack and gift shop, lounge, classroom, snack bar and locker rooms. Serious horse riders will note that this was the first American equestrian centre to be approved by the British Horse Society, and it operates the BHS test programme. Inevitably, this five-star facility does not come cheap, but, especially for children, it is a highly worthwhile experience. Private lessons are $45 per half hour or $75 per hour, while a week's package of eight half-hour lessons is $270. Young Junior Lessons (15-minute supervised rides for under-12s) are $25, while the Western Trail Ride (an hour's excursion for novice riders) is $30 per person and the Advanced Trail Ride $45. The centre is open from 8am to 5pm daily and can be found by taking exit 27 on I4 on to Route 535 north, turning left after half a mile at the traffic lights and then following the road north for a mile (past the entrance to the Hyatt Regency Grand Cypress Hotel) until the equestrian centre is on your right. For more details and to book rides (which are most popular from late November through to March), call 407 239 1938. On a smaller scale and none the less charming is the

The Orlando Arena

## Spectator events

When it comes to **Spectator events**, Orlando is not quite so well furnished as other big American cities, but there is always something on offer for the discerning sports fan who would like to sample the local version of the big football or cricket match. There are no top-flight American Football or baseball teams in Orlando, but there is an indoor version of gridiron, called Arena Football, plus two Minor League baseball teams. The big sport in town, though, is **Basketball** and the Orlando Magic, who are one of the best-supported teams in the NBA. The basketball season runs from November to May (with exhibition games in October), and the only drawback is that the Magic are so popular that the state-of-the-art, 16,000-seat Orlando Arena where they play (on Amelia Street, exit 41 off I4, turn left, then left again) is nearly always fully booked for home games. The Arena box office (407 649 3245) can always tell you if there

Tampa Bay Stadium

**Horse World Riding Stables** on Poinciana Boulevard, just 10 minutes south of Highway 192. This gets you more out into the wilds as it is further away from the main tourist areas, and you can spend anything from an hour to a full day enjoying the different rides and lessons on offer. Their two main trail rides are the Nature Trail ($29.95), a 45-minute to one-hour ride for beginners through 750 acres of untouched Florida countryside (no reservations required), and the Private Trail Ride, a 90-minute trip for advanced riders with a private guide ($39.95, reservations required). There is also a picnic area with fishing pond, playing fields, pony rides for under 8s and farm animals to pet. There is no charge for just looking around, and the stables are open from 9am to 5pm daily. Call 407 847 4343 for details and reservations.

8

Florida Citrus Bowl

are any tickets left, although you need to call in person to buy them (from $16 up in the gods to $58 courtside), or you can try calling Ticketmaster on 407 839 3900 for credit card bookings. The Orlando Predators, one of America's top **Arena Football** teams, are also popular at the same venue (from May to August, ticket prices from $10–$30) and you would need to call several days in advance to avoid missing one of their lively home games that feature some great entertainment as well as their fast, hard-hitting version of indoor American Football in the magnificent Arena. For the Real Thing in gridiron terms, the nearest teams in the **National Football League** are the Tampa Bay Buccaneers, 75 miles to the west, the Miami Dolphins, some 3 ½ hours drive to the south down the Florida Turnpike or the Jacksonville Jaguars way up the east coast past Daytona, a three-hour drive up I4 and I95. Again, Ticketmaster can give you ticket prices (they vary from $20 to $40) and availability. College American Football is also a big draw in America and Orlando's **Citrus Bowl Stadium**, which staged four World Cup games in 1994, is home to one of the biggest annual games, the New Year's Day Citrus Bowl, which pits two of the season's top college teams in an end-of-season play-off. However, tickets are again hard to come by as it is nearly always a sell-out, so call the Stadium (which is in the downtown area, just off the North Orange Blossom trail, take exit 36 off I4, turn left then right) on 407 423 2476 at least a month in advance if you are interested.

# Disney's Wide World of Sports

The newest sports facility in the area is inevitably a Disney project to bring in some world-class events and competitors. **Disney's Wide World of Sports** is a 200-acre, state-of-the-art complex, featuring more than 32 sports and is quite awesome to wander round even when no-one is playing! A recent addition is a permanent version of the **NFL** (American Football) **Experience**,

> BRIT TIP: Disney's Wide World of Sports provides the official winter training headquarters for the British Olympic Association, so you may bump into some of our top athletes here at times.

which gives you the chance to test your skills as a gridiron star in an interactive playground for adults and kids alike. The complex's main features are a 7,500-seater baseball stadium, a softball quadraplex, an 11-court tennis complex, beach volleyball and the **All Star Café** with a massive array of sports memorabilia and even themed food. The baseball stadium is home for spring training of the mighty **Atlanta Braves**, and the crowds positively flock in for their pre-season games. Other stand-outs include the US Men's Clay Court Tennis Championship (in April), Harlem Globetrotters basketball and international beach volleyball. The facilities alone should inspire world-class performances in any athlete. Standard admission is $8 (increased for the big events, but free with an All-in-One Hopper Pass) and the

Wide World of Sports can be found off Osceola Parkway, between World Drive and I4. Call 407 363 6100 for current events and ticket prices.

**Baseball** is, of course, America's traditional sporting pastime, and, if the Braves' games are sold out, you can still get a taste of the action with two other spring training outfits and

> BRIT TIP: Spring training is a big deal in baseball. Games can be extremely competitive as players are battling to make their team's squad for the coming season.

two Minor League teams. **Baseball City** (just off exit 23 of I4 going [south] west) is home to the Kansas City Royals for spring training (March and April) while the Houston Astros set up their pre-season HQ at impressive **Osceola County Stadium** on Bill Beck Boulevard on east Highway 192. The Astros' Minor League team, the **Kissimmee Cobras,** then play here from April to September, while the **Orlando Rays**, a Minor League offshoot of the new Tampa Bay Devil Rays, play at Tinker Field, next to the Citrus Bowl on Tampa Avenue. Both the Cobras and Rays usually have several games a week, priced $3.50, $4, $5 and $7 (tickets always available at the gate) and are well worth checking out for a little extra Americana.

**Ice hockey** is also new in town with the Orlando Arena home to the International Hockey League's Orlando Solar Bears. It is a real family atmosphere and the season runs from September to April, with tickets from $5–$24 available from Ticketmaster on 407 839 3900 or the Bears office 407 872 7825, with special offers often available.

## Rodeo

For another all-American pursuit straight out of the Old West, go and see the twice-yearly **Silver Spurs Rodeo** at Osceola County Stadium. This is the biggest event of its kind in the south-east United States and is held the first week in July and the last week in February every year, but it sells out fast so you need to call at least a month in advance for tickets on 407 677 6336. The event features some classic bronco and bull riding and attracts top rodeo competitors from as far away as Canada.

On a slightly smaller scale but still worth a visit, the **Kissimmee Rodeo** is held every Friday (except when the Silver Spurs is on) at the Kissimmee Sports Arena, on Hoagland Boulevard two miles south of Highway 192. Events include calf roping, steer wrestling and bull riding, and admission is $10 for adults and $5 for children 12 and under. Children especially seem to enjoy the live action, which can be surprisingly rugged (not to mention downright dangerous), and there is even a special kids' contest – grab the ribbon from the calf's tail. It goes down a storm!

## Motor Sport

For the guaranteed ultimate in high-speed thrills, Walt Disney World has its own speedway oval which is home to the **Richard Petty Driving Experience**, taking you out in one of their 650bhp stock cars as either driver or passenger at up to 145mph. The programmes have been devised by top NASCAR driver Richard Petty and offer the three-lap **Riding Experience**; a three-hour **Rookie Experience** (with tuition and eight laps of the speedway); the **Winston Experience** (tuition plus 16 laps in two sessions); and the **Experience of**

8

a **Lifetime** (an intense 30-lap programme in three sessions). The Riding Experience will probably appeal to most, three laps of the 1.1-mile circuit with an experienced, race-proven driver lasting just 37 seconds a lap but an unbelievable blast all the way. Your initial take-off from the pit-lane takes you from 0–60 in a couple of seconds and you are straight into Turn One with your brain some distance behind. It is a bit like flying at ground level, it is hot and noisy and you must wear sensible clothes (you have to climb into the makeshift passenger seat through the window), but it is definitely the Real Thing in ride terms and a bigger thrill than anything else in Walt Disney World® Resort. You don't need to book for the Riding Experience from mid-February to the end of September, just turn up and blast off. There is also no admission fee, so you can come along just to watch others going through their paces and see if it might appeal to you. The three driving programmes all require reservations, while the track is occasionally closed for race testing from October to February. However, before you get carried away with the idea of being the next Nigel Mansell, wait for the prices: $89.99 for the

**Daytona Speedway**

Riding Experience, $329.99 for the Rookie Experience, $699.99 for the Winston and $1,099.99 for the Lifetime Experience. For more details, or to book, call 407 939 0130.

The Walt Disney World Speedway also hosts an Indy 200 race and the Chevy Truck Challenge in the last two weekends of January, and these are NOT good times to visit the next door Magic Kingdom® Park.

Race fans will also want to check out the **Daytona Speedway** (take I4 east, then I95 and Highway 92) for more big-league car and motorcycle thrills, notably the Daytona 500 on the first Sunday in July, while the **World Center of Racing** is a fascinating interactive museum. Call 904 253 7223 for details.

**The Richard Petty Driving Experience**

# Orlando by night

When it comes to night-time fun 'n' frolics, Orlando again has a dazzling array of attractions, particularly in its four purpose-built entertainment complexes, but also its range of dinner shows, bars and night-clubs.

The original development in this sequence was **Church Street Station** in the heart of the downtown area, which opened in 1974 with Rosie O'Grady's Goodtime Emporium and added six more clubs or restaurants in the next 12 years to become an unmissable source of family fun for its elaborate settings. Disney opened **Downtown Disney Pleasure Island** in 1987 to provide an even greater range of entertainment with its clubs, discos and restaurants, and is still adding new venues and up-dating existing ones. This was greatly enhanced in 1997 with the growth of the area into Downtown Disney and the addition of the **Downtown Disney West Side** complex. **Disney's**

**Boardwalk**, new in 1996, also added to their entertainment options. International Drive opened its own source of night-time fun at the end of 1997 with **The Pointe*Orlando**, a combination of lively restaurants, night clubs, speciality shops and a 21-screen cinema complex, and, towards the end of 1998, Universal Studios Escape is due to open **CityWalk**, the very latest in all-round entertainment and sophisticated amusement.

These represent yet another slick opportunity to be dazzled and relieved of your cash in the name of tourism, but you should count on visiting at least one if your wallet can take the strain.

## Church Street Station

This converted old railway depot has quickly become the focal point of Orlando nightlife, with a number of bars, night clubs, restaurants and other minor attractions springing up

**8**

**Church Street Station at night**

all around it. Its combination of shops, restaurants and bars has its highly sophisticated touches, but this is largely a lively, occasionally raucous, centre that caters for contrasting musical tastes from jazz, country and western to rock.

It is open all day, but from 5pm there is an admission charge of $17.95 for adults and $11.95 for children (4–12) to the Station (children must be accompanied by their parents, but Phineas Phogg's disco is 21 and over only). If the attractions of New Orleans-style trad jazz and Can-Can girls, live country and western music with line dancing, or 60s and 70s rock classics played by the resident band do not appeal, visit Church Street during the day just to browse in the shops, look inside each of the venues and marvel at the magnificent interior architecture and furnishings. The Cheyenne Saloon, in particular, is visually stunning with its intricate oak railings and panelling. Be warned, however, Church Street Station is NOT a cheap place to eat or drink, even after you have paid your admission fee. A simple beer will set you back $4 (plus tip) and dinner for two at Lili Marlene's or Crackers is likely to be a $50–$60 touch. They also serve a couple of howitzer house cocktails, but, at $9 a time (including souvenir glass), it's a one-off rather than an oft-repeated experience! Here's a full rundown of the entertainment: **Rosie O'Grady's Good Time Emporium** (formerly the dilapidated Orlando Hotel) is the centrepiece of Church Street and a must-see venue for its Dixieland saloon setting, lively jazz music and trademark Can-Can girls who dance on the bar. Rosie's also serves deli sandwiches and hot dogs. The **Cheyenne Saloon** hosts the country and western scene, but if you're not a fan of the music don't let it put you off as the magnificent setting and atmosphere are definitely worth

sampling, while the sight of the locals doing their line-dancing is equally fascinating (and there are Country dance lessons on Saturdays and Sundays from 2–5pm). The Cheyenne restaurant also offers barbecue chicken, ribs and beef. The **Orchid Gardens** belies its peaceful-sounding name by hosting the rock 'n' roll scene in another superb setting of ironwork and glass in a mock-Victorian style. **Phineas Phogg's Dance Club** (8pm–1am, 2am Fri and Sat) is the youngest end of the spectrum, a loud, lively disco that doesn't really get going until at least 11pm (don't forget your photo ID to prove you are 21 or over). For all four of these night clubs, you need to pay the one-off admission charge, but if you just want to go shopping in the Church Street Exchange (11am–11pm), sit for a drink in **Apple Annie's Courtyard** (11am–1am) or visit one of the restaurants – **Lili Marlene's** (5.30–11.30pm) for excellent prime rib and seafood (and a kids' menu at $6.95), **Cracker's Oyster Bar** (4pm–11.30pm) for Cajun specialities and some of the best seafood in town (and a kids' menu $6.95) or the **Wine Cellar** (4pm–11pm, 12pm Fri and Sat) for a huge selection of (expensive) European and New World wines with food available from Cracker's – you are free to wander around.

At the weekends there is live entertainment in the cobbled street that connects the two buildings of Church Street Station, but expect the crowds to be at their highest then, too. For a romantic half hour (or to keep all the family amused), take one of the horse-drawn carriage rides from outside Church Street Station around the whole of the downtown area and its lakes, which are all magnificently lit at night. Church Street does make up for its rather high prices with some weekly specials. Wednesdays at Phineas

Phogg's (6.30–7.30pm) is Nickel Beer Nite (that's five cents a time, and the place gets PACKED); the Cheyenne Longneck Night on Thursdays (4.30–7.30pm) offers $2.00 BBQ sandwiches and cheap beer; the Backyard Barbeque is Fridays (11am–3pm) at the Cheyenne Saloon with an unlimited buffet for $7.95; and Sundays at Lili Marlene's is their special brunch buffet (10.30am–3pm) at $12.95 for adults and $6.95 for kids. Daytime historical tours of the Station are also available, call for reservations on 407 422 2434.

If you are planning more than one visit to Church Street Station it is worth knowing their annual pass ($24.95) is less than the price of two single night admissions, while the Dixie Double Pass ($44.95 for you and a guest) and VIP Pass ($74.95 for four of you) work out cheaper still (and offer discounted drink prices plus discounts at many of the shops). To get to the Station, take Exit 38 (Anderson Street) off I4, turn left on to Boone Street, left again on South Street and right on to Garland Avenue. There are no less than five parking locations in the vicinity. For anyone staying on International Drive, there is also an excellent **shuttle service** from eight hotels four evenings a week to save you the drive. Check out the ticket desks of Universal Studios Escape Travel or Suncoast Services in your hotel foyer for details.

The surrounding areas of Church Street can be equally lively, with a (slightly cheaper) range of restaurants and bars. Look out in particular for **Pebbles, Scruffy Murphy's Irish Pub** and **Mulvaney's** (for a touch of the Emerald Isle, especially on St Patrick's Day), **Tanqueray's Bar and Grill** (another Cheers-style venue), **Fat Tuesday** (for an amazing range of daiquiris and frozen specialities), **Martinis** and the pure fun of **Sloppy Joe's**, a full-service restaurant and bar with a Key West/Ernest Hemingway flair (look out for their 4–7pm happy 'hour' and live entertainment). For those who like a bit of spice with their evening entertainment, there is also **Terror on Church Street** (as revealed in Chapter 7).

## Downtown Disney

The large-scale development of what is now **Downtown Disney** (the old Village Marketplace and Pleasure Island) has evolved into a three-part complex (Downtown Disney Marketplace, Pleasure Island and West Side) doubling the size of the old site and providing two key evening entertainment sources.

**Downtown Disney Pleasure Island:** this is the traditional night-club zone which packs the locals in as well as the tourists and where every night is New Year's Eve. The Island (which forms the centrepiece, or linking part, of Downtown Disney) comprises the **Rock 'n' Roll Beach Club**, a live music venue featuring 40 years of classic rock (and some outrageous DJs); the **Pleasure Island Jazz Company**, for excellent modern jazz and blues in a 30s-style nightspot; **Mannequins Dance Palace** (21s and over), a huge, popular disco featuring a revolving dance floor and live entertainment from the Explosion Dancers; **Comedy Warehouse**, improvised acts from up-and-coming comics and occasional big-name acts; **8Trax**, a homage to 70s music, dance and styles (again over-21s); the **West End Stage**, which hosts the Island's resident band and occasional big-name acts and is the focus for the street party and midnight fireworks; the unmissable **Adventurers Club**, a multi-level live entertainment lounge where the place comes to life all round you (watch the animal heads and masks!)

8

**Church Street Station**

and the stars of the show are as likely to be next to you as on stage; **BET Soundstage Club**™, new in 1998, with an interactive VJ/DJ and featuring the best of R&B, soul and hip-hop sounds; and the **Wildhorse Saloon**®, another brand new venue which showcases live country & western acts and dancing, as well as an American barbecue restaurant. As well as the clubs, the Island also has a range of shops, including **Music Legends** for rock memorabilia, **DTV**, an upscale Disney fashion store and **Avigators Supply**, offering some stylish men's and women's clothing. There is also a fine choice of eating outlets either on or next to the Island. **Planet Hollywood**® (the largest of this worldwide movie-themed chain) is the busiest restaurant in all Walt Disney World and therefore draws big queues in the evening, while the **Portobello Yacht Club** offers excellent northern Italian cuisine in smart, lively surroundings and **Fulton's Crab House** serves up some of the best seafood in Orlando (although at a price – average $35 for a three-course meal – and with serious queues from 6pm). You can also enjoy **Captain Mickey's Character Breakfast** here at 8am and 10am daily for $13.95 adults and $8.95 kids 11 and under. Downtown Disney Pleasure Island is free before 7pm when the entertainment kicks off, then there is an $18.95 charge

with strict age restrictions (under-30s should take passports as ID). The eight shops here, plus the outstanding ice cream and coffee bar **D-Zertz**, are all open from 11am, and the 7pm admission is, of course, free for the duration of an All-in-One Hopper Pass.

**Downtown Disney West Side** is the newest element of the Downtown expansion and incorporates the **AMC® Theater Complex**, which has been increased to 24 screens, with 5,400 seats in state-of-the-art cinema surroundings. Due to open

BRIT TIP: For the full run-down of Downtown Disney's Marketplace, see page 223 in the shopping chapter. Wallets beware!

in December 1998 will be a permanent home for the acrobatics, dance and outrageous costumes of **Cirque du Soleil**® in a 70,000-square foot, 1,650-seat theatre, which will stage two shows five days a week in one of Walt Disney World's most imaginative venues.

The other elements are a fantastic mix of live music, fine dining, eye-catching shopping and the ultimate in interactive game arcades, Disney-Quest. The cavernous **House of Blues**®, in backwoods Mississippi

**Rosie O'Grady's Good Time Emporium at Church Street Station**

© Disney

**Downtown Disney**

style, is a must for anyone even vaguely interested in blues, rock 'n' roll, R&B, gospel, jazz and Brazilian rock. Check out their magnificent Gospel Brunch on Sundays (8.30am, 1pm and 3.30pm), Wednesdays and Fridays (8.30 and 10.45am) or the 500-seat restaurant next door to the stunning main hall for some fine food, including catfish, jambalaya and a host of delicious Cajun dishes. The inevitable gift shop stocks some quality merchandise.

Similarly, **Bongos Cuban Café**™ (co-owned by Gloria and Emilio Estefan) brings the sights, sounds and tastes of Old Havana to another imaginative setting (check out the bongo-drum bar stools!), with red-hot Latin music and some of the best Cuban food in America. The **Wolfgang Puck® Café** also offers a rich experience from the renowned Californian chef, with no less than four dining options: Wolfgang Puck Café, gourmet food in a casual setting; Wolfgang Puck Express, the fast-food version; B's Bar for sushi, seafood, pizzas and micro-brew beers; and The Dining Room, the upscale restaurant.

The shopping is also original and engaging, from the basic sweet shop **Candy Cauldron** that still resembles a fairytale dungeon, through the one-off outlets like **Sosa Family Cigars, Celebrity Eyeworks' Studio** and the stylish art in glass and ceramics of **Hoypoloi**, to the more predictable souvenir stores of **All Star Gear, Copperfield Magic Underground – The Store** and **Wildhorse Saloon®** and finally the truly mega **Virgin**™ **Megastore**, the largest music store in Florida, with 300 listening stations, a full-service café, hydraulic outdoor stage and a mean sound system!

The most unusual element opened in June 1998 and brought yet another novel idea to life. **DisneyQuest**™ is described variously as 'an immersive, interactive entertainment environment', the latest in arcade games, a series of state-of-the-art adventure rides or, as one employee told me, 'a theme park in a box'. It houses 11 major adventures, like CyberSpace Mountain (design and ride your own roller-coaster!),

8

Virtual Jungle Cruise (shooting the rapids, prehistoric style) and Aladdin's Magic Carpet (more virtual reality, riding in best cartoon fashion), a host of old-fashioned video games in the Replay Zone (do you remember Asteroids and Galaxian?), the latest sports games, a test of your imagination in Animation Academy and two futuristic cafés, one with computers and Internet tables, the other, Food Quest, straight out of a space-age comic book. The almost surreal, futuristic setting is enhanced by the method of pay 'n' play, with a 'credit card' of units you buy at the entrance booth to use at each game or attraction. Big adventures use 8–20 units, while video games vary from 2–8. You can add units to your card inside at any time. A Quest 60 ticket (giving you 60 units) costs $15, Quest 90 costs $20 and the Ultimate Quest (100 units a day for three days) is $40, while there is an additional $2 entry fee. Disney reckon you will spend 2–3 hours here, but I can see someone going through a Quest 60 ticket in under an hour, so watch your spending! DisneyQuest is open from 10am–2am daily, but, if you want to avoid the queues (the building admits only 1,500), go during the day.

Finally, the whole of West Side is characterised at night by outstanding lighting and special effects and a vibrant, thrilling atmosphere that is almost intoxicating. Words alone do not do it justice – go see it!

Disney's other big evening entertainment offering is **Disney's BoardWalk** resort, where the waterfront entertainment district contains two notable venues for non-residents (three if you count the excellent micro-brewery of the Big River Grille and Brewing Works). **Jellyrolls** is another variation on the duelling piano bar, with the lively pianists conjuring up a raucous evening of audience participation

songs, while the **Atlantic Dance Club** offers more mainstream dance sounds, plus a Martini bar. Both have a $3 admission charge ($5 at weekends) and you MUST be 21 or older to enter, so remember your passports for ID as they are strict.

## The Pointe*Orlando

This eye-catching new development on International Drive, almost opposite the Convention Center, is a mix of unique shops, cinemas, restaurants and the WonderWorks science centre. It is open all day, but is most likely to appeal at night.

The big-name stores are all upscale and include some hugely imaginative touches that make them stand out from mere shops. Witness the massive toy shop **FAO Schwarz**, with its huge teddy bear entrance, leading into a world of kiddie fun, like the interactive Monopoly game built into the floor, a Star Wars area of laser screens, and a giant key-board which children can play with their feet! There are another 45 tempting outlets like **A/X Armani Exchange, Foot Locker Interactive, Disney Worldport, Gap** and **Gap Kids** and the imaginative gift shops of **Yankee Candle, Bath and Body Works** and **Florida Wild**. It's worth stopping by just for a look, but keep your wallet

BRIT TIP: The Pointe's dazzling evening entertainment consists of the multi-venue **Graham Central Station**, home to six different clubs (8pm–2am), from the high-energy dance of Zazoo, to country and western in Memphis Lights. Entrance fee to the Station is $18.

under strict control!

The collection of restaurants strive to be different too, with **Lulu's Bait Shack** leading the way for New Orleans-style cuisine and entertainment (it looks like an old shack blown in from Bourbon Street), **Johnny Rockets** 50s-style diner, **Adobe Gila's**, a fine Mexican cantina stocking more than 100 different tequillas (ouch!), **Monty's Conch Harbor**, for fine seafood, and **Dan Marino's Town Tavern**, sports-themed dining with the great Miami Dolphins quarterback. My personal favourite, though, is the elegant **Players Grill** (see Chapter 9, Eating Out).

The 21-screen **Muvico Cinema** is another unusual experience as it includes a six-storey IMAX 3-D Theater where the film practically comes to life around you.

## Universal Studios CityWalk

From the end of 1998, there is yet another multi-faceted entertainment complex to demand your attention. And, if the plans are anything to go by, it should be quite awesome. It is Universal's answer to Downtown Disney, a 30-acre array of live music, dance clubs, restaurants and creative shopping all in an extravagant setting of rich architecture and lavish landscaping, right down to the lagoon-side setting.

The central hub of the mushrooming Universal Studios Escape development, CityWalk will be free to enter for shopping and dining at such one-off eateries as **Jimmy Buffet's Margaritaville**, an island homage to Florida's laid-back musical hero, **Emeril's Restaurant Orlando**, a fine-quality culinary creation built round an open kitchen, **Pat O'Brien's**, the famous Irish-tinged New Orleans watering hole imported in every detail (including their knockout speciality drink, the Hurricane), the **NASCAR**

**Café**, for motor racing fans, **Motown Café**, a combination of legendary music and slow-cooked 'homestyle' food, **Bob Marley – A Tribute to Freedom**, a re-creation Jamaican 'live museum' to the man and his music, and, in early 1999, an **NBA restaurant** for basketball fans.

Anchoring one corner of CityWalk is the all-new **Hard Rock Café**, the largest in the world (taking over from the one next door to the Universal Studios Florida® theme park, which will become a hotel), with the addition of a concert venue **Hard Rock Live** that promises to bring in top-name acts. Another stand-out feature for music fans is **City Jazz**, which consists of the Down Beat Jazz Hall of Fame, the Thelonius Monk Institute of Jazz and a live performance venue.

Breathless yet? Well, there's still the **Universal Cineplex**, a 20-screen cinema complex with a 5,000 capacity and the latest in stadium seating, curved-screen visuals and high-tech sound systems. There there is **E! Entertainment Television**, a US TV network that won't mean a lot to us but will offer live programmes in the making and similar entertainments.

And for the disco-minded? Well, how about **The Groove**, a multi-format night club that combines classical theatre architecture, high-tech refurbishments and a huge dance floor surrounded by individually-themed secluded retreats where guests can catch their breath and chat in quiet comfort (what a change that will be). Sophisticated visual effects, audio systems and state-of-the-art lighting are taken as read. I'm exhausted and I'm only *writing* about it!

The proof of this particular entertainment pudding will definitely be in the tasting, but I fully expect it to be a thrilling alternative to all the other major evening centres.

8

# Disney shows

Walt Disney World® Resort's other night-time extravaganzas are often overlooked by visitors unless they are staying at one of the main hotel resorts within Walt Disney World. The most popular with those in the know (and it's free!) is the nightly **Electrical Water Pageant** on Bay Lake and the Seven Seas Lagoon in front of the Magic Kingdom® Park. It lasts just 10 minutes (from around 9pm) so it is easy to miss, but it is almost a waterborne version of the SpectroMagic parade in the Magic Kingdom® itself, with thousands of twinkling lights on a floating cavalcade of boats and mock sea creatures. The best points to see it are outside the Magic Kingdom® (in high season only), Disney's Polynesian Resort and the shores of Disney's Fort Wilderness, but it can also be seen from Disney's Contemporary Resort, Disney's Grand Floridian and Disney's Wilderness Lodge. For a night of South Seas adventure and entertainment, try the **Polynesian Luau Dinner Show** (open to non-residents at Disney's Polynesian Resort). It's a bit expensive at $38 for adults, and $19.50 for under 12s (SeaWorld's version is slightly better value at $30 and $20), but the entertainment is quite thrilling (fire jugglers, hula-drum dancers and clever musicians) even if the food, in keeping with most of Orlando's dinner shows, is nothing out of the ordinary. For reservations (usually necessary), call 407 939 3463. The **Hoop-Dee-Doo Musical Revue** at Disney's Fort Wilderness Resort is an ever-popular nightly dinner show that carries on where the Diamond Horseshoe Saloon Revue in the Magic Kingdom® leaves off. Especially loved by young children, it features the joking, dancing, singing Pioneer Hall Players in a merry American hoedown-style show, with barbecued ribs, chicken and corn on the cob while you're watching. Okay, it's corny and a tad embarrassing to find yourself singing along with the hammy action, but you're on holiday, remember! The Revue plays three times a night (5, 7.15 and 9.30pm) at the Pioneer Hall, admission $37 for adults, $19.50 for under 12s, and reservations are ALWAYS necessary (tel 407 939 3463).

Having stumbled into the topic of themed dinner shows, it would be appropriate here just to outline this particularly Orlando-based type of attraction for first-time visitors. As the name suggests, it is live entertainment coupled with dinner in a fantasy-type environment where even the waiters and waitresses dress in costume and act out roles. The staging is always of a large-scale, elaborate nature, the acting on the hammy side and the food hearty, plentiful but distinctly ordinary, usually accompanied by unlimited beer, house wine or soft drinks. There is always a strong family appeal and they nearly all seat you on large tables where you can get to know other folks, too, but, at an average of $30 for adults, they are not cheap (especially when you add on the taxes and tips). If you think of the price as $15 for the entertainment and $15 for the food, you get a better idea of what you're paying for, and if you go in with a willing suspension of disbelief and the attitude of being prepared to join in come what may, you WILL enjoy yourself! However, **beware** the almost constant attempts to shake an extra few dollars out of you with photos, souvenirs, flags, etc. Every show has its variation on this theme, but you shouldn't be rail-roaded into parting with more cash (apart from a tip for your server).

There are a whole range of different shows vying for your attention, and it is hard to recommend just one, so take your pick from the following:

## Arabian Nights

This lovingly-maintained, family-owned attraction is the largest-scale production and one of the most popular with locals as well as tourists. It's a real treat for horse lovers, but you don't need to be an equestrian expert to appreciate the spectacular stunts, horsemanship and marvellous costumes as more than 50 highly-trained horses perform a 25-act show loosely based on the celebration of Princess Scheherezade's engagement to Prince Khalid in the huge, covered arena at the centre of this 1,200-seater Palace. The magnificent close-quarter drill of the Lipizzaner stallions, the daring riding and the

**Arabian Nights**

BRIT TIP: NEVER pay full price for the dinner shows as there are always discounts to be had. Watch out for discount coupons among all the tourist brochures and magazines, or ask your holiday company.

thrilling chariot race all add up to a memorable show that kids, in particular, adore. The recent addition of new characters, costumes and special effects, plus the

incorporation of a bumbling Genie, have given Arabian Nights a real boost and helped to keep their appeal fresh. The food – green salad, oven-roasted prime rib with new potatoes, and a dessert (vegetarian meals on request) – is above average, but so is the price at $36.95 for adults and $23.95 for kids three to 11. Arabian Nights, which is located just half a mile east of I4 on Highway 192, (it's on the left, just to the side of the Parkway shopping plaza, or just past Water Mania if you are coming from the eastern end of 192) runs every evening at 7.30 or 8.30 pm, with occasional matinees, lasting about two hours, and tickets may be purchased at the box office between 10am and 6pm or by credit card if you phone 407 239 9223.

**8**

### Pirates Dinner Adventure

This new show in one of the most spectacular settings is still finding its feet after several changes from the unsuccessful original. The basic premise of the audience being hi-jacked by a pirate crew is a sound

**Arabian Nights**

one, but the show is still uneven and the food could be better. On the plus side, there is heaps of audience participation, the drink flows freely and the cast perform with gusto, right down to the post-show disco party. There are plenty of stunts and special effects and ticket prices are $38.10 for adults and $21.15 for three to 11s (but watch out for discounts especially here). The Pirates can be found on Carrier Drive between International Drive and Universal Boulevard at 7.30pm Tuesday–Sunday. Call 407 248 0590 for reservations.

## Mark II Dinner Theater

This variation on the dinner show theme offers a full-scale Broadway musical or comedy after you have been able to dine well on another well-stocked buffet and salad bar, with home-made desserts and an (extra) full cocktail service and wine list. The quality productions change every six weeks or so, but include works like *Fiddler On The Roof, La Cage Aux Folles* and *Cabaret*. The interior is tastefully designed with tables of two or four in tiered ramps surrounding the stage. An additional feature after Friday and Saturday evening performances is the Afterglow, a chance to meet the performers in the lobby, enjoy a few drinks and join in with a few well-known songs or even have a go in the spotlight yourself! There are eight performances a week, with prices ranging from $27.50–$35 for matinees (11.30am, Wed, Thur and Sat), and $32.50–$40 for evening shows (6pm, Wed–Sat, 4.30 p.m. Sun). Call 407 843 6275 for details of the current show and reservations. The Theater can be found off exit 44 travelling (north) east on I4, turn left on to Par Avenue and one mile on the left in the Edgewater Plaza.

## Medieval Times

Eleventh-century Spain is the entertaining setting for this two-hour extravaganza of medieval pageantry, sorcery and robust horseback jousts that culminate in furious hand-to-hand combat by the six knights. It is worth arriving early to appreciate the clever mock-castle design and costumes of all the staff as you are ushered into the pre-show hall and then taken into the arena itself with banks of bench-type seats flanking the huge indoor battle-ground. The weapons used are all quite real and there is a lot of skill, not to mention hard work, involved, plus some neat touches with indoor pyrotechnics and other special effects. You need to be in full audience participation mode as you cheer on your own knight and boo the others, but kids get a huge kick out of it (not to mention a few adults) and they also love the fact that eating is all done without cutlery – don't worry, there are handles on the soup bowls! The elaborate staging takes your mind off the fact that the chicken dinner is only average, but there is plenty of it and the serfs and wenches who serve you make it a fun experience. Admission (inclusive of Medieval Life also) is $37.95 for adults and $22.95 for kids three to 12 and the doors open 90 minutes prior to each performance, the times of which vary according to the season, so call 407 396 1518 for details. The castle is located on Highway 192, five miles east of the junction with I4. If you have 45 minutes to spare before the show, the adjoining **Medieval Life** exhibition makes an interesting diversion. This mock medieval village re-enacts the life and times of 900 years ago, with artisans demonstrating the crafts of pottery and tool-making, glass-blowing, spinning and weaving. There is also a Chamber of Horrors that might be a touch gruesome for small children.

## King Henry's Feast

Continuing the theme of Middle Ages entertainment, this castle setting offers more deeds of derring-do, but the accent is more on the humorous than the epic. A hilarious court jester acts as MC for the evening with a rather underfed King Henry VIII making regular appearances in search of another wife (ladies beware!). The entertainment is provided by strolling players, singers and some eye-popping speciality acts like jugglers, fire-eaters and trapeze artists (you will find your mind boggled in particular by the balancing act, served up as it is with lashings of good humour), and woe betide anyone who doesn't enter into the spirit of the evening! The chicken dinner is again pretty ordinary but the performers will have your attention fully engaged and always seem to get the audience going in great style long before the end, and no-one ever goes home hungry. King Henry's Feast is located in the heart of International Drive (you can't miss its huge castle-like structure next to Race Rock restaurant) and tickets are $36.95 for adults and $22.95 for kids three to 11. Showtimes vary, so call 407 351 5151 for details.

## Wild Bill's

Operated by the same people who run King Henry's, this show is more likely to appeal to us Brits as its Wild West theme is more what we associate with a holiday in America. It's located at the magnificently built Fort Liberty in the heart of Highway 192's tourist area and features two hours of western-style entertainment and hearty food all served by cavalry troopers in full gear. Rope tricks, knife throwing, Native American acts, Can-Can girls and a country and western hoedown (with special audience 'victims'!) are the featured entertainment, served up with stacks of gusto, while the meal comprises vegetable soup, fried chicken and barbecued ribs, corn on the cob, baked potato, biscuits, salad and apple pie. It's one of the most popular shows for foreign tourists and goes down well with kids too. Tickets are $36.95 for adults and $22.95 for three to 11s, and showtimes again vary so call 407 351 5151 for information and reservations. The Fort is also home to a 22-acre **Trading Post**, complete with authentic Western shops and photo spots, open from 10am to 10pm daily.

## Sleuth's

Here's another fun variation, a real live version of Cluedo acted out before your eyes in hilarious fashion while you enjoy a substantial meal and unlimited beer, wine and sodas. The setting is an English drawing room for one of seven murder mysteries, with the action taking place all around you and even with some cameo roles for various audience members. The quick-witted cast keep things moving well and keep you guessing during the 40-minute show, then you have the main part of dinner to formulate some questions to interrogate the cast (but be warned, the real murderer is allowed to lie!). If you solve the crime you win a prize, but that is pretty secondary to the overall enjoyment – and this is a show I do enjoy a lot. Prices are $34.95 for adults and $22.95 for children 3–11 and again showtimes vary, so call 407 363 1985 for details. Sleuth's Mystery Dinner Theater is located in Republic Square, on Universal Boulevard, just off International Drive (turn right past Wet 'n' Wild).

8

**Al Capone and his gang**

## Capone's

Song, dance, comedy and a personal invitation from Al himself to make sure you really enjoy yourself in this mock Speakeasy diner where the threat of a raid from 'the Feds' is ever-present. A big, all-you-can-eat Italian buffet, plus the addition of Sangria and Rum Runners to the free drinks list, make this as much an invitation to stuff yourself silly as to enjoy the rather hammy musical revue. It's all good, harmless, knockabout fun though, and, at $31.99 for adults and $16.99 for kids 12 and under, pretty good value. Capone's runs every night and is located on Highway 192 just past its junction with Poinciana Boulevard heading east. Call 407 397 2378 for reservations and showtimes.

## Night Clubs

Orlando is also blessed with a huge variety of other nightlife, from common or garden discos to elaborate live music clubs and new features like Blazing Pianos,

although the majority are situated in the downtown area, i.e., away from the main tourist centres. The local paper, the *Orlando Sentinel*, has a regular Friday listing section called 'Calendar' which details every local nightspot worth knowing about as well as individual events and one-off concerts, and it is worth checking out as there is an amazing turnover in the success/failure rate of bars and discos. Alternatively, the freebie *Orlando Weekly*, available in most tourist areas, offers a more off-beat look at the area's attractions, with a full rundown of alternative ideas and the week's events. Don't be surprised if a night club suddenly

BRIT TIP: Downtown Orlando is really the heart of the night club scene, with a host of clubs within walking distance along Orange Avenue between Church Street and Jefferson Street.

undergoes a complete change of name and personality, as this is fairly common too. The basic distinctions tend to be **Live Music** clubs, **Mainstream Discos**, which can also have the occasional live band, **Alternative** or **Progressive Clubs** and then **Bars** which specialise in evening entertainment.

## Live Music

The following should give you a representative taste of the most popular venues (for those 21 and over only in most cases), starting with the Live Music clubs.

**Blazing Pianos**, at the Mercado Centre on International Drive is currently the 'in' place for the young, trendy crowd, a raucous cavern of a place featuring three duelling, fire-red pianos pounding out audience participation rock songs and regular contest spots (open 7pm–midnight Sun–Thur, 7pm–1am Fri and Sat, cover charge $5 and $7 and it's PACKED at weekends, when it's 21 and overs only). The rock 'n' roll piano idea was pioneered here, though, by the

**Wild Bill's Dinner Extravaganza**

wonderfully-named **Howl At The Moon Saloon** on west Church Street and is equally popular there (Sun-Thur 6pm–2am, Fri and Sat 5pm–2am). Classic rock 'n' roll, show tunes, current hits, the Saloon's duelling pianists play them all, with full audience involvement and non-stop banter. There is no cover charge on Sunday to Tuesday, while on Wednesday and Thursday it is $3 after 7.30pm, on Friday it's $5 after 6pm and Saturday is $5 after 5.30pm, and the live piano action begins at 8pm every night.

Country music fans – and others in search of the 'in' crowd – will want to check out **:08 Seconds**, a huge, multi-level entertainment centre. It earns its 'unique' tag by hosting live bull riding(!) and monster truck wars as well as having a huge dance hall with live bands, line-dancing lessons, 12 bars, a pool hall, game room and classic country BBQ. On West Livingston Street in the heart of downtown, it has bags of style, but call 407 839 4800 for the latest details.

Blues and Jazz are the staples of the new **Sapphire Supper Club**, at 54 North Orange Avenue, where resident DJs, bands and special guest acts vary from week to week. Call for details on 407 246 1419. (This was the hippest place to be seen at in 1998, with a terrifc range of live acts. Will it still be hot in '99?)

**Medieval Times**

Not exactly a music attraction but nonetheless a very 'live' one is **The Comedy Zone**, in the Holiday Inn on International Drive, which puts some top American comedians on stage twice a night at 8.30pm and 10.30pm (Friday and Saturday, just 10.30 on Wednesday and Thursday) as well as serving light snacks and drinks ($8 admission, $18.95 includes a full meal, and you must be at least 18 to get in). Call 407 645 5233 for details.

## Discos

For out-and-out, boppy, good-time discos, the huge **Embassy**, on Adanson Street (at the end of the Lee Road shopping plaza, just west of I4 exit 46, Lee Road, turn left), is one of the trendiest in town, with two state-of-the-art dance floors, a Games Room and a quiet VIP lounge (check for details on 407 629 4779). Cover charge varies from $5–$10, and it's open from 8pm to 2am nightly).

Borrowing from the success of

BRIT TIP: The local music radio stations – of which there are many – regularly advertise the different nightly sessions at most clubs. The various inducements include free entry for ladies, live bands and 'all-you-can-drink' nights (which are unsurprisingly popular!). Don't think you have to confine your night club attentions to the weekend, either. There is usually something happening EVERY night, hence Sunday or Monday can be as busy as Saturday.

American radio stations come in a vast number of types and styles that conform to fairly narrow musical tastes. Here is a quick guide to finding the main ones in your car:

| | |
|---|---|
| **ADULT CONTEMPORARY** | **CLASSICAL** |
| 94.5 FM (WCFB) | 90.7 FM (WMFE) |
| 98.9 FM (WMMO) | 91.5 FM (WPRK) |
| 99.3 FM (WLRQ) | |
| 100.3 FM (WSHE) | **CHILDREN** |
| 105.1 FM (WOMX) | 950 AM (WZKD) |
| | |
| **POP** | **JAZZ** |
| 99.9 FM (WFKS) | 89.9FM (WUCF) |
| 106.7 FM (WXXL) | 103.1 FM (WLOQ) |
| | |
| **OLDIES** | **COUNTRY** |
| 105.9 FM (WOCL) | 92.3 FM (WWKA) |
| 790 AM (WLBE) | 97.5 FM (WPCV) |
| | 98.1 FM (WGNE) |
| **NEWS/TALK** | 102.7 FM (WHKR) |
| 90.7 FM (WMFE) | |
| 104.1 FM (WTKS) | **ROCK** |
| | 91.5 FM (WPRK) |
| **SPORT** | 96.5 FM (WHTQ) |
| 540 AM (WQTM) | 101.1 FM (WJRR) |

Embassy and going for the same mass-market appeal is the **Zuma Beach Club**, on North Orange Avenue, just up from Church Street. Zuma Beach goes for a beach theme throughout, complete with palm trees, lifeguards and girls in bikinis. Its mainstream top 40 music

BRIT TIP: Can't find the Calendar section among the zillion supplements with the *Orlando Sentinel*? It's the one tabloid section of this huge newspaper.

approach is popular with the 25–30-somethings and there is a different attraction most evenings. Music themes include retro-progressive and acid jazz, with guest radio DJs, call 407 648 8363 for the latest info. Cover charge is $5 most nights.

## Progressive

The alternative scene can boast several lively clubs that offer what the Americans term 'progressive' music but in real terms is more likely to be a techno-dance or even rave style. **Barbarella**, on Orange Avenue on the corner of Washington Street, offers alternative and new wave music from 9pm–3am most nights. Again, it is more of a techno-dance sound, but with various retro-progressive, old wave and 'Bad Disco' nights. Cover charge varies from $3–$6, call 407 839 0457 for details. **The Club at Fivestone** is almost impossible to categorise as it ranges from mainstream disco to acid jazz lounge, with something different each night from Wednesday to Saturday (including gay nights on Wednesday and Saturday). About half a mile north of Church Street on the corner of Orange Avenue and Concord Street, it is open from 9pm–3am with the cover charge ranging from $5–$9 according to the night. Free beers, live progressive bands, go-go dancers and no cover charge for ladies are additional attractions, and the sounds run the full mixture of the progressive label. Call 407 426 0005 for night-by-night information. Other current hot-spots at the time of writing include the high-energy dance of Club Volcano on Orange Avenue (9pm–3am, Latin Night Wed, College Night Thur, call 407 999 0033 for details) and the eclectic sound of the **Blue Room** on West Pine Street (10pm–2.30am Wed, 8pm–2.30am Thur–Sat, ladies drink free Thursdays).

## Bars

Bars of all types simply abound in Orlando, but there are again several which offer a particular tourist appeal, especially to newcomers to the scene. Live entertainment, extrovert barmen, sports-themed bars and raw bars (offering seafood, often by the bucket!), the choice is, as ever, wide-ranging, but here are a few of the best.

**Fat Tuesday** (on Church Street next to the market) advertises the 'world's largest selection of frozen drinks' and we're not talking lemonade! Open seven days a week from 11am–2am it is a fun, lively bar for the younger crowd with live entertainment and no cover charge. **Chillers**, on Church Street, is another young and trendy venue, basically a lively bar that serves, among other things, 20 varieties of frozen cocktails, plus bar snacks (5pm–1am, no admission charge). The neighbouring **Mulvaney's Irish Pub** is another good-time emporium with its flavour straight from the Emerald Isle (hence Guinness on tap!). Shepherd's pie and bangers and mash are the menu staples, while Irish folk singers add regular live entertainment and it is positively shoulder-to-shoulder at weekends. No cover charge, and hours from 11.30am–2am. Similarly, **Scruffy Murphy's Pub** offers an authentic Irish flavour three blocks north on Washington Street. Again, no cover charge and a real good-time atmosphere when it is busy (which is most nights).

### Sports bars

Finally, with the multitude of sports bars that are another particularly American pastime, **Friday's Front Row Sports Grill** on International Drive (just south of the Sand Lake Road junction) really sticks out as a major tourist trap which even the

8

locals enjoy. Here you can catch ALL the action (and, yes, they do show soccer as well) on 84 TV screens, plus enjoy some 100 beers from around the world (and bar features like $1 domestic 12oz drafts!), as well as try out their basketball nets, pool tables and shuffleboard, and rub shoulders with the local sports stars from time to time. The food is good, standard American diner fare and there is plenty to keep the kids amused, too (like crayons to colour in the paper table-cloths and a huge range of video games). The atmosphere varies

> BRIT TIP: Want to shoot a few hoops of basketball, or play darts, shuffleboard or pool? Friday's has all this and more. (Don't miss their foot-long hot dogs, too!)

according to the time of day and the sports event (VERY rowdy for Orlando Magic basketball games!), so call 407 363 1414 for up-to-the-minute info. There is never a cover charge, reservations are not accepted and it is open from 11am–2am Monday to Saturday, 11am–midnight on Sunday.

Other choices for the sports bar experience include the massive

**Sports Dimension** on Curry Ford Road – some 87 TV screens, with 12 of the big-screen variety – which is open from 11am–2am every day (tel 407 895 0807) and **Headlightz Sports Bar** on East Colonial Drive, which also offers live music (tel 407 273 9600). Another *Brit's Guide* favourite (so, I happen to like sport, what's wrong with that!) is **The Ale House** on Kirkman Road, just opposite Universal Studios (tel 407 248 0000). Boasting more than 30 TVs, a raw bar and some great seafood, it also carries an above-average range of beers. **Kenny Wallace's Motorsports Grill**, on Caravan Court, opposite Universal, is a must for motor racing fans (tel 407 248 0012), while Walt Disney World® Resort can boast the excellent **ESPN Club** at Disney's BoardWalk Resort, a full-service restaurant with sports broadcast facilities, video games, more than 70 TV monitors, giant scoreboards and even a Little League menu for kids. No sports fan should miss it.

Right, if that doesn't give you enough to keep you occupied for the next fortnight, I'll be very surprised (it takes me all year just to check the information!). But it's all very well giving you the low-down on the attractions, you will also want to know a lot more about where, when and how to tackle that other holiday essential – FOOD. So, read on …

# 9

# Eating Out
*(or, Watching the Americans at Their National Sport)*

If eating was an Olympic event, the Americans would take gold, silver and bronze every time. Forget baseball, basketball or American Football: eating is their national sport! To say they take meal times seriously would be the understatement of the year.

I know I am doing a vast disservice to the majority of the inhabitants of their huge country, but it is hard to dispel the notion of the average American as a walking food intake, especially when so many of the local tourists you will encounter are so, well, not to put too fine a point on it, fat.

## Variety

As a consequence, the variety, quantity and quality of restaurants, cafés, fast-food chains and hot dog stalls is in keeping with this great tradition of eating as much as possible, as often as possible. It is not out of the question to be able to eat around the clock, i.e., 24 hours a day, and at first glance the full selection of food is rather overwhelming (hence this chapter). Cruising along either of the main drags of International Drive or Highway 192 will quickly reveal a dazzling array of different eating houses, the choice of which can be quite bewildering.

As a general rule, food is plentiful, relatively cheap, readily available and nearly always appetising and filling. You may not encounter many gourmet establishments (although Orlando DOES possess some outstanding high-quality restaurants), but you will get good value for money and you probably won't need to eat more than two proper meals a day, unless your appetite is of a similar transatlantic nature. Put simply, portions tend to be large, food of a heavily steak-, chicken- or pizza-based variety, service of an efficient, friendly character, and it is ultimately hard to come by a really BAD meal.

## Exceptional deals

In keeping with the climate, most restaurants tend towards the informal (T-shirts and shorts are usually acceptable) and cater readily for families. This also leads to two exceptional deals for budget-conscious tourists, especially those with a large tribe to keep happy. Many of the main hotels now offer 'Kids Eat Free' deals, provided they eat with their parents. The age restrictions can vary from under 10s to under 14s, but it obviously represents good value for money if you are staying there. The second item of interest is the 'All You Can Eat' buffet, another common feature of many of the large chain restaurants in particular, and, when you consider they are catering for the American appetite, it means you can have a pretty hearty meal for not too much and probably eat enough at, say, breakfast, to keep you going until dinner! A few establishments also offer 'Early Bird' specials, a dinner discount if you dine before 6pm. Don't be afraid to ask for a doggy-bag if you have a fair amount left over (and even if you haven't brought the dog!). It is common practice to take away the half of that

> BRIT TIP: A buffet break-fast at Ponderosa, Sizzler or any other similar establish-ments will probably keep you going until tea-time and is a good way to start the day if you are tackling one of the Magnificent Seven theme parks.

pizza you couldn't finish, or those chicken legs or your leftover salad. The locals do it all the time and, again, it is wallet-friendly. Just ask for the leftovers 'to go'. (PS. It's not usually a bag, either!) Don't hesitate to tell your waiter/waitress if something isn't quite right with your meal. Americans will readily complain if they feel aggrieved, so restaurants are keen to make sure everything is to your satisfaction. And, please, don't forget to tip. The basic wage rate for waiters and waitresses is low, so they rely heavily on tips to supplement their wages. Unless service really is shoddy, in which case you should mention it, the usual rate for tips is 10 per cent of your bill at buffet-style restaurants and 15 per cent at full-service restaurants. However, it is usually worth checking to see if service has already been added to your bill. It is a common practice in many British restaurants nowadays, but not so common in America.

Having implied that the majority of eating outlets tend to be of a hearty rather than quality- and variety-conscious kind it is still quite easy to encounter a monumental array of food types. Florida is renowned for its seafood, which also comes at a much more reasonable price than in the Mediterranean. Crab, lobster, shrimp (of a size which we would call king prawns), clams and oysters can all be sampled without fear of breaking the bank, as well as several dozen varieties of fish, many of which you won't have come across before.

Cuban, Cajun/Creole and Mexican are other more local types of cooking which are well represented here (if you haven't eaten Mexican food, try fajitas – pronounced faheetas – they're delicious!), and you'll also be spoiled for choice of Oriental fare, from the more common Chinese and Indian to Japanese, Thai and even Vietnamese.

The big shopping complexes and malls also offer a good choice of eateries in their food courts, and again they often represent particularly good value for money. Cracker cooking is original Floridian fare, and the more adventurous will want to try the local speciality –

> BRIT TIP: Another way to save money given the large portions usually on offer is to share an entree, or main course, between two. Your waiter/waitress will be happy to oblige (provided you keep their tip up to the full rate).

alligator meat. This can be stewed, barbecued, smoked, sautéed or braised. Fried gator tail 'nuggets' are an Orlando favourite, while barbecued gator ribs are the 'unofficial' food of Central Florida, according to the local press.

## Ordering

Ordering your food can also be an adventure in itself. The choice for each item is often the cue for an inquisition of exam-type proportions from your waiter/waitress. You can never order just 'toast' – it has to be white, brown, wholegrain, rye, muffin or bagel; eggs and bacon come in a baffling variety of types; an order for tea or coffee usually provokes the response 'Regular or decaf? Iced, lemon or English?'; and salads have more dressings than the National Health Service. Whenever I've finished ordering I'm tempted to ask 'Have I passed?' after the barrage of questions. (NB: American bacon is always streaky and crisp-fried and sausages are chipolata-like and on the spicy side.) Don't be worried about going in to a restaurant and asking to see their menu if it isn't prominently displayed. It is no big deal to Americans and the restaurant won't feel insulted if you decide to look elsewhere.

## Vegetarian options

In a culinary country where beef is king, vegetarians often find themselves hard done by, and Orlando is little different to the general American rule. However, there are a couple of bright spots, plus a handy hint when all seems lost. Firstly, there is *one* speciality vegetarian restaurant in Orlando, The Lower East Side at 3401 L. B. McLeod Rd (tel 407 648 4830), while the tapas-style Café Tu-Tu Tango on International Drive serves a number of veggie dishes. Most of the upscale restaurants should be able to offer a vegetarian option and will be happy for you to ask in advance. Walt Disney World® Resort is slightly more enlightened in that the California Grill (in Disney's Contemporary Resort), Citricos (Disney's Grand Floridian Resort

**Elegant dining in Orlando**

and Spa) and Spoodles (Disney's BoardWalk) feature vegetarian dishes, while all the full-service restaurants (notably Bongos Cuban Café™ and Wolfgang Puck's® Café in Downtown Disney, plus some of the counter-service ones) are usually keen to try to cater for non-menu requests. It is always worth asking.

## Drinking

Drinking is another matter altogether. Most British towns now have their share of American bars and diners and they give you a pretty good idea of what to expect, only there is a lot more of it here. The biggest complaint of Brits on holiday in the USA is of the beer. With the exception of a handful of English-style pubs (see below), American beer is always lager, either bottled or on draught, and ice-cold. It goes down great when it's really hot, but, as a general rule, it is weaker and fizzier than we're used to. Of course, there are exceptions and they are worth seeking out (try Killian's Red,

**9**

BRIT TIP: If there are several of you, ordering a pitcher of beer will work out cheaper than by the bottle or glass.

© Disney

**Delicious foods at End Zone Food Court at Disney's All Star Resort**

Michelob Amber Bock or Dos Equis for a fuller flavour), but if you are expecting a good, old-fashioned British pint, forget it. But I would suggest if you can't do without your pint of Tetley's, or whatever, for a couple of weeks, then you're probably going on the wrong kind of holiday here! Spirits (always called 'liquor' by Americans) come in a typically huge variety, but beware ordering just 'whisky' as you'll get bourbon instead. Specify if you want Scotch whisky or Irish whiskey and demand it 'straight up' if you don't want it deluged under a mountain of ice! If you fancy a cocktail, there is a

BRIT TIP: Watch out for all the different free tourist magazines and brochures that can be found in the information centres, hotels and shopping areas. They all carry valuable money-off coupons for many of the restaurants and can save you lots of $s.

massive choice and most bars and restaurants have lengthy happy hours where prices are very consumer-friendly (hic!). Californian wines also work out much better value than imported European ones (and are usually of equally good quality). If you are sticking to soft drinks ('sodas') or coffee, most bars and restaurants will give you free refills. You can also run a tab in most bars and pay when you leave to avoid having to shell out for each round.

Another few words of warning. Florida licensing laws are stricter than ours and you need to be **21 or over** to enjoy an alcoholic beverage in a bar or lounge. Even if you are over 21 you will often be asked for proof of your age before you are served (or allowed in entertainment complexes like Downtown Disney Pleasure Island) and this means your passport as it contains a picture of you (Americans use their driving licences as proof of ID because it also has to carry a photo of the owner). It's no good arguing or trying to reason with a reluctant barman. Local licensing laws are strict and they cannot afford to take any chances. No photo ID, no beer! Anyone under 21 may NOT sit or stand near a bar either.

Right, that gives you the inside track on HOW to eat and drink like the locals, now you want to know WHERE to do it, so here's a handy guide to that veritable profusion of culinary variety. At the last count there were 3,515 restaurants in the metro Orlando area, with new ones being added and some biting the dust all the time, and, while it would be a tall order to try to list every one, the following section will cover the main tourist areas and all the chain groups, as well as provide an insight into the more specialist, one-off establishments.

As a simple reference to the types of restaurants you will encounter, I have grouped them into four types, with the price scale gradually increasing through each one. They are: **Fast Food** outlets (McDonald's, etc); **Family Restaurants** (for example, Denny's, the American version of the Little Chef or Happy Eater); **American Diners** (the typical US-style establishment like the Hard Rock Café); and **Speciality Restaurants** (as a general rule, the one-off, more expensive places and 'foreign' food, like Chinese, Japanese and Italian).

## Fast food

If you are a **McDonald's** fan you are coming to the right place as there are no less than 57 outlets in the greater Orlando area, varying from small drive-in types to the mega, 24-hour-a-day establishment on Sand Lake Road (near the junction with International Drive) that also has the biggest play area for kids of any McDonald's in the world and a number of differently themed eating areas. **Burger King** is also well represented, with 42 outlets, as is another familiar American franchise in Britain, **Wendy's**, which has 22 restaurants. If you're a burger freak and want to sample a variation on the theme, give **Checkers** (10 outlets) or **Hardees** (9) a try.

Kentucky Fried Chicken (or KFC as it now likes to be known) has no less than 15 restaurants around the area, but you might like to try the local variations on the chicken theme at **Popeye's Famous Fried Chicken** (10) or **Kenny Roger's Roasters** (5).

If it's pizza you're after there is also a wide choice, from the well-known **Pizza Hut** (with 37 restaurants) to the local varieties of **Flipper's Pizza** and **Domino's**, who all offer a local delivery service, even to your hotel room.

A particularly American form of take-away is the Sub, or French-bread-type sandwich. This is what

**End Zone Food Court at Disney's All Star Sports Resort**

you will find at any one of the 36 local branches of **Subway**, or the 11 of **Sobik's** or 12 of **Miami Subs**. They're a rather more healthy option than yet another burger, and offer some mouth-watering varieties. Two other minor variations on the fast-food theme are **Arby's** (with 10 outlets), which offers a particularly appetising roast beef sandwich and other beefy delicacies, and **Taco Bell** (27 outlets), which does for Mexican food what McDonald's does for the hamburger. If you've never had Mexican food before, this is not the place to start, but for anyone familiar with their tacos, nachos and tortillas, it's a quick and cheap spicy meal.

Practically all of these establishments will also have drive-through windows which are fun to try at least once on your Orlando visit. Simply drive around the side of the building where indicated and you will find their takeaway menu with a voice box that will take your order. Please, don't wait for the food to be miraculously produced from the voice box! Carry on around the building and your food will be served from a side window where the cashier will also take your money. You will probably find your car has a slide-out tray from the central dashboard area that will take your coffee or soda cup and you can drive along with your meal and really pretend to be American!

© Disney

9

## Family restaurants

This is a section that may, at first appearance, seem similar to the American Diner type, but there are two quite major differences. First, they are only restaurants. You usually won't find a bar here and some don't serve alcoholic drinks at all. And second, they make a big effort for family groups in terms of kids' menus and activities (in many cases the kids' menu doubles up as a colouring and puzzle book) and budget-conscious prices. They also all serve breakfasts, and you will find the best of the all-you-can-eat buffet deals here. Nearly all are chain groups in the same way as you find Little Chef and Happy Eaters all over Britain, but there are one or two individuals worth knowing about.

Leading the way in terms of popularity with British tourists are the **Ponderosa Steakhouse** group and **Sizzler**. Whether it's breakfast, lunch or dinner, you will find great value and good, reliable food. In terms of style they are almost indistinguishable: you order and pay for your meal as you enter and are then seated, before being unleashed on some of the biggest buffet and salad bars you will have seen. Ponderosa have the rather flashier style, but you'd be hard pushed to tell whose food was who's. Expect to pay about $4–$5 for their breakfast buffets and $6–$9 for lunch and dinner (there IS a difference in price depending on location, with the International Drive area tending to be a dollar or two dearer than elsewhere). Standard fare includes chicken wings, meatballs, chili, ribs, steaks and fresh seafood, while their immense salad bars in particular represent major value for money. Both are open from 7am until late evening and are handily located in all the main tourist spots.

A more homely touch can be found at the following selection of restaurant chains, with equally good if not better value for money. To my mind the best of the bunch are **Friendly's** restaurants for their exceptionally friendly service (naturally), well laid out and extremely appetising menus, hearty portions and positively mouthwatering desserts. They also do kids' fun menus that will keep the young 'uns amused and contented for the duration of the meal. They're open from 6am every morning with breakfast served until midday. **Bob Evans** restaurants (open 6am–10pm, or 6am–11.30pm Friday and Saturday) traditionally specialise in American down-home breakfasts, with all manner of pancakes, omelettes and egg platters guaranteed to fill you up without breaking the bank. They also do the inevitable burgers and hot sandwiches and a special dish of the day that might be shepherd's pie, roast turkey or hickory-smoked ribs. Their restaurant on Canadian Court, just off International Drive, is entered through a delightful General Store where you can buy country crafts and some of the homestyle foods on their menu. If it's a hearty breakfast you want at any time of day, then the **International House of Pancakes** (otherwise known as IHOP) or the **Waffle House** will both appeal to you. You will struggle to spend more than $5 or $6 on a full meal, whether it be one of their huge breakfast platters or a hot sandwich with fries. Waffle Houses are also open 24 hours a day, while IHOPs open at 6.30am right through to 1.30am. Another traditional American 24-hour family diner is **Denny's**, the nearest thing to our Little Chefs. Again, they make a traditional bacon 'n' egg breakfast seem ordinary with their wide selection, and they do an excellent range of hot, toasted sandwiches and some imaginative dinner meals, like grilled catfish, as well as a Senior Selections menu, featuring smaller portions at reduced prices for the over-55s. Similarly, **Perkins Family Restaurant** is also open around the clock with a lookalike menu. For a really hearty breakfast try Perkins Eggs Benedict (two eggs and bacon on a toasted muffin with hash browns and fresh fruit), while their bread-bowl salads are an equally satisfying meal. A new chain who impress for their clean, fresh style are **Golden Corral**, who offer a delicious Carver's Choice of hand-carved meats in addition to the usual buffet deals and a terrific dessert bar.

Continuing the theme of American country cooking is the **Black Eyed Pea** group, where Mom's Meatloaf and fresh vegetables are the order of the day, along with huge salads and daily specials like chicken and dumplings and roast turkey. Their weekend breakfast buffet is also a highlight, as is their kids' menu with puzzles. **Shoney's** is another buffet specialist, offering an impressive breakfast bar and a range of different dinner buffets that include soup, salad and fruit bar. Their country buffet, boasting Cajun jambalaya and barbecue chicken, is a particular favourite, and Shoney's also do a neat little Just 4 Kids menu and fun book. Another 'homestyle' 24-hour establishment is the oddly-titled **Kettle**, otherwise known as America's Kitchen. Features include the Kettle Snippets menu, which is also a kids' activity book, some tasty snacks for the smaller appetite, a big breakfast choice and a hearty range of country dinners. If you are travelling on the major highways of Florida one of the 29 branches of **Cracker Barrel** may catch your attention, in which case you should definitely check out their delightful Old Country Store style, with mountainous breakfasts, well-

balanced lunch and dinner menus, Kid's Stuff choices and a real old-fashioned charm that is a nice change from the usual tourist frenzy.

One of the most popular one-off restaurants for wide family appeal is **Captain Nemo's**, on Highway 192 opposite Fort Liberty. It serves breakfast from 8am–noon, lunch until 3pm and dinner until 11pm, and its seafood and steak menu means mum and dad can try oysters, lobster, salmon, swordfish or grouper while the kids still get their burger fix. Prices are also budget-orientated, with daily specials and a Happy Hour from 3–7pm.

For a real fun family treat, (and the biggest crossover into the diner-type restaurant) take the clan to one of the two **Jungle Jim's** in the Orlando area (at Crossroads of Lake Buena Vista, and West Church Street). From the parrots that welcome you to the restaurant, you know you are in for an unusual dining experience, and sure enough you will eat in an entertaining jungle setting, with the menu promising 'An epic dining adventure of lost legends, forbidden pleasures and ancient rituals'. There are 63 (count them, 63!) choices of burger, including the World Famous Headhunter, a one-pound burger, with ham, bacon and cheese and a full pound of fries – polish off the lot and your next one is free! The alternatives are ribs, steak or chicken, but it would be a shame not to try at least one of the 63 varieties. The kids' menu is suitably varied, and there is a huge range of cocktails served by Dr S'Tiph Shotta Likker (ouch!). They are open 11am–1.30am Sun–Thur, 11am–2am Fri–Sat.

## British

To complete this section, it would probably be appropriate to mention the handful of British pubs and

© Disney

**Planet Hollywood at Downtown Disney**

diners which seek to attract the UK visitor. All offer a fairly predictable array of pub grub along the lines of pies, pasties and fish and chips and a few imported British beers (Guinness has become very popular since the Irish were here for the World Cup in 1994!). You'll find the odd Brit or two working behind the bars, and you can happily take the kids into all of them, providing they don't sit at the bar. First and foremost among them is the **Cricketers Arms** in the Mercado Mediterranean Village on International Drive. This has become a favourite haunt for many British visitors due to the large selection of beers, appetising food, live evening entertainment and (soccer fans take note) live Premiership matches on their giant TV screen on a Saturday morning (from 10am – remember the time difference). It gets busy in the evenings, their live music is usually pretty good, and many of the staff are Chelsea fans, but we won't hold that against them!

Highway 192 in Kissimmee sports a number of fairly derivative pubs all keen to appeal to the home market. The best of them are **Harry Ramsbottom's** at Fort Liberty (between Markers 10 and 11), which also has its own fish 'n' chippie, and the wonderfully kept **Stage Door**, six miles west of the junction with I4 (and west of Marker 4, just past Lindfields Boulevard). This restaurant gets full marks from the locals too.

## American diners

This section is the one where it would be easiest to go OTT. Not surprisingly, there are so many American-style restaurants of one kind or another it would be a full-time job just to keep track of them all. Therefore, I will limit this particular survey to the main tourist areas of International Drive and Highway 192, plus a couple off the beaten track that are well worth finding. The **$ price listings** are intended only as a rough guide for a three-course meal in each case.

| | | |
|---|---|---|
| $ | = | $10–$15 |
| $$ | = | $15–$20 |
| $$$ | = | $20–$25 |
| $$$$ | = | $25–$30 |
| $$$$$ | = | $30 plus. |

**Steak and Ale** is a popular choice and can be found at eight locations around Orlando (11.30am–10pm Mon–Thur, 11.30am–11pm Fri, 12noon–11.30pm Sat, 12noon–10pm Sun; **$$**). They do some great steaks and ribs, plus tempting seafood and chicken dishes, with early bird specials of a three-course set meal from 4–7pm (4–6pm November–March), and two-for-one drink specials at the same time. **TGI Friday's** will already be well-known from their outlets springing up all over Britain and their fun style of lively mealtimes is served up in exactly the same way in their seven Orlando restaurants. (11am–1am; **$$**). They do a great range of burgers, plus Mexican dishes, pizza, pasta, steak, ribs and seafood. The nationwide chain **Bennigan's** has six outlets in

BRIT TIP: reader Mrs Gillian Austin from Horsham in West Sussex, recommends **JT's Prime Time** (at the western end of Highway 192 out towards Highway 27), a down-to-earth, good value locals' eatery, with a good kids' menu, early bird dinner specials (before 6.30pm for $6), offering barbecue chicken, steaks and 'wonderful burgers. It knocked the spots off TGI Friday's.' Ouch!

Orlando and is a particular personal favourite for their friendly, efficient service, smart decor and tempting menu, especially at lunchtime (11am–2am; **$$**). They make the ordinary seem appetising and have a bar atmosphere straight out of the TV programme *Cheers!* Their Irish flavour really comes into its own on St Patrick's Day (17 March), and they have a happy hour (!) every day from 2–7pm and 11pm–midnight. Another enjoyable dining experience can be found at the two branches of **Darryl's** (one on International Drive, the other at Fort Liberty on Highway 192). Their weird and wonderful decor is totally original; they also have a great bar area and a nicely varied menu with some interesting choices, like Cajun-fried shrimp (11am–1am; **$$**). Thick, wood-fired steaks, delicious burgers and Southern-style dishes are their main fare, but they also offer some tasty soups and quiches.

**Hooters** makes no bones about its style. 'Delightfully tacky yet unrefined' declares the menu proudly, and sure enough here is a relatively simple, lively

establishment, especially popular with the younger crowd for its beach-party atmosphere (11am–midnight Mon–Thur, 11am–1am Fri–Sat, noon–11pm Sun; **$**). Their five restaurants have a truly entertaining menu featuring great value seafood, salads, burgers and Hooters Nearly World Famous Chicken Wings that come in five strengths: mild, medium, hot, 3 Mile Island or Wild Wing. You have been warned!

By contrast, **Pebbles** (five restaurants) goes for the casual but sophisticated style, with a genuinely imaginative menu that will appeal to the amateur gourmet and won't cost you a fortune (11am–midnight; **$$$**). You can eat burgers or roast duck, salad or steak and be sure of an individual touch with every meal. Their pastas are particularly appetising and they also do a kids' menu. **Uno Chicago Pizzeria** is the place to go if Pizza Hut has become *passé*. Their five outlets offer great deep-dish pizzas with the addition of pastas, chicken dishes, steaks and salads (11am–midnight; **$$**). The **Olive Garden** restaurants (10 of them) are one of America's big success stories in recent years as they have brought Italian food into the budget, mass-market range (11am–10pm Sun–Thur, 11am–11pm Fri–Sat; **$$**). Their light, airy restaurants make for a relaxed meal and, while they don't offer a huge choice, what they do they tend to do pretty well and in generous portions. Pastas are their speciality, but they also offer chicken, veal, steak and seafood and some great salads, and there are unlimited refills of garden salad, garlic breadsticks and non-alcoholic drinks that add to their good value. What the Olive Garden does for Italian cuisine, **Chilis** does for Mexican. Actually, it's an Americanised version of Mexican cooking with the emphasis more on

**9**

steak and ribs and less on tortillas and hot spices (11am–1am Mon–Sat, 11am–11pm Sun; **$**). Service is frighteningly efficient, and, if you are looking for a quick lunch or dinner, you'll be hard-pushed to find a quicker turnaround. Atmosphere is lively and bustly and they do a good kids' menu that is also a colouring/puzzle book.

**East Side Mario's** on International Drive in front of the Visitor Center, brings a little piece of New York to Orlando in the form of this wonderfully innovative 'street festival'. The American-Italian style and cuisine (burgers, pasta, chicken, ribs and steak) is ideal for the family market and delivers a casual yet up-beat atomsphere. Step in for a look around and you'll be hooked (11.30am–11pm; **$$**)

**Jack's Place** (in the Clarion Plaza Hotel on International Drive) refuses to be easily categorised. Here in this lively eatery you dine surrounded by 'the stars' – dozens of signed celebrity caricatures by the famous New York artist Jack Rosen. The menu is pretty good, too – grilled yellow fin tuna, rosemary roasted pork and slow-roasted prime rib, as well as some more delicious pasta and steak dishes (5.30–11pm; **$$$**).

The **Bahama Breeze** on International Drive is a must for its striking Caribbean styling – and its packed car park and queues (up to an hour's wait at peak periods!). As the Bahamas are not strictly in the Caribbean, their theming is a little suspect, but we'll forgive them as it makes for a memorable experience with well above average food for a typical diner. Try West Indies Patties or Creole Baked Goat Cheese as a starter, while the main courses (primarily pastas, seafood, chicken, beef or pizza) feature outstanding items like Black Pepper Seared Tuna or the Cuban beef stew Ropa Vieja, with every dish coming

up immaculately fresh. The plantation-room styling, delightful outside wooden deck for enjoying a pre- or post-dinner drink and live music most nights fully endorse their own slogan of: 'At Bahama Breeze there are no worries, just happy, friendly people and island hospitality!' (4pm-2am Mon-Sat, 4pm-midnight Sun; **$$$**).

## Ribs

When it comes to steaks, ribs and all manner of barbecue food, Orlando has a magnificent array of one-off restaurants that all proudly proclaim some kind of 'world famous' variety. In many instances they are right, and here's a good selection of the best on offer. **Austin's** (on International Drive, just south of the Mercado centre) does everything in good cowboy style, with an inviting gas-lit saloon-style bar and live country and western music (11am–midnight; **$$$**). Ribs are their stock-in-trade, and portions are huge, but they also do very acceptable pasta, chicken and seafood as well as some massive steaks.

**Lazy Bones Ribs** (on Highway 192, just past the junction with State Road 535 going east), is an authentic barbecue diner that also has a kids' playroom. Baby back pork ribs, prime beef ribs, steaks, chicken and seafood are all succulent choices, plus there are gator ribs for the really brave (4pm–11.30pm, with the Riverboat Bar and Lounge open until 2am; **$$**).

While in the Mercado centre, you may decide to try **Damon's**, which pronounces itself The Place For Ribs. While they also do salads, chicken, seafood and burgers, their rib platters are simply humongous. (11am–10pm; **$$$**). Try their onion loaf as a starter as it is rightly 'famous', while their lunch selections are particularly good value and, they promise, served within 15 minutes with their 'express' label.

**Cattleman's Steak House** (on Vineland Road, Kissimmee, near the junction with Highway 192) goes for the cowboy approach once again, with a neat saloon bar (happy hour 4–7pm), early bird specials from 4–6pm and the Little Rustlers' Roundup menu for the kids. Steaks are again the order of the day, but you can also order chicken and seafood, while their Heavenly Duck is worth trying for something different (4–11pm, saloon open until 2am; **$$$**). The up-market version

> BRIT TIP: Don't miss Wild Jack's jalapeño mashed potatoes, their dynamite chicken wings, cowboy baked beans and the Jack Daniels chocolate cake for dessert!

of this type of establishment is **Wild Jack's** (on International Drive, just north of Sand Lake Road) where you are greeted by the most magnificent wood-smoked barbecue aroma as you walk in the door. The huge, western-themed interior features a big, open pit-barbecue where you can watch your food being cooked (11.30am–11pm; **$$$**). Steaks, ribs, chicken and turkey represent your main choices and they are all served up with bags of panache and a big helping of Wild West style. There is happy hour from 4–7pm, kids eat free with a full-paying adult and you can even buy yourself a Wild Jack's souvenir boot-shaped beer mug!

**The Magic Mining Co** (at the western end of Highway 192's main tourist drag) is another fun-themed restaurant where you can imagine you are inside a gold mine while you eat. The menu is the usual array of

steaks, ribs, chicken and seafood, and an extra feature is the adjoining gold mine mini-golf (5–10.30pm; **$$$**).

I can also heartily recommend any of the six restaurants of **Tony Roma's,** which pronounce themselves Famous For Ribs, and rightly so. The airy but relaxing decor and ambience, clever kids' menu (the Roma Rangers Round-up, full of puzzles and games), junior meals, (and their melt-in-the-mouth ribs (try their Original Baby Backs if you don't believe me!) all add up to a winning combination. You can still get chicken, burgers and steaks, but why ignore a dish when it's done this well? The Rib Sampler is a great platter, and there are also chicken and shrimp-rib combos. (11am–midnight Sunday-Thursday, 11am–1am Friday and Saturday, **$$**).

## Mexican

Back at the Mercado center on International Drive you'll find the excellent Mexican food of **Jose's**, a neat, relaxed restaurant that won't blow your taste buds if you're new to this type of food. In fact, it's an excellent introduction to Tex-Mex cooking with a fine array of fajitas, enchiladas and beef and chicken dishes, while their salads are big enough for two (11.30am–10pm Sun–Thur, 11pm Fri & Sat; **$$$**). Similarly, **Fajita Grill** (on State Road 535, just north of Highway 192) offers a tempting slice of Mexican along with the biggest margaritas you have seen! Sizzling fajitas, enchiladas and chimichangas are served in huge amounts, along with steak, ribs and seafood (4–11pm; **$$**). The newest and most elaborate Mexican offering is the cavernous **Don Pablo's**, next to the Visitor Center on I-Drive. Clever theming, lively atmosphere (especially around the Cantina bar!) and a classic, well-explained menu

9

**Morton's Steakhouse**

add up to a real fun experience (4–10pm Sun–Thu, 4–11pm Fri & Sat; **$$**). Another one-off restaurant that has a lot of Brit appeal is **Café Tu Tu Tango** on International Drive, next to Austin's. The accent is artist-colony Spanish (whatever that means), with a really original menu, live entertainment and art-work all over the walls that changes daily. Vegetarians will find themselves well catered for here, while you can also try some particularly succulent pizzas, seafood, salads and paella. Mexican and Chinese dishes also make an appearance, and there is a thoughtful kids' menu (11.30am– midnight; **$$**). The overall style is based more on a tapas bar, so you order a number of different dishes rather than a starter and main course. Ultimately, it is as much an artistic experience as a meal, and the fun atmosphere perfectly complements the rich array of dishes.

## Steakhouses

Serious steak lovers will have to pay a visit to **Ruth's Chris Steak House** (999 Douglas Avenue in the suburb of Altamonte Springs just to the north of the city) where prime beef in a mouth-watering variety of choices is the order of the day. It isn't cheap, but you'll be hard-pushed to get a better steak anywhere (5–11pm Mon–Sat, 5–10pm Sun; **$$$$$**). 'Only the

best', proclaims the restaurant's slogan. 'Come judge for yourself, but come hungry.' Nuff said. Similarly, the **Butcher Shop** (in the Mercado center on International

> BRIT TIP: Don't miss the Butcher Shop's skillet-fried mushrooms in garlic and butter sauce!

Drive) offers steaks, steaks and more steaks. Hugely impressive is the cold counter where you can select your own piece of meat, and the hickory charcoal open grill where you can actually cook your steak to the desired degree (of course, there is also a chef to do it for you or offer advice). (5-10pm Sun–Thu, 5–11pm Fri & Sat; **$$$$**).

**Charley's Steak Houses** (of which there are three, the biggest on International drive just north of the Mercado centre) continue the theme of excellent steaks, cooked over a specially built pit woodfire. It's not cheap, but the decor and bar area are splendidly furnished, and if you don't fancy steak, which you can watch being grilled on their large, hardwood grill, there are seafood choices as well (5–11pm; **$$$$$**). Another new and imaginative choice is the **Buenos Aires Argentine Grill**, on Golden Sky Lane next to the Florida Mall, for an elegant South American-tinged dining experience featuring a full range of steaks plus chicken, veal and lamb. The Buenos Aires bar offers happy hour on weekdays from 5–7pm with a free buffet (5pm–1am; **$$$$**).

For more steak-induced hedonism, **Morton's** of Chicago (on The Market Place at Dr Phillips Boulevard) is hard to beat. Its rather more up-market (and sometimes pretty smoky) style is offset by a lively ambience that fully adds to the enjoyment of their trademark steaks, which you can watch cooked on an open range. You are provided with a fully exhibited menu (they bring examples to the table!) and invited to enjoy some of the biggest, most succulent steaks it has been my pleasure to sample. The Porterhouse is an inspired choice, as is one of the principal alternatives, Shrimp Alexander. Needless to say, this homage to bovine cuisine does not come cheap, especially as your vegetables are extra, but it is a thoroughly memorable experience (5pm–midnight Mon–Sat, 5pm–11pm Sun; **$$$$$**). **Black Angus** and **Western Steer** complete the line-up of steakhouses along more budget lines as they also serve breakfasts and aim for the family market. Black Angus (down at the east end of Highway 192) offers an all-you-can-eat breakfast buffet as well as a typical range of steaks, and also has a nightly Karaoke session (hours 7am–11.30pm; **$$**). Western Steer (on Palm Parkway, just north of Lake Buena Vista, and International Drive, opposite Wet 'n' Wild) offers a breakfast buffet as well as a dinner buffet. Steaks are still the main fare, and with a large tribe to feed it's great value (7am–11.30pm; **$$**).

## Seafood

After that exhausting trek through the steakhouses of Orlando, you won't be surprised to learn that the choice of seafood restaurants is equally large. **The Crab House** (locations on Goodings Plaza on International Drive and Palm Parkway) should be self-explanatory. Garlic crabs, steamed crabs, snow crabs, Alaskan king crabs, etc. Yes, this is THE place for crab. You can always try their prime rib, pasta or other seafood, but it would be a shame to ignore the house speciality when it's done this well

**The fabulous Planet Hollywood**

(11.30am–11pm Mon–Sat, noon–11pm Sun; **$$$**). **Red Lobster** (nine restaurants) is from the same company that has made a success of the Olive Garden chain. This is seafood for the family market, with a varied menu, lively atmosphere and one of the best kids' menus/activity books you'll find. And, while lobster is their speciality, their steaks, chicken, salads and other seafood are equally appetising, and they do a great variety of combination platters (11am–10pm Sun–Thur, 11am–11pm Fri and Sat; **$$$**). **Charlie's Lobster House** (on International Drive at the Mercado center) has a similar menu, with nightly fresh fish specials and reservations recommended. The bar areas are immaculately finished and

**9**

**Race Rock**

service has that extra bit of charm (4–10pm Sun–Thur, 4–11pm Fri and Sat; **$$$$**). Completing the chain restaurants here are the three outlets of the **Boston Lobster Feast**, with elaborate nautical decor and an unlimited lobster and seafood buffet (hence the Feast, you see). They have early bird specials from 4.30–6.00pm Mon–Fri, 2.00–4.30pm Sat–Sun (and that represents excellent value), while their 40-item Lobster Feasts are guaranteed to stretch the stomach more than a little (4.30pm–10pm Mon–Fri, 2–10pm Sat and Sun; **$$$$**).

Of the one-off restaurants, **The Ocean Grill** (on International Drive, just north of the Sand Lake Road junction) represents great seafood at moderate prices. Daily specials, including the early bird variety from 4–6pm, jostle with the likes of fried clams, Southwestern swordfish, fried catfish, shrimp creole and seafood lasagna. Their plain old fish and chips would put most British chippies to shame, and for the really hearty appetite they do a magnificent surf 'n' turf (lobster or shrimp and steak), although admittedly at a hearty price (4pm–11pm; **$$$**).

The **Atlantic Bay Seafood Grill** (on Highway 192, just east of I4) surprisingly offers a breakfast buffet on top of its full range of well-priced seafood dishes, early bird specials from 4.30–6.30pm, and steaks, ribs and pasta. It's not gourmet fare but it is hearty and good value, especially their all-you-can-eat seafood bar (4–11pm; **$$**).

Inside the new Omni Rosen hotel on International Drive is the **Everglades Restaurant**, an up-market seafood and steak choice which again combines unusual decor (an environmental look at the Everglades, complete with manatee, swamp scenery, tropical music and a 12ft aquarium) with fine cuisine. The daily seafood specials jostle with the likes of wild boar, venison and buffalo steak, while the gator chowder is a must-try starter. There is a relaxing adjacent bar area in this cavernous hotel, and diners at the Everglades also enjoy complimentary valet parking (5.30-11pm seven days a week; **$$$$**).

New at The Pointe*Orlando is **Monty's Conch Harbor**, where Key West is the relaxed, casual theme and the specialities include conch chowder, clams, oysters, stone crabs and Cajun-spiced tuna. Their fresh fried seafood baskets are also a real treat and key lime pie is a must for dessert (11.30am–11pm; **$$$$**).

For a selection of all the above – and more – visit **Marriott's Orlando World Center** on World Center Drive. Here you will find no less than FIVE distinctive restaurants that beautifully encapsulate Orlando's dining choice. **Allie's American Grill** (6.30am–2pm and 5–10pm; **$$**) is a versatile diner, **Champions Sports Bar** (4pm–2am Mon–Fri, midday–2am Sat and Sun; **$**) boasts 18 televisions, **JW's Steakhouse** (11.30am–10pm Mon–Fri, 7am–10pm Sat and Sun; **$$$$**) offers indoor or outdoor dining overlooking the magnificent golf course, **Tuscany's** (6–10pm; **$$$$**) is an elegant Italian option and the **Mikado** (6–10pm; **$$$$**) goes for Japanese style and flavouring.

## Six of the best

It could be said I've saved the best for last in this American Diners section as there are six other restaurants that sort of fit into this category but are really delightful, one-off restaurants in their own right. All six will provide a genuinely exciting dining experience in novel settings that will linger long in the memory, and without costing you a fortune.

**Hard Rock Café**: Okay, if you've been to the one in London (or elsewhere around the world) you'll know what to expect, but even so Orlando's Hard Rock Café (adjacent to Universal Studios, and with a separate entrance and free car park) is still a wonderfully fun place for a loud, lively meal. Their burgers are hard to beat (especially their trademark 'Pig Sandwich'), while they also do ribs, steaks and sandwiches, and pop music fans will be able to study the dozens of pop mementos and memorabilia that line the walls. Their Hard Rock merchandise is also a lot cheaper here than in London (10.30am–2am; **$$**). A new Hard Rock Café, even bigger and with a live music revue, is due to replace this one at Universal's CityWalk in 1999.

**Planet Hollywood®**: The largest restaurant in the rapidly-expanding worldwide chain of this glitzy, showbiz-style venture is next door to Disney's Pleasure Island and is just a pure fun entertainment venue. The food is fairly predictable diner fare, although everything is served up with pizazz, but the cavernous interior lends itself to a real party atmosphere, complete with numerous film clips and a stunning array of movie memorabilia. Some memorable house cocktails, too, but visit either mid-morning or mid-afternoon to avoid the serious queues! (11am–2am; **$$$**).

**B-line Diner**: Inside the Peabody Hotel on International Drive lurks an amazing Art Deco homage to the traditional 50s-style diner, faithful to every detail, including the outfits of the staff. You sit at a magnificent long counter or in one of several booths, with a good view of the chefs at work, and with a rolling menu that changes four times a day (which isn't bad when it is open around the clock!). The food is way above usual diner standard, but the prices aren't, so you can munch away on catfish in a papaya-tartare sauce or pork chops with apple-sage chutney, as well as the traditional favourites of burgers, steaks and ribs, happy in the knowledge you won't break the bank. Their desserts are displayed in a huge glass counter and I defy you to ignore them! (open 24 hours; **$$**).

**The Players Grill**: New at The Pointe*Orlando on I-Drive, it would be a mild insult to call this American Football-themed restaurant a mere diner. The ground floor level, with its bar and gift shop, is diner-orientated, but the real business of the Players Grill – jointly run with the NFL Players' Association – is the upscale dining room upstairs which also serves as a Football hall of fame with a host of memorabilia. The under-stated elegance of the restaurant, the fascinating range of exhibits, attentive service and an outstanding full menu (created by top New Orleans chef Ralph Brennan) and kids' choice, not to mention an excellent wine list, combine for one of the most surprising and enjoyable dining experiences in Orlando. Try the clam chowder, buffalo chicken or spicy chicken and sausage gumbo for starters, then progress to pasta jambalaya, stuffed pork chops or wasabi-crusted salmon and finish with fudge chocolate soufflé and you'll see why the Players Grill is a genuine cut above. You will also rub shoulders (if you're tall enough) with many players too, so have an autograph book handy! (11am–11pm Mon–Wed, 11am–1am Thu–Sat; **$$$$**).

**Rainforest Café:** This volcano-topped (!) restaurant in the heart of Downtown Disney Marketplace has to be seen to be believed. You don't dine, you go on a 'safari adventure' in a rainforest setting amid audio-animatronic animals (including elephants and gorillas), thunderstorms, tropical birds, waterfalls, aquariums and some of

**9**

the cleverest lighting effects I have seen. It is an amazing experience, especially for children, and the food is well above average. Try the Rasta Pasta or Mo' Bones ribs, but the menu alone will take a while to negotiate. Unless you arrive before midday, you will have to wait for a table, but that is no hardship with the shops of the Marketplace all around. Beware the café's huge gift shop, too! The same goes for their new site, even larger, topped by a waterfall at Disney's Animal Kingdom™ Theme Park (open 11am–11pm daily; **$$$**).

Another unmistakable landmark on International Drive is the super-charged, super-large restaurant of **Race Rock**, packed with rare motor-

**Inside Race Rock**

racing memorabilia and eye-catching machines of all kinds. This does for motor sport what the Hard Rock does for music, and how! Two giant car transporters line the entrance, which also boasts a giant-wheeled buggy, two dragsters and a hydroplane speedboat, welcoming you in to the circular, 20,000-square

foot restaurant itself. Giant TV screens and a host of regular TVs, video games, virtual reality racing machines and loud, loud music and chequered flag tables complete the atmosphere, while the central bar sports an upside-down racing car circulating as the world's biggest ceiling fan! The food is traditional diner fare given a few tweaks like Start Your Engines (the starter selections), Circle Tracks (pizza), Stock and Modified (burgers and sandwiches), Pole Position Pastas and The Main Event (ribs, chops, chicken and salmon – I rate the Road Runner chicken, marinated in lime juice, olive oil and garlic and char-grilled). There is a Quarter Midget menu at $4.99 for children 12 and under (11.30am-midnight; **$$**).

## Speciality restaurants

This final section requires least preamble as the type of fare is fairly obvious. As I have already mentioned, the food on offer varies enormously from American to Japanese, through all kinds of Asian, to the Middle East, through Europe and back again. Here are the main varieties.

### Chinese

Chinese food is well established in America and well represented in Orlando. **Ming Court** on International Drive, just south of King Henry's Feast, is the Rolls Royce of local Chinese restaurants. With the magnificent setting and live entertainment you could easily convince yourself you had been transported to China itself. The menu is extensive and many dishes can be had as a side order rather than a full main course to give you the chance to try more (11am–2.30pm and 4.30pm–midnight; **$$$**). **Bill**

**Wong's Famous Super Buffet** (yes, they really do call it that) on International Drive offers a cross between Chinese and diner-type fare. Their all-you-can-eat buffet features jumbo shrimp (and they mean Jumbo!), as well as crabs, prime rib, fresh fruit and salad (11am–10pm; **$$**). Similarly, the **Sizzling Wok**, on Sand Lake Road, just across from the Florida Mall, offers an opportunity to get stuck in to a massive Chinese buffet at a very reasonable price (11am–10pm Sun–Thur, 11am–10.30pm Fri and Sat; **$$**). Out on Highway 192 you'll find a number of fairly predictable, budget-priced outfits, the best of which is **Peking Gardens**, which goes slightly more up-market with a tempting range of Szechuan, Hunan and Cantonese cuisine (noon–11pm Sun–Thur, noon–midnight Fri and Sat; **$**). **Trey Yuen** and **China Jade Buffet** complete the tourist area Chinese offerings, and are fairly typical of Chinese restaurants in Britain. Both are located on the northern stretch of International Drive, with Trey Yuen specialising in the appetising small bite Dim Sum selections and offering a local delivery service (11am–midnight; **$**) and China Jade sticking to a more limited range of specialities but again at a sound all-you-can-eat price (11am–11.30pm; **$**).

## Japanese

The more adventurous among you (and those already familiar with their cuisine) will want to try one of the fine Japanese restaurants with which Orlando is blessed. **Shogun Steakhouse**, on International Drive under the International Inn, is ideal for those who can't quite go the whole hog and get stuck into sushi (raw fish). If you decide to 'chicken' out, you can still order a no-nonsense steak or chicken, but their full Japanese menu is well explained and vividly demonstrated by their chefs in front of you at long, bench-like tables (6–10pm Mon–Thur, 6–10.30pm Fri–Sun; **$$**). **Kobe** also brings a touch of Americana to its dining content. With six locations around the area, Kobe go for the mass market appeal but still achieve individual style with the chef preparing your food at your table in a style that is as much showmanship as culinary expertise (11.30am–11pm; **$$**). **Ran-Getsu**, on International Drive opposite the Mercado centre, does for Japanese cuisine what the Ming Court does for Chinese, i.e., it's stylish, authentic and as much an experience as a meal, and it is still reasonably priced. The setting is simple and efficient, and you can choose to sit at conventional tables or their long, S-shaped sushi bar (5pm–midnight; **$$$**). **Benihana** completes a formidable quartet of outlets, situated in the Hilton Hotel at Walt Disney World Village, Lake Buena Vista. Again, it's a memorable experience, with everything cooked right in front of you by their expert chefs, and their steaks are among the most tender you will ever taste (5–10.30pm; **$$$**).

## Indian

If you have come all this way and still fancy a curry, believe it or not you will be able to get one as good as any you have tried back home. There are already more than a dozen Indian restaurants around the Orlando area and they all maintain a pretty fair standard, from the up-market **Far Pavilion**, at the intersection of International Drive and Kirkman Road, to the budget-price **New Punjab** at the upper end of International Drive and on West Vine Street, Kissimmee, with its excellent lunch and dinner specials. For a medium-range restaurant, **Passage To India** (also on International Drive) gets the locals'

9

vote as best Indian restaurant and is a cut above the average, too, with unusual dishes like Chicken Kadhai, the exotic Chicken Hyderabadi and vegetarian Sabzi Dal Bahar (11.30am–midnight; **$$$**). It is a particular personal favourite for its attentive service and relaxed atmosphere, and you will probably find yourself dining with a few fellow Brits, too. Rock band The Cure and cricketer Imran Khan have also eaten here and left the photos to prove it!

### Thai and more

For other types of Oriental cooking, the **Siam Orchid** (on Universal Boulevard, just around the corner from Wet 'n' Wild) offers exceptional Thai food in a picturesque setting overlooking Sandy Lake (5–11pm all week; **$$**). If you'd like to try another variation, **Little Saigon** (on East Colonial Drive) will introduce you to Vietnamese cuisine and a whole new array of soups, barbecue dishes, fried rice variations and other interesting treats that take up where Chinese food leaves off (10am–9pm; **$**). Cuban food is a Floridian speciality and you will find some of the best examples at **Rolando's** (on Semoran Boulevard, in the suburb of Casselberry, head east from I4 exit 48). Try the red snapper or pork chunks and find out why the *Orlando Sentinel* rates this the best Cuban food north of Havana (11am–9pm Tue–Thur, 11am–10pm Fri & Sat, 1–8pm Sun; **$**).

### Italian

No survey of Orlando's restaurants would be complete without mention of its fine tradition of Italian cooking. **Pacino's** on Highway 192, opposite Old Town, goes for the family market and scores a big hit with value for money, friendly atmosphere and Sicilian style, with

clever animated puppet operettas, a fountain that occasionally spouts flame and a relaxing open-air feel that is enhanced by the clever use of the differently arranged seating areas (4pm–midnight daily; **$$$**). **Bergamo's**, in the Mercado centre, is actually German-owned but nonetheless authentic for all that. Don't be surprised if your waiter suddenly bursts into song – it's all part of the unique charm of this extremely tempting and ultimately highly entertaining restaurant (5–10pm Sun–Thu, 5–11pm Fri and Sat; **$$$$**). **Italianni's** (on International Drive just south of its Sand Lake Road junction), won't hurt your wallet quite so much and does a great pizza among a typical selection of Italian fare. Don't miss their homemade cheesecake for dessert (11am–11pm; **$$$**). **Donato's** keeps up the budget appeal and adds the attractions of an Italian market, pizzeria and deli that make dining there a very appetising experience. No frills, but very good food, and its location just south of the Belz Factory Outlet at the top of International Drive makes it a handy retreat after a shopping frenzy (11.30am–11.30pm; **$$**). The five-star version of Italian cuisine here belongs to two contrasting restaurants, **Christini's** on Dr Phillips Boulevard, and **La Sila** on Kirkman Road. Strolling musicians, elegant surroundings and a 40-year history of award-winning cuisine characterise Christini's, where their homemade pasta and filet mignon are as good as anything you will find in Italy (5–11pm; **$$$$$**). La Sila, just north of Universal Studios in Turkey Lake Village, promotes a candlelit atmosphere with live music in the cocktail lounge, formal, dinner-jacketed staff and a northern Italian cuisine that features delicious veal, snapper and pasta delicacies. Their pasta, bread and desserts are all homemade and it is all presented in an old-world style that is a million miles away from the tourist hurly-burly of the theme parks (6–11pm, 6pm–2am in the bar; **$$$$$**).

## Splashing out

Finally, if you fancy really splashing out, there are two notable restaurants I would always recommend for a memorable occasion. The **Park Plaza Gardens** is part of the Park Plaza Hotel on Park Avenue, Winter Park and this beautiful courtyard restaurant gives you the feel of outdoor dining with the air-conditioned comfort of being indoors. Attentive service is coupled with an elegant, versatile menu that offers the choice of a relatively inexpensive lunch or a three-course

BRIT TIP: If you have something to celebrate, or are considering a romantic engagement, book a table for two in the evening, tel 407 645 2475.

adventure featuring escargot, pasta with salmon, medallions of beef or one of several tempting fish dishes. Cuisine is distinctly nouvelle rather than American, but nonetheless satisfying for all that. Its setting becomes even more intimate and charming in the evening with lights scattered among the foliage. Enjoy a very pleasant happy hour in the lounge 5–7pm (with complimentary buffet Thursday and

Friday), while their popular three-course Sunday brunch features unlimited champagne and live jazz (11.30–3pm Mon–Sat and 11am–3pm for Sunday brunch, 6–10pm Mon–Thur, 6–11pm Fri and Sat, 6–9pm Sun; **$$$$$**).

If you made the mistake of bringing your glad-rags with you only to find they are not required anywhere you go, **Peter Scott's**, an up-market new dinner-dance establishment, may be the place for you. The old-fashioned supper-club atmosphere is enhanced by live music that may be big band, blues or jazz, with plenty of opportunity to take a spin round the dance floor. Equally impressive is the menu, featuring Dover sole, veal and immaculately-cooked steaks. The price goes with the style however (expect to pay around $25 for a main course), and men are expected to wear jacket and tie. Alternatively, try the swinging Dixieland Sunday brunch. Peter Scott's can be found just north of downtown Orlando, take Exit 49 off I4 and head west a short distance on SR 434 to the Longwood Village Shoppes (tel 407 834 4477 for reservations; open from 6pm–2am Tue–Sat, 11am–2pm Sun; **$$$$$**).

Now on to another of my favourite topics. As already mentioned, and in keeping with the area's great diversity of attractions, the other main way in which Orlando will seek to separate you from your hard-earned money is in shopping. The choice is suitably wide-ranging …

9

# 10 Shopping

## (or, How to Send Your Credit Card into Meltdown)

The vast area that constitutes metropolitan Orlando is a positive shopper's paradise, with a dazzling array of specialist outlets, malls and complexes, flea markets and discount retailers. It is also one of the most vigorous growth markets, with new centres springing up seemingly all the time, from the smartest of malls to the cheapest and tackiest of tourist gift shop plazas (and you can hardly go a few yards in the main tourist areas without a shop insisting it has the best tourist bargains of one sort or another).

You will be bombarded by shopping opportunities every way you turn, and the only hard part is avoiding the temptation to fill an extra suitcase or two with the sort of goods that would cost twice as much back home. As a general rule you can expect to pay in dollars what you would pay in pounds for items like clothes, books, records and CDs, while there are real bargains to be had in jeans, trainers, shoes, sports gear and T-shirts.

But beware! Your duty free allowance in the catch-all duty category of 'gifts' is still only £145 per person, and it is perfectly possible to exceed that sum by some distance. Paying the duty and VAT is still often cheaper than buying the same items at home, however, so it is worth splashing out, but remember to keep all your receipts and go back through the red 'goods to declare' channel on your return. You will pay duty of up to 19 per cent on the total purchase price (i.e. inclusive of Florida sales tax, see below) once you have exceeded your £145 allowance, and then VAT at 17.5 per cent. Unfortunately, you can no longer pool your allowances to cover one item that exceeds a single allowance. Hence, if you buy a camera, say, that costs £200, you have to pay the duty on the full £200, taking the total to £213.20, and then the VAT on that figure. However, if you have a number of items that add up to £145, and then

> **BRIT TIP:** If you are tempted to use 'doctored' receipts to show a lesser value – don't, it is illegal. Your goods will be confiscated and there are heavy fines. Also, you can't escape the duty by saying the items have been used (in the case of golf clubs, for example) or that they are gifts for someone else.

**Park Avenue is Winter Park's sophisticated main thoroughfare**

# KEY TO ORLANDO – SHOPPING CENTRES

A = CHURCH STREET EXCHANGE
      AND CHURCH STREET MARKET
B = OLD TOWN
C = KISSIMMEE HISTORIC DISTRICT
D = SEMINOLE TOWNE CENTER
E = FORT LIBERTY TRADING POST
F = THE PARKWAY SHOPS
G = DISNEY'S MARKETPLACE
H = MERCADO MEDITERRANEAN VILLAGE
I = GOODINGS INTERNATIONAL PLAZA
J = CROSSROADS OF LAKE BUENA VISTA
K = BELZ FACTORY OUTLET
L = QUALITY OUTLET CENTER
M = KISSIMMEE MANUFACTURER'S OUTLET MALL

N = FLEA WORLD
O = OSCEOLA FLEA AND FARMERS' MARKET
P = FLORIDA MALL
Q = ALTAMONTE MALL
R = OSCEOLA SQUARE MALL
S = COLONIAL PLAZA MALL
T = ORLANDO FASHION SQUARE MALL
U = COLONIAL PROMENADE
V = LAKE BUENA VISTA FACTORY SHOPS
W = THE MARKETPLACE
X = THE POINTE*ORLANDO
Y = PARK AVENUE
Z = BELZ INTERNATIONAL OUTLET CENTER

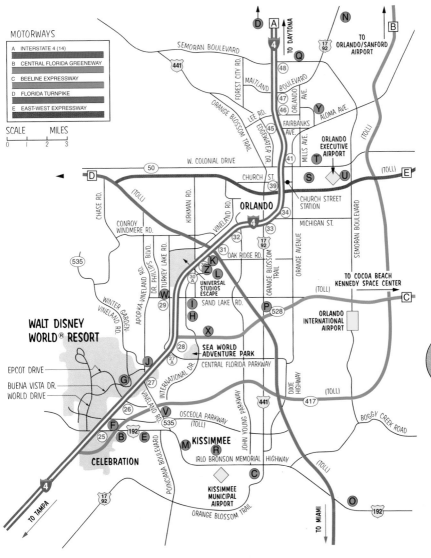

MOTORWAYS

A  INTERSTATE 4 (14)
B  CENTRAL FLORIDA GREENEWAY
C  BEELINE EXPRESSWAY
D  FLORIDA TURNPIKE
E  EAST-WEST EXPRESSWAY

SCALE        MILES
0     1     2     3

10

another which exceeds that, you pay the duty and VAT only on the excess (and the customs officers will usually give you the benefit of the lowest rate on what you pay for). To give you some examples of duty rates (which fill three volumes and are updated regularly), golf clubs are charged at 3.4 per cent, cameras at 4.8 per cent and mountain bikes at a whopping 15.4 per cent, all plus VAT. If you have any queries about your allowances or the duty on specific items, consult the Customs and Excise office located in the departure lounge before you leave your home airport.

Your ordinary duty free allowances from America include 200 cigarettes and a litre of spirits or two litres of sparkling wine and two litres of still wine. Alligator products, which constitute an endangered species, require a special import licence, and you should consult the Department of the Environment first.

Be aware, also, of the hidden 'extras' of shopping costs. Unlike our VAT, the local version in Orlando, the Florida State sales tax, is NOT added to the displayed purchase price, so you should add 6 or 7 per cent (depending on which county you are in) to arrive at the 'real' price. This frequently catches visitors out as they are convinced the wrong price has been rung up or that some clever con is being

BRIT TIP: As with the theme parks and restaurants, there are special coupons and discounts in the various tourist hand-outs for some of the shops. A few are worth keeping but the majority are pretty tacky.

worked. The sales tax is added to everything you buy in Orlando, from your theme park tickets to a beer at the hotel and all meals (but not supermarket groceries, which are classed as 'essentials').

Here is a rundown of the main shopping attractions and the sort of fun and bargains that can be had, divided into four categories. First, the purpose-built speciality shopping complexes, specifically out to catch the tourist; second, Orlando's speciality flea markets and discount outlets; third, the large, typically American shopping malls; and finally a few specific shops with the bargain-hunter in mind.

## Shopping complexes

Top of the first category must come **Church Street Exchange** and **Church Street Market**, two separate but similarly intentioned restorations full of one-off gift shops in downtown Orlando. The Exchange is part of the Church Street Station entertainment complex, but there is no admission charge to go shopping here. It is a grand, eye-catching old railroad station conversion now housing three levels of gift shops, cafés and restaurants, split into two sides, with live entertainment and sideshows in the evenings and at weekends. Open from 11am to 11pm every day, it also features Commander Ragtime's Midway of Fun, Food and Games, a floor of antique, carnival-style games and a usually uncrowded food court. Stores vary from the exclusive and expensive to typical tourist fare, but all with a distinctly stylish, Victorian flavour. Look out for the Bumby Emporium, Church Street Station's elaborate gift shop, and the Buffalo Trading Company, for all things Western. Although the two tend to merge into each other, the two-storey Market is separately owned and run, built around a large brick courtyard, and consists of another two dozen specialist stores (check out Laser Magic for some clever holograms and Brookstone for all manner of useful and useless gadgets), craft stalls and street performers, plus restaurants like the young and trendy Hooters and the excellent budget Italian eatery the Olive Garden. The Market is open until 10pm (6pm on Sundays) and for both take exit 38 off I4. Parking is available and well signposted all around Church Street in either multi-storey or ground-level facilities.

Kissimmee's version of the purpose-built tourist shopping centre is **Old Town**, an antique-style offering in the heart of Highway 192. Some 75 shops – from standard souvenirs, novel T-shirt outlets, Disney merchandise and sportswear to motorbike fashions – line the brick-built streets, along with eight restaurants, a haunted house attraction, the Yellow Submarine play area (great for letting the youngsters loose for a while!) and a host of fairground rides, including the 60ft tall Century Wheel, the Windstorm roller-coaster, go-karts, a Kids' Town area of junior rides and even bungee-jumping. Allow for up to four hours here and try to take in the weekly **Saturday Nite Cruise** at 8.30pm, a drive-past of 300-plus vintage and collector cars from all over America (and a new **Friday Nite Cruise** featuring cars built from 1973–85, live music and prizes). Parking is free and Old Town is open from 10am–11pm seven days a week.

Other Kissimmee tourist-orientated shopping centres include the recently revamped **Historical District of Kissimmee** on Broadway, which can be found two blocks south of Highway 192 on Route 17–92. These are a number of restored turn-of-the-century homes featuring gift shops, a children's boutique, country store and Chef's Pantry restaurant. The Historical District shops are open 10am–5pm (10am–3pm on Saturdays).

## Downtown Disney

Not to be outdone, Disney have embarked on a major expansion of what used to be the Village Marketplace and is now one of the three elements of Downtown Disney (discussed in Chapter 6). **Downtown Disney Marketplace** is typical Disney, a beautiful location, imaginative building and landscaping and a host of one-off elements that make shopping here a pleasure. Don't miss the awesome **World of Disney** store, the largest of its kind in the world (and with a range of products you will find nowhere else), the new **Lego Imagination Center**® (an inter-active playground and shop), **Summer Sands** for swimwear and accessories and **Team Mickey's Athletic Club**. Dancing fountains and squirt pools (where kids tend to get VERY wet), the lakeside setting and boating opportunities all add to the appeal. Restaurants include the wonderfully relaxed and exclusive yacht club feel of **Cap'n Jack's** (don't miss their Maryland crab cakes), the new **Rainforest Café** and the first **McDonald's**® in Walt Disney World® Resort. Once you have taken in Downtown Disney Marketplace, stroll over to **Downtown Disney West Side** and see a film or visit the world's largest **Virgin**™ **Megastore** (with 300 listening posts!). The whole complex is open from 9.30am–11pm every day. It is found off exit 26A of I4 and is well signposted (avoid exit 27 for the increasing traffic congestion).

Similarly cleverly built to attract the eye of passing tourists is the **Mercado Mediterranean Village** in the heart of the southern

10

**Mercado Mediterranean Shopping Village**

International Drive tourist drag, with more than 60 speciality shops, some superb restaurants (including Bergamo's, Charlie's Lobster House, Jose's and The Butcher Shop), the Blazing Pianos night club, live evening entertainment and an impressive international food court (especially for the budget-conscious). The wonderful Spanish architecture encourages browsing along the 'streets', lined with one-off shops. The Mercado is open 10am–10pm daily (longer at the bars and restaurants), and will amuse you and your wallet for several hours.

Almost next door to the Mercado

> BRIT TIP: A word of warning on videos. If you are tempted to buy those souvenir videos – beware! American video tapes are **NOT** compatible with European VCRs, so you will be wasting your money unless the video is marked **PAL**, which signifies European use.

is **Goodings International Plaza**, another tourist shopping centre featuring discount stores like Denim World and Skips Western Wear.

Handily, the supermarket here is a 24-hour operation, while the rest of the plaza is open from 10am–10pm. Likewise, **Crossroads of Lake Buena Vista**, the less expensive neighbour of Downtown Disney Marketplace, offers a similar collection of 25 busy shops and some fun restaurants, and is open all week long from 10am to 10pm.

The newest shopping centre, of course, is the hugely elaborate **Pointe*Orlando** (already discussed in Orlando by Night in Chapter 8), which is as much an evening adventure as mere shopping. The stores here are all distinctly more up-market than usual tourist fare, and you can indulge your passion for fashion at places like Ocean Drive Fashion, Abercrombie & Fitch and Armani Exchange.

## Discount outlets

**Belz Factory Outlet** is by far the most impressive of the second category of shops, the 'factory' or discount outlet, and is a positive Mecca for all serious shoppers. Actually, it almost defies description as it is too widespread to be a full shopping mall, too elaborate to be a flea market and too down-to-earth to be a straightforward tourist trap (the locals do a lot of shopping here, too). Belz can be found on West Oak Ridge Road at the top of International Drive and consists of more than 160 shops arranged in two indoor malls (both with lively food courts and one with a vintage carousel to amuse the kids), plus four separate annexes that all require a separate journey by car (unless you want to wear out a lot of shoe leather!). Avoid Belz at weekends, if you want to beat the crowds. The aim is to sell name brands at factory-direct prices and, while you may have to wade through a fair amount of stuff you wouldn't want if they were giving it away, you will find shoes, clothes, books, jewellery, electronics, sporting goods, crockery and much more at bargain rates. Check out the Calvin Klein outlet

> BRIT TIP: For the best value genuine Disney merchandise, try the Character Warehouse in Belz Mall 2.

(Annex 2), Reebok footwear (Annex 4), the Van Heusen factory store (Malls 1 & 2), OshKosh kidswear, the Umbro store and Guess Jeans (all Mall 2). Serious shoppers will want to spend several hours here, and Belz is conveniently open 10am–9pm Mon–Sat and 10am–6pm on Sundays. **Quality Outlet Center** (9.30am–9pm Mon–Sat, 11am–6pm Sun) further down on International Drive offers much of the same,

although not in quite the same quantity. (Disney Gifts for heavily discounted Disney merchandise is worth a look here.) For a slightly classier version, the **Belz Designer Outlet Center**, just south of Belz on I-Drive has a more up-market range of shops, including Donna Karan, Rocky Mountain Chocolate Factory and Westpoint Pepperell for fine linens (10am–9pm Mon–Sat, 11am–6pm Sun). Kissimmee's version of the discount outlet is the **Kissimmee Manufacturers' Outlet Mall** on Old Vineland Road (just off the central drag of Highway 192, between Markers 13 and 14). Again featuring name brands like Nike, Levis and London Fog, it is open 10am–9pm Mon–Sat and 11am –5pm on Sunday.

The new **Lake Buena Vista Factory Stores** offer another range of big-name products at discount prices, from Adidas, Reebok and

10

**Shopping in the Old Town**

Starter Athletic Wear to OshKosh B'Gosh and (the better-priced) Carter's Childrenswear, plus a lively food court and a kids' playground. They can be found on SR 535 (two miles south off Exit 27 of I4) and are open 10am–9pm Mon–Sat,

> BRIT TIP: Despite the attractive prices, avoid the temptation to collect a house-load of electrical goods as they are geared to run on American 110–120 volt supplies and not our 220, and you would have to buy special adapters to use them back home.

10am–6pm Sun. Another recent development (and worth a look because they are off the beaten tourist path) are the shops and restaurants of Disney's town of **Celebration**, a unique collection of speciality stores, an ice cream and candy shop, cinemas, lakeside dining and Saturday Farmers' Market, plus boat and bike rentals. Follow the signs to downtown Celebration down Celebration Avenue, just off Highway 192 ¼-mile east of its junction with I4. The shops are open 10am–9pm Mon–Sat, 12noon–6pm Sun.

## Flea markets

**Flea World** boasts America's largest covered market, with 1,700 stalls spread out over 104 acres, including three massive, themed buildings, plus a seven-acre amusement park, Fun World, that will keep the kids amused for a good hour or two. It is open Friday, Saturday and Sunday only from 9am to 6pm and can be found a 20-minute drive away on Highway 17–92 (best picked up from exit 47 of I4) between Orlando and Sanford (to the north). The stalls include all manner of market goods, from fresh produce to antiques and jewellery and a whole range of arts and crafts (try Rag Shoppe USA for some real bargains in materials and lace), while there is a full-scale food court and a 300-seat pizza and burger eatery, the Carousel Restaurant, plus free entertainment on the Fun World Pavilion stage.

On a slightly smaller scale is the **Osceola Flea and Farmers' Market** at the eastern extremity of the tourist area of Highway 192 in Kissimmee.

## Malls

The inevitable indoor malls are all big, efficient and much of a muchness, offering rather run-of-the-mill shopping compared to the tourist-orientated centres. However, there are a few exceptions to this rule which are worth seeking out for a couple of hours. The **Florida Mall** has a much more stylish appearance than most of its counterparts, featuring some 200 shops in three themed areas, with several large department stores and an excellent food court offering a choice of 19 speciality restaurants, plus the lively bar-restaurant, Ruby Tuesday. It is located on the South Orange Blossom Trail, on the corner of Sand Lake Road, and is open 10am–9.30pm Mon–Sat, 11am–6pm on Sunday. A recent addition is the up-market (but expensive) Saks Fifth Avenue, while OshKosh baby gear can be bought, usually at reduced prices, at J.C. Penney. Florida's oldest (and biggest) department store, Burdine's, is due to open a branch here in 1999.

The huge two-storey **Altamonte Mall**, on Altamonte Avenue in the suburb of Altamonte Springs (take exit 48 on I4 and head east for half a mile on Route 436), is also well above average. It is one of the largest in America, featuring 175 speciality shops, four major department stores, a choice of 15 eating outlets in Treats food court, plus another three restaurants, including Ruby Tuesday, and an elegant overall design with marble floors that makes visiting a pleasure. You can also get away from the usual tourist hordes here to do some serious shopping from 10am–9pm Monday to Saturday and from 11am–6pm on Sunday (weekdays are best, though). Out-of-town visitors can benefit from the mall's Visitor Savings shopping programme, which offers discounts in many of the stores. Simply show your hotel room key or your driving licence or passport at the Customer Service Center in the middle of the lower level to pick up your Savings Passport.

One of the most extensive mall developments is the new and hugely spacious **Seminole Towne Center** just off I4 to the north of Orlando on the outskirts of Sanford. This vast complex offers another two-storey wonderland of designer shops, boutiques and department stores (like Burdine's and J.C. Penney) as well as craft stalls and a wide-ranging food court. Turn right off exit 51 of I4 and you are there, and it makes a handy place to while away your last few hours if you have an afternoon flight from the nearby Orlando/Sanford Airport.

The large and spacious **Osceola Square Mall** (where Highway 192 mysteriously becomes Vine Street along its central stretch) is the only enclosed mall in Kissimmee, with 50 shops and a 12-screen cinema complex (open 10am–9pm Mon–Sat, noon–6pm on Sun), while also worth a look if you are in the vicinity are the series of malls and shopping plazas along East Colonial Drive (Exit 41 off I4), including **Colonial Plaza Mall, Orlando Fashion Square Mall, Colonial Promenade, Herndon Plaza** and

**Herndon Village Shoppes**, all of which offer more leisurely browsing, especially during the week. New plazas are being added all the time, while the shops of **Park Avenue** remain a healthy alternative to the main tourist fare. Open from 9am–5pm (Mon–Sat), they include fine jewellery, antiques, wine, fine art and boutiques like Chico's and Jacobson's (see also Off the Beaten Track, Chapter 8).

Apart from the big chemist chain stores, Eckerd and Walgreens, already mentioned, there are a few more typical large-group stores. The main supermarkets you will find are Publix and Goodings, which are comparable with Asda, Safeway or (in the case of Goodings) Marks and Spencer, while for clothes, DIY, home furnishings, souvenirs, toys, electrical goods and other household items the big discount stores are K-Mart, Wal-Mart (open 24 hours for serious shopaholics!) or Target

> BRIT TIP: If you are planning on raiding the Duty Free booze shelves before you head home, the chances are that the liquor stores in the big supermarkets will offer you better prices and more variety.

(like a big version of Tesco's, but without the food department, if that makes sense). If there is anything you have forgotten to bring, the chances are you can get it at K-Mart or one of the other two. For photographic supplies and film processing you should try one of the many branches of Eckerd Express Photo. Kids will also want to know Orlando is home to the biggest Toys 'Я' Us shop in the world! It can be found on Florida Mall Avenue, just off Sand Lake Road and the Orange Blossom Trail.

## Specialist shops

Finally, a few worth making a note of for specific items are the various outlets of **Denim World** (no explanation necessary), **The Sports Authority** and **Sports Dominator**, the former on Sand Lake Road and the latter north of Sand Lake Road, on International Drive, which both offer all manner of sporting goods

> BRIT TIP: Need a good book? Make a beeline for **Barnes & Noble** by the Florida Mall or opposite the Colonial Plaza for a magnificent array of titles (especially travel) and a wonderful coffee shop to sit in and contemplate your purchases. A truly world-class shop!

and apparel, while serious sportsmen and women will also want to visit the magnificent range of the five **Edwin Watts Golf** shops, including their national clearance centre on International Drive, or any of the

five **Special Tee Golf & Tennis** shops. On golf clubs in particular you can pick up some great deals and save pounds on the same equipment back home. **Skips Western Outfitters** (on International Drive, just south of the junction with Sand Lake Road) and **The Great Western Boot Co** (in the Quality Outlet Centre on International Drive and opposite the Altamonte Mall) both offer the chance to get yourself fully kitted out in the latest cowboy fashions, while for an alternative statement in local fashion visit the **Orlando Magic Fanattic** (on the corner of Colonial Drive at its junction with I4) for an amazing range of clothing and souvenirs all bearing the colours or logo of the city's basketball heroes (including their mascot, 'Stuff' the Magic Dragon. I kid thee not!). Another novelty is **Shell World**, by Marker 13 on Highway 192, Kissimmee, and on International Drive (on the corner of Kirkman Road), one of the world's oldest and largest retailers of exotic sea shells and coral. They even have a free museum dedicated to the subject in their Kissimmee store (9am–10pm daily).

Now you should be completely familiar with all the delights in store, let's move on to some practical advice on safety …

# 11 Safety First

*(or, Don't Forget to Pack Your Common Sense!)*

**F**rom the coverage Florida has received in our media you would be forgiven for thinking any holiday to Orlando could be the equivalent of signing up for a vacation in Crime City, USA. This is simply not the case.

Make no mistake, America is a more violent, crime-worried country than ours, but the newspaper and TV images of Orlando as a mugger's paradise are a long way from the truth. If we were talking about New York or even Miami, there would be serious considerations of personal safety, especially for families. But, in pure statistical terms, you have more chance of being mugged in your local High Street than in Orlando. The only tourist destination in America with a LOWER crime rate than Orlando is Sante Fe in New Mexico, and that handles only a fraction of the numbers that central Florida does. Of course there have been incidents of violent crime in the city, no one could pretend otherwise, but on the whole these have been isolated and unusual, and have drawn so much publicity simply because they are the exception rather than the norm. Again, in terms of the most recent statistics, crimes against visitors to Orlando account for 0.04 per cent of the total crime figures for the area, or something in the region of 4,000 incidents for every 13 million tourists. The area has its own Tourist Oriented Policing Service (or TOPS), centred on International Drive, with more than 70 officers patrolling purely the main tourist areas, arranging crime prevention seminars with local hotels and generally ensuring that Orlando takes good care of its visitors. You will often see the local police in these areas out on mountain bikes, and they are a polite, helpful bunch should you need assistance or directions. Tourism is such a vital part of the local economy that the authorities cannot afford not to be seen to be taking an active role against crime, hence the area has an extremely safety-conscious attitude.

This is most evident in the use of state-of-the-art methods of crime prevention that have gone a long way towards driving tourist crime out of the area. These include the fitting of electronic locks on hotel

**The security-featured Omni Rosen Hotel**

rooms, designing new hotels with crime prevention criteria, like special landscaping, lighting and the use of particular colours, and putting extra police patrols on duty in motorway areas where tourists encounter difficulties through bad sign-posting or avoiding the tolls.

Having said all that it would be foolish to behave as if the villainous element did not exist and therefore there are a number of guidelines which all visitors to America in general, and Orlando in particular, should follow. Put simply these are all a question of common sense. For example, just as it would be inadvisable to walk around the darker corners of Soho in London late at night alone, so it would in parts of Florida.

## Emergencies

**General**: In an emergency of any kind, for police, fire department or ambulance, dial 911 (9–911 from your hotel room). It is a good idea to make sure your children are aware of this number, while for smaller-scale crises (mislaid tickets or passports, rescheduled flights, etc) your holiday company should have an emergency contact number in the hotel reception. If you are travelling independently and run into passport or other problems that require the assistance of the British Consulate in Orlando, their office is located in Sun Bank Towers, 200 South Orange Avenue, with walk-in visitors' hours from 9.30am–noon and 2–4pm, or phone between 9.30am–4pm on 407 426 7855.

### Hotels

While in your hotel, motel or guest house, you should always use door peepholes and security chains whenever someone knocks at the door. DON'T open the doors to strangers without asking for

identification, and check with the hotel desk if you are still not sure. It is stating the obvious, but keep your room doors and windows

BRIT TIP: If your room has already been cleaned before you go out for the day, hang the 'Do Not Disturb' sign on the door.

locked at all times and always use deadlocks and security chains. It is still surprising how many people simply forget basic precautions when they are on holiday (the local police also never cease to be amazed at how many people leave their common sense behind when they leave home!). Always take your cash, credit cards and car keys with you when you go out, and don't leave the door open at any time, even if you are just popping down the corridor to the ice machine. Lock your suitcases so they can't be used to carry property out of the room and report any suspicious-looking characters to the hotel desk. And make a point of asking the hotels about their safety precautions when you make your reservation. Do they have electronic card-locks (which can't be duplicated) and do they have their own security staff?

Don't be afraid to ask reception staff for safety pointers in the surrounding areas or if you are travelling somewhere you are not totally sure about. Safety is a major issue for the Central Florida Hotel/Motel Association, so hotel staff are usually well briefed to be helpful in this area. Keep a regular inventory of your belongings during the holiday so you won't get home and suddenly realise you have mislaid your spare handbag/camera/ trainers. Using a bumbag (the Americans call them fanny packs!) is a better bet than a shoulder bag or handbag, and if you carry a wallet try to keep it in an inside pocket.

Nothing is guaranteed to get the local police shaking their heads in disbelief and disgust than the tourist who goes round looking like an obvious tourist. The map over the steering wheel is one obvious giveaway, but other no-nos are wearing large amounts of ostentatious jewellery, carrying masses of photographic equipment or flashing wads of cash around. The biggest single giveaway of all is leaving your camera or camcorder on the front seat of the car. In 1995, Orlando had fewer instances of tourist car crime in the year than Las Vegas on an average day, but it still doesn't pay to put temptation in a

> BRIT TIP: A handy idea for your journey over is to use a business address rather than your home address on all your luggage. It is less conspicuous and safer should any item be stolen or misplaced.

criminal's way. If you want to look a bit more like one of the locals, wearing the ubiquitous baseball cap is a good way of blending in, and wearing a hat is a good idea anyway given the local climate.

Finally, and this is VERY strong police advice, in the unlikely event of being confronted by an assailant, DO NOT resist or try to 'have a go', as it more often than not will result in making the situation more serious.

N.B. If you want to be extra safety conscious, you can hire mobile phones, pagers and even two-way radios from as little as $20 a week from **All Cellular**, tel 407 843 7716.

## Money

Following on from the advice about bumbags and wallets, it is completely inadvisable and totally unnecessary to carry large amounts of cash around with you. US travellers' cheques are accepted almost everywhere as cash and can be readily replaced if lost or stolen, as can credit cards, which are another widespread form of currency. Visa, Mastercard and American Express are almost universally accepted, but don't take unnecessary bank or credit cards with you. The Sun Bank in Disney's Magic Kingdom® and Epcot® is open seven days a week should you need extra help with any financial transactions. It is also worth separating the larger notes from the smaller ones in your wallet to avoid flashing all your money in public view. Losing £200 worth of travellers' cheques shouldn't ruin your holiday – but losing £200 in cash might.

In addition, most hotels will offer the use of safes and deposit boxes for your valuables, and many rooms now come equipped with mini-safes in which it is a good idea to leave your passports, return tickets, cameras etc, when you don't need them. Always keep your valuables out of sight, whether in the hotel room or the car. Use the car boot if you're leaving a jacket or camera.

> BRIT TIP: Be forewarned that all American banknotes are EXACTLY the same green colour and size. It is only the picture of the president and the denomination in each corner which change.

## Driving

Car crime is one of the biggest forms of criminal activity in America and has led to some of the most lurid headlines, especially in the Miami area. Once again, it pays to make a number of basic safety checks before you set off anywhere. The first thing is to be SURE of the car's controls before you drive out of the hire company's car park. Which button is the air-conditioning, which side of the steering wheel are the indicators

BRIT TIP: American freeways, highways and expressways (with the exception of the Florida Turnpike) do not have service stations, so if you need petrol you will have to get off the motorway (although not very far in most cases).

and where are the windscreen wipers? Check BEFORE you leave! Also, make sure you know your route in advance, even if it is only a case of memorising the road numbers. Most of the car hire companies now give good directional instructions on how to get to your hotel from their car park so read them before you set off.

Just about the main item on the list of local police Dos and Don'ts is to use your map BEFORE you set off – trying to drive with the map over the steering wheel is just asking for an accident, let alone marking you out as an obvious tourist. Make sure, too, you put your maps and brochures away in the glove compartment when you leave the car to avoid leaving the obvious sign that says 'Tourist Parked Here'! Check that the petrol tank is full and never let it get near empty. Running

out of 'gas' in an unfamiliar area holds obvious hazards.

If you stray off your pre-determined route, stick to well-lit areas and stop to ask directions only from official businesses like hotels and garages or better still, a police car or station. Always try to park close to your destination where there are plenty of street lights and DO NOT get out if there are any suspicious characters lurking around. Always keep your doors and windows closed (if it's hot, you've got air-conditioning, remember?), and don't hesitate to lock the doors from the inside if you feel threatened by unlikely-looking pedestrians (larger cars have doors that lock automatically as you drive off). As a general rule, be wary of car parks and get into the habit of glancing around your car before you get in. And, please, don't forget to lock it when you leave it!

Miami crooks have developed the habit of trying to get cars to stop by trying to look official or deliberately bumping into obvious hire cars from behind. The easily-identified hire car plates have now been phased out by most companies, but still NEVER stop for a non-official request. Go instead to the nearest garage or police station, and always insist on identification before unlocking your car and getting out of it for an official. It is comforting to know that a unique aspect of driving in Orlando is that none of the main tourist areas have any sort of no-go areas to be avoided. The nearest is the portion of the Orange Blossom Trail south of downtown Orlando. This houses a selection of strip clubs and 'adult bars' that are not particularly attractive and can be downright seedy at night.

Should you require any further information on being safe in Orlando, contact the Community Affairs office of the Orange County Police on 407 836 3720.

# 12 Going Home
## *(or, Where Did the Last Two Weeks Go?)*

And so, dog-tired, financially crippled but (hopefully) blissfully happy and with enough memories to last a lifetime, it is time to deal with that bane of all holidays – the journey home.

If you have come through the last week or two relatively unscathed in terms of the calamities that can befall the uninformed or the plain unlucky, there are still one or two more little pitfalls that can catch you out.

## The Car

First and foremost is the hire car. It has to be returned from whence it came – and that can take time if you had to use an off-airport car depot. Remember how long it took to get mobile in the first place? Well, it can take just as long to return your vehicle, complete any necessary remaining paperwork, pay any outstanding bills and catch the hire company's courtesy bus back to the airport (if their operation is off-airport). The process tends to be quicker with the firms who operate directly from the two airports.

## Orlando International

For reference purposes, the International Airport is 46 miles

Orlando International Airport – Great Hall

12

from Cocoa Beach and 54 from Daytona Beach on the east cost, 84 miles from Tampa and 110 from Clearwater and St Petersburg to the west, 25 from Walt Disney World® and 10 from Universal Studios; always allow yourself plenty of time for the journey.

As with all of the major tourist activities in Orlando, car hire return is a well-organised, highly efficient matter, but the simple numbers involved usually determine that here is one more queue to be negotiated, especially if you leave it until the last minute. Allow a good hour for this process ON TOP of the two hours you are advised to leave for checking in at the airport, and you should sail through.

Having automatically tipped the bus driver for dropping you off at the terminal, you are now back where you started in terms of your Orlando adventure – in the impressively large, clean confines of the International Airport (there are also two local, domestic airports, Orlando Executive, just east of the city, and Kissimmee Airport, just south of Highway 192, and should you end up at either of these you may have a long wait for the flight home!).

**Orlando International** is officially the fastest-growing airport in the world, handling an average of 1,000 flights and some 60,000 passengers per day at peak periods. The terminal complex covers 854 acres (and the whole airport a massive 15,000 acres), so it can swallow a lot of people comfortably, but its modern expanses can still get seriously busy. It handles almost half of the traffic of Heathrow, the same as Gatwick and comfortably more than our other regional airports, so be prepared for one final battle with the crowds if there are several British charter flights scheduled at the same time. However, at all but peak periods, this is one of the most comfortable and relaxing airport

terminals you will find anywhere in the world, and it was recently rated No 1 in America for customer service. Its provision of services and other facilities, like shops and restaurants, is second to none, and its airy, open concourses will make you feel you are in a top-quality hotel rather than an international airport (perhaps this is not too surprising when one end of the terminal is taken up by the airport-run Hyatt Hotel, a beautifully appointed and magnificently equipped establishment that is also open to airport passengers).

Ramps, restrooms, wide lifts and large open areas throughout the airport ensure easy access for wheelchairs, and there are special features like TDD and amplified telephones, wheelchair-height drinking fountains, braille lift controls and companion-care rest rooms to assist disabled travellers.

You will also find plenty to do here to while away that final hour or two, and, should you have more than a couple of hours to spare, it is worth knowing you can leave your carry-on bags at the Baggage Checkroom and take the 15-minute taxi ride to the Florida Mall for any last-minute shopping, or take in a film at the big cinema complex just to the north of the airport (a five-minute journey by taxi). The airport's two information desks (both on Level Three) keep all the cinema timetables, so if you think you have time, consult them and hail a cab!

In keeping with the Orlando area, the International Airport has some wide-ranging plans for staying a step ahead. A recent addition is the **Shipyard Pub and Brewery** in the centre of the terminal, which has bags of Brit appeal. REAL beer (albeit still a little on the cold side), excellent bar meals and the option of a tour of the micro-brewery add up to an above-average airport experience. Similarly, the airport is in the middle of a $1.2 billion expansion programme, to add the fourth satellite terminal, improve public parking and traffic flow, add more check-in facilities (notably for Disney's cruise operations), tackle the double luggage retrieval system for international arrivals and start work on a major new terminal complex to the south. The car hire operations should also be improved, although there may be some small-scale inconvenience to passengers while the work is carried out.

## Landside

As with all international airports, you have a division between **LANDSIDE** (for all visitors to the airport) and **AIRSIDE** (beyond which you need to have a ticket). Orlando's **LANDSIDE** is divided into three levels: **One** is for ground transportation, parking, buses and the car rental agencies; **Two** is the Baggage Claim level (you will probably hardly have noticed it on your way in); **Three** is where you should enter the airport on your return journey as it holds all the check-in desks, plus shops, restaurants, lockers, bank and information desks. Level Three is effectively sub-divided into four sections: **Landside 'A'** is the check-in section for Gates 1–29. Here you will find American Airlines, Continental, TWA and Pan Am. **Landside 'B'** is home to the check-in desks for Gates 30–99 and the other main airlines, including Northwest, United, USAir, BA, Delta and Virgin.

Then, once you have checked in, you can choose to explore the **East** and **West** sections of the main concourse which occupies the centre of Level Three. The **West** end houses the Great Hall, around which are the main shopping and eating areas. Inevitably, Disney & Co make one last attempt to part you from

what's left of your money, so here you will find some more highly impressive, not to mention large, gift shops for Walt Disney World®, SeaWorld and Universal Studios (and there is no airport mark-up either), Benjamin Books, Tie Rack, Sunglass International, The Grove Sweet Shop (great pic 'n' mix!), two newsagents, a highly-varied food court (including Burger King, Pizza Hut, Nathan's Famous frankfurters and chili dogs and Cinnabon) and, up the escalators in the centre of the hall, a new restaurant of the lively Chili's chain, a Tex-Mex diner and bar.

The **East** end of Level Three tends to be quieter and more picturesque as it is dominated by the eight-storey Hyatt Hotel atrium, featuring palm trees and a large fountain, and there are fewer

> BRIT TIP: Overlooked by many travellers, McCoy's Bar and Grill in the Hyatt Hotel is the perfect little sanctuary to while away that final hour or two before the flight.

departure gates and shops down here (until the fourth satellite terminal opens). Universal and SeaWorld both have secondary shops (and they're different, too!), while the Paradies Shop is also worth a look for other gift items. For food and drink there is a Starbuck's coffee shop and the new Shipyard Pub. There is also, up the escalator, the entrance to the Hyatt Airport Hotel if you fancy seeing out your visit in style. McCoy's Bar and Grill (up the escalator, turn right) is one of the smartest bar-restaurants you will find in Orlando, and it has the bonus of a grandstand view of the airport runways to watch all the comings

**12**

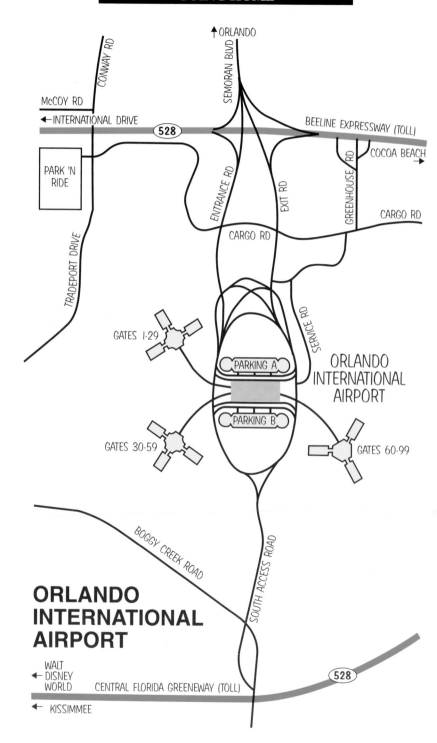

# ORLANDO INTERNATIONAL

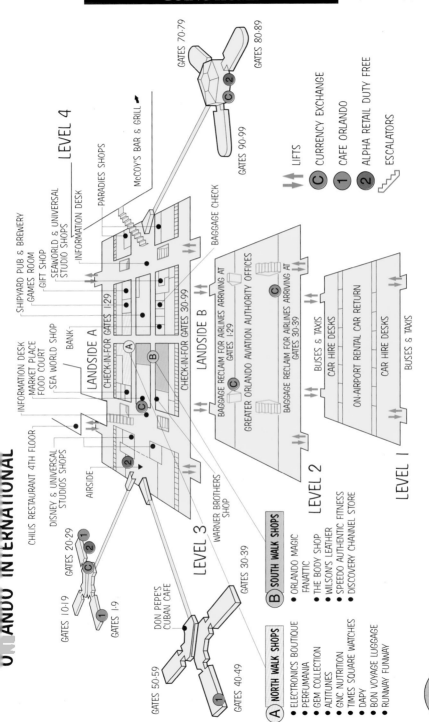

CHILIS RESTAURANT 4TH FLOOR

GATES 70-79

GATES 80-89

**LEVEL 4**

McCOY'S BAR & GRILL

PARADIES SHOPS

GATES 90-99

SHIPYARD PUB & BREWERY
GAMES ROOM
GIFT SHOP

SEAWORLD & UNIVERSAL
STUDIO SHOPS
INFORMATION DESK

BAGGAGE CHECK

INFORMATION DESK
MARKET PLACE
FOOD COURT
SEA WORLD SHOP
BANK

LANDSIDE A

CHECK-IN-FOR GATES 1-29

CHECK-IN-FOR GATES 30-99

LANDSIDE B

BAGGAGE RECLAIM FOR AIRLINES ARRIVING AT
GATES 1-29

GREATER ORLANDO AVIATION AUTHORITY OFFICES

BAGGAGE RECLAIM FOR AIRLINES ARRIVING AT
GATES 30-39

BUSES & TAXIS

**LEVEL 2**

CAR HIRE DESKS

ON-AIRPORT RENTAL CAR RETURN

CAR HIRE DESKS

BUSES & TAXIS

**LEVEL 1**

DISNEY & UNIVERSAL
STUDIOS SHOPS

AIRSIDE

WARNER BROTHERS
SHOP

**LEVEL 3**

GATES 10-19

GATES 20-29

GATES 1-9

DON PEPE'S
CUBAN CAFE

GATES 50-59

GATES 40-49

GATES 30-39

**A NORTH WALK SHOPS**

- ELECTRONICS BOUTIQUE
- PERFUMANIA
- GEM COLLECTION
- ALTITUNES
- GNC NUTRITION
- TIMES SQUARE WATCHES
- DAPY
- BON VOYAGE LUGGAGE
- RUNWAY FUNWAY

**B SOUTH WALK SHOPS**

- ORLANDO MAGIC
  FANATIC
- THE BODY SHOP
- WILSON'S LEATHER
- SPEEDO AUTHENTIC FITNESS
- DISCOVERY CHANNEL STORE

**LIFTS**

**C** CURRENCY EXCHANGE

**1** CAFE ORLANDO

**2** ALPHA RETAIL DUTY FREE

**ESCALATORS**

12

and goings. The surroundings are immensely stylish and a long way removed from the average airport lounge. If you want to go really up-market in your Orlando farewell, go up the escalator, turn left and take the lift to the ninth floor and Hemisphere Restaurant. Not only do you have an even more impressive view of the airport's workings, its northern Italian cuisine provides some of the best fare in the city. It's slightly on the pricey side, but the service and food are five-star.

The central access corridors between the East and West ends, which already house some service facilities like a bank, travel agent, post office, baggage checkroom and hair salon, now also contain a mini shopping parade with some more impressive stores like Warner Brothers, Body Shop and a Magic Fanattic souvenir store and a family entertainment games and playroom.

If you still have time to kill after visiting all these establishments and buying those final gift items, wander round the concourse and examine some of the airport's magnificent art collection or view the large aquarium next to the SeaWorld shop at the East end.

## Airside

Once you have decided it is time to move on to your departure gate, you have to be aware of the three satellite arms that make up the airport's **AIRSIDE**.

These are divided into **Gates 1–29, 30–59** (both at the West end of the main terminal) and **60–99** (at the East end). ALL the departure gates are here, plus the duty free shops, more restaurants, lockers and nursery services.

The airport is ultimately designed to have four separate satellite arms, each connected to the main building by a mono-rail shuttle service (as exists between the North and South terminals at Gatwick), so you need to keep your wits about you when it comes to finding your departure gate. As is increasingly the case these days, there are no tannoy announcements for flights, so you must remember to ask your departure gate and time when you check in on Level Three. However, there are three monitor boards in the main terminal which display all the necessary departure information. As a general rule, British Airways and Virgin use **Gates 60–99**, as do Delta. NorthWest, United and USAir usually use **Gates 30–59**, while Pan Am departs from **Gates 1–29**, along with American, Continental and TWA.

In most airports, once you have moved Airside it is not possible to return to the Landside area again. However, that is not the case here, and, if you find the crowds milling around your departure gate too much to bear, you can always return to one of the terminal hostelries, for a bit of peace and quiet.

Having said all that, you will find the Airside areas just as clean and efficient as the main terminal, with the added bonus of three duty free shops just in case your credit card hasn't already gone into meltdown.

As you pass through the ticket and baggage check at the West end of the terminal you will find the Alpha Retail Duty Free immediately on your right. This is the biggest of their three shops and is open only to departing international passengers, so you will need to have your boarding card handy. Unlike the duty free shops in Britain, you don't carry your purchases out with you. Instead, they are delivered to your departure gate for collection as you get on the plane. This is because the international flights are mixed in with the domestic ones and, of course, duty free shopping does not apply to internal flights.

Having taken the shuttle to **Gates**

**1–29**, you will find another duty free shop (they're DETERMINED to get your money!), plus a newsagents (The Keys Group News and Gifts), a currency exchange, two bar/lounges of the Café Orlando and another mini-food court, featuring Burger King, Mrs Field's Cookies and TCBY (which really does stand for The Country's Best Yoghurt). **Gates 30–59** is the only satellite arm NOT to have its own duty free shop, so remember to bag your duty frees back at their main store just past the Airside ticket check. However, you will still find a Café Orlando lounge bar, Don Pepe's Cuban Café, a food court and a WH Smith's. Travelling from **Gates 60–99** gives you the options of another duty free shop, a Fenton Hill newsagents, currency exchange and food court containing Burger King (inevitably – it's always the busiest, too), Nathan's Famous frankfurters, etc, TCBY and the Shipyard Brewport for that final beverage.

Just like back at your home departure airport, you still have to be near your departure gate a little before time so you can hear the rows being called for embarkation.

## Orlando/Sanford Airport

Returning to what is now the main Orlando gateway for British charter flights should be a relatively simple experience, providing you retrace your route on the Central Florida Greeneway and come off at Exit 49. You go across one set of traffic lights then turn right at the second set on to Lake Mary Boulevard and follow it all the way back into the Airport. New signs have been posted along all the main routes to make the return journey very straightforward, and the wonderfully efficient ease of the Dollar car rental return adds to this simplicity.

By way of a little more explanation, Orlando/Sanford was created as a full international airport only in the spring of 1996 as an initiative between the airport

> BRIT TIP: You do not want to be based in the Sanford area for an Orlando holiday. You would have at least an hour's journey in to Walt Disney World® in the morning along I4, probably longer with the traffic at that time.

authorities and several of the main British tour operators. The relatively slow processing of international passenger arrivals at the International Airport, with its double baggage retrieval system, long queues at the Immigration Hall and congested car hire operations (with many of them having to bus people to off-airport depots) led to the inevitable cries of 'Can't we do it better/quicker/more efficiently?' And so the British charters (Leisure Air, Airtours, Britannia, Monarch and Air 2000) decided to see if they could speed up their passenger through-put by using the alternative, i.e. Orlando/Sanford. With its small, simple design (straight off the plane into Immigration, one baggage carousel and then a walk across the road into the Dollar or Alamo car hire offices) it DOES get you mobile appreciably quicker. Of course, you are that much further to the north to start with, so your journey time is a good 40–45 minutes longer and you have to pay an extra $4–$5 in tolls, BUT, providing you follow the simple directions to the main tourist areas, you can save as much as an hour in overall time taken.

**12**

# ORLANDO/SANFORD AIRPORT

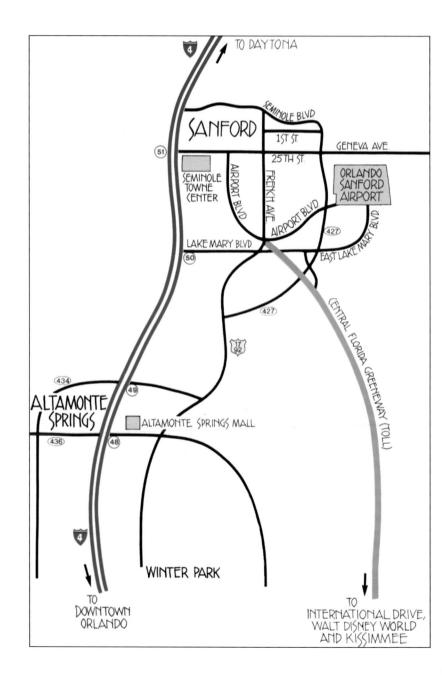

**The Airtours children's lounge at Orlando/Sanford airport**

However, while this new charter gateway is a much simpler operation, it stands to reason that you lose out on the extra facilities of the International Airport, which can be a drawback if there is a delay in the flight home for any reason.

At peak holiday periods, there have been hold-ups on the busiest days (Thur–Sat) as the check-in desks struggle to cope with the numbers involved, while the departure lounge can get crowded, too. The one departure gate access can also create a bit of a bottleneck, but the airport authority has recently announced a major expansion plan to take care of these growing pains. And, when the airport is not at full capacity or subject to unforeseen delays, its facilities are perfectly adequate for a comfortable stay, with a British-style pub, a restaurant, snack bar, cafeteria and ice cream shop, a video games room, a well-stocked duty free shop and a fully supervised (free) child care centre. More facilities are being added all the time, and there are some useful changing rooms which allow you to turn up in your shorts and T-shirt before switching to something more sensible for arriving back home in the early hours. The addition of extra departure gates later in 1999 should go a long way towards alleviating the pressure of sheer numbers, and ultimately help to make Orlando/Sanford as smooth a proposition on the way out as it is on your arrival.

After all that, you can expect your return flight to be somewhat shorter than the journey out thanks to the Atlantic jetstreams that provide handy tail-winds to high-level flights. Differences of more than an hour in the two journey times are not uncommon.

Finally, you will land back at Heathrow, Manchester, Glasgow, etc rather more jet-lagged than on the trip out. This is because the time difference is more noticeable on eastward flights, and it may take a good day or two to get your body's time-clock back on to local time. It is therefore even more important not to indulge in alcoholic beverages if you are driving home.

And, much as it may seem like a good idea, the best way to beat Florida jet-lag is NOT to go straight out and book another holiday to Orlando!

**But, believe me, the lure of this great theme park wonderland will ultimately prove impossible to resist again.**

**Come back soon, now!**

**12**

# 13

# Your Holiday Planner

You can design your own holiday schedule on pages 246–247 with the aid of the Theme Park busy day guide on page 248.

## Example 1: with 5-day Walt Disney World® Pass

| DAY | ATTRACTION | NOTES |
|-----|------------|-------|
| **SUN** | DAY | |
| | EVE | |
| **MON** | DAY | |
| | EVE | |
| **TUE** | DAY | |
| | EVE | |
| **WED** | DAY | |
| | EVE | |
| **THUR** | DAY Arrive 2.40pm local time Orlando/Sanford Airport | *N.B. 50 mins to drive to hotel* |
| | EVE Check out local shops and restaurants | |
| **FRI** | DAY Welcome meeting/SEAWORLD | |
| | EVE | |
| **SAT** | DAY Fantasy of Flight and Splendid China | |
| | EVE | |
| **SUN** | DAY THE MAGIC KINGDOM® PARK | *(Open until 10pm today)* |
| | EVE | |
| **MON** | DAY Disney's Blizzard Beach/Discovery Island | |
| | EVE Downtown Disney Pleasure Island | |
| **TUE** | DAY KENNEDY SPACE CENTER | |
| | EVE Fort Liberty Wild Bill's Dinner Show | |
| **WED** | DAY BUSCH GARDENS | |
| | EVE | |

(N.B. Five-Day All-in-One Hopper gives 5 full days unlimited access to all Disney attractions; there may be a separate charge for big events at Disney's Wide World of Sports.

# Example 1: with 5-day Walt Disney World® Pass

| DAY | | ATTRACTION | NOTES |
|---|---|---|---|
| **THUR** | DAY | Balloon Flight/Wet 'n' Wild | |
| | EVE | Skull Kingdom/Belz Shopping Centre | |
| **FRI** | DAY | UNIVERSAL STUDIOS® FLORIDA | |
| | EVE | Universal Studios CityWalk | *(until late!)* |
| **SAT** | DAY | Winter Park Lakes/Shopping | |
| | EVE | | |
| **SUN** | DAY | DISNEY'S ANIMAL KINGDOM™ THEME PARK | *(7am start)* |
| | EVE | Relax! | |
| **MON** | DAY | EPCOT® | *(open until 9pm)* |
| | EVE | | |
| **TUE** | DAY | Aquatic Wonders Tours? | |
| | EVE | Church Street Station | *Holiday company trip* |
| **WED** | DAY | DISNEY-MGM STUDIOS/Disney's Typhoon Lagoon | |
| | EVE | Downtown Disney | *(Final fling)* |
| **THUR** | DAY | Gatorland/Back to Airport | |
| | EVE | | *Flight 6pm; return car at 3.30pm* |
| **FRI** | DAY | Return Gatwick 7am | |
| | EVE | | |
| **SAT** | DAY | | |
| | EVE | | |
| **SUN** | DAY | | |
| | EVE | | |

# Example 2: with 7-day Walt Disney World® Pass

(N.B. Seven-Day All-in-One Hopper Pass gives 7 full days unlimited access to all Disney attractions; there may be a separate charge for big events at Disney's Wide World of Sports.

| DAY | | ATTRACTION | NOTES |
|---|---|---|---|
| **SUN** | DAY | | |
| | EVE | | |
| **MON** | DAY | | |
| | EVE | | |
| **TUE** | DAY | | |
| | EVE | | |
| **WED** | DAY | | |
| | EVE | | |
| **THUR** | DAY | Arrive 2.40pm local time Orlando/Sanford Airport | *N.B. 50 mins to drive to hotel* |
| | EVE | Check out local shops and restaurants | |
| **FRI** | DAY | Welcome Meeting + SEAWORLD | *(Open until 7pm)* |
| | EVE | | |
| **SAT** | DAY | Fantasy of Flight/Spendid China | |
| | EVE | Fort Liberty Dinner Show | *Holiday company trip* |
| **SUN** | DAY | THE MAGIC KINGDOM® PARK | *(Open until 11pm today)* |
| | EVE | | |
| **MON** | DAY | Disney's Typhoon Lagoon/Discovery Island | *(Open until 8pm)* |
| | EVE | Downtown Disney/Pleasure Island | |
| **TUE** | DAY | DISNEY-MGM STUDIOS | |
| | EVE | Polynesian Luau | *(6.30–8.30pm)* |
| **WED** | DAY | Disney's Blizzard Beach | |
| | EVE | Church Street Station | *Holiday company trip* |

# Example 2: with 7-day Walt Disney World® Pass

| DAY | | ATTRACTION | NOTES |
|---|---|---|---|
| **THUR** | DAY | EPCOT® | *(Open until 10pm)* |
| | EVE | | |
| **FRI** | DAY | THE MAGIC KINGDOM® PARK | *(Arrive later (open until 10pm today)* |
| | EVE | | |
| **SAT** | DAY | Winter Park Lakes or Silver Springs | |
| | EVE | Relax! | |
| **SUN** | DAY | DISNEY'S ANIMAL KINGDOM™ THEME PARK | *(7am start)* |
| | EVE | EPCOT® | *(Open until 10pm)* |
| **MON** | DAY | UNIVERSAL STUDIOS® FLORIDA | *(Open until 7pm)* |
| | EVE | | |
| **TUE** | DAY | BUSCH GARDENS | |
| | EVE | Wet 'n' Wild | *(Open until 10pm)* |
| **WED** | DAY | KENNEDY SPACE CENTER | |
| | EVE | Universal Studios CityWalk | *(Final fling!)* |
| **THUR** | DAY | Gatorland/Back to Airport | *Check-out by midday* |
| | EVE | | *Flight 6pm; return car at 3.30pm* |
| **FRI** | DAY | Return Gatwick 7am | |
| | EVE | | |
| **SAT** | DAY | | |
| | EVE | | |
| **SUN** | DAY | | |
| | EVE | | |

# Blank form: Your Holiday!

| DAY | ATTRACTION | NOTES |
|-----|-----------|-------|
| **SUN** | DAY<br>———————————<br>EVE | |
| **MON** | DAY<br>———————————<br>EVE | |
| **TUE** | DAY<br>———————————<br>EVE | |
| **WED** | DAY<br>———————————<br>EVE | |
| **THUR** | DAY<br>———————————<br>EVE | |
| **FRI** | DAY<br>———————————<br>EVE | |
| **SAT** | DAY<br>———————————<br>EVE | |
| **SUN** | DAY<br>———————————<br>EVE | |
| **MON** | DAY<br>———————————<br>EVE | |
| **TUE** | DAY<br>———————————<br>EVE | |
| **WED** | DAY<br>———————————<br>EVE | |

# Blank form: Your Holiday!

| DAY | ATTRACTION | NOTES |
|---|---|---|
| **THUR** | DAY<br>————————<br>EVE | |
| **FRI** | DAY<br>————————<br>EVE | |
| **SAT** | DAY<br>————————<br>EVE | |
| **SUN** | DAY<br>————————<br>EVE | |
| **MON** | DAY<br>————————<br>EVE | |
| **TUE** | DAY<br>————————<br>EVE | |
| **WED** | DAY<br>————————<br>EVE | |
| **THUR** | DAY<br>————————<br>EVE | |
| **FRI** | DAY<br>————————<br>EVE | |
| **SAT** | DAY<br>————————<br>EVE | |
| **SUN** | DAY<br>————————<br>EVE | |

| | BUSIEST | AVERAGE | LIGHTEST |
|---|---|---|---|
| **MON** | MAGIC KINGDOM® <br> DISNEY'S ANIMAL KINGDOM™ THEME PARK | EPCOT® <br> DISNEY-MGM STUDIOS <br> UNIVERSAL STUDIOS | BUSCH GARDENS <br> SEAWORLD <br> KENNEDY SPACE CENTER <br> CYPRESS GARDENS <br> WATER PARKS |
| **TUE** | EPCOT® <br> UNIVERSAL STUDIOS <br> DISNEY'S ANIMAL KINGDOM™ THEME PARK | MAGIC KINGDOM® <br> DISNEY-MGM STUDIOS | BUSCH GARDENS <br> SEAWORLD <br> KENNEDY SPACE CENTER <br> CYPRESS GARDENS <br> WATER PARKS |
| **WED** | UNIVERSAL STUDIOS <br> WATER PARKS <br> EPCOT® | DISNEY-MGM STUDIOS <br> MAGIC KINGDOM® <br> BUSCH GARDENS <br> DISNEY'S ANIMAL KINGDOM™ THEME PARK | SEAWORLD <br> KENNEDY SPACE CENTER <br> CYPRESS GARDENS |
| **THUR** | MAGIC KINGDOM® <br> UNIVERSAL STUDIOS <br> WATER PARKS <br> DISNEY'S ANIMAL KINGDOM™ THEME PARK | EPCOT®   WATER PARKS <br> DISNEY-MGM STUDIOS <br> BUSCH GARDENS <br> SEAWORLD <br> KENNEDY SPACE CENTER | CYPRESS GARDENS |
| **FRI** | WATER PARKS <br> EPCOT® <br> SEAWORLD <br> KENNEDY SPACE CENTER <br> DISNEY-MGM STUDIOS | BUSCH GARDENS <br> CYPRESS GARDENS <br> DISNEY'S ANIMAL KINGDOM™ THEME PARK | MAGIC KINGDOM® <br> UNIVERSAL STUDIOS |
| **SAT** | MAGIC KINGDOM® <br> BUSCH GARDENS <br> SEAWORLD <br> CYPRESS GARDENS <br> WATER PARKS | DISNEY-MGM STUDIOS <br> KENNEDY SPACE CENTER | UNIVERSAL STUDIOS <br> DISNEY'S ANIMAL KINGDOM™ THEME PARK |
| **SUN** | DISNEY-MGM STUDIOS <br> BUSCH GARDENS <br> SEAWORLD <br> CYPRESS GARDENS <br> WATER PARKS | KENNEDY SPACE CENTER | MAGIC KINGDOM® <br> EPCOT® <br> UNIVERSAL STUDIOS <br> DISNEY'S ANIMAL KINGDOM™ THEME PARK |

The author and publisher gratefully acknowledge the provision of the following photographs.

Cover: Spaceship Earth, Copyright 1995 The Walt Disney Company.
Catastrophe Canyon, Copyright 1990 The Walt Disney Company.
Blizzard Beach, Copyright 1995 The Walt Disney Company.
The Big Parade, Copyright 1995 The Walt Disney Company.

Airtours: 241. Arabian Nights: 193. Busch Gardens: 4, 24, 128, 132, 133, 136, 137. Capone's: 196. Church Street Station: 185, 188. Clarion Plaza: 60. Cypress Gardens: 12, 37, 144, 145. Daytona Speedway: 184. Delta Orlando: 61. Fantasy of Flight: 156, 157. Gatorland, 41, 149. The Holiday Inn Sunspree Resort: 53. Kennedy Space Centre: 12, 140. Medieval Times: 197. Morton's Steakhouse: 212. Omni Rosen Hotel: 229. Orange Blossom Balloons: 172. Orlando Convention and Visitors' Bureau: 9, 20, 21, 33, 169, 176, 177, 180, 181, 203, 220, 224, 225. Orlando International Airport: 233. Peabody Orlando: 56. Planet Hollywood: 208, 213. Race Rock: 213, 216. The Richard Petty Driving Experience: 184. SeaWorld: 121, 124, 125, 167. Seminole County: 29. Silver Springs: 145. Skull Kingdom: 156. Splendid China: 148, 149. Universal Studios: 104, 108, 109, 112, 113, 116, 117, 118, back cover. Water Mania: 165. Wet 'n Wild: 164. Wild Bill's Wild West Dinner Show: 197, 241. WonderWorks: 157.

**Page 9:** An animation program at the Disney Institute, Copyright 1996 The Walt Disney Company. **Page 16:** The Touchdown Hotel at Disney's All Star Sports Resort, Copyright 1997 The Walt Disney Company. The baseball stadium at Disney's Wide World of Sports, Lake Buena Vista, Copyright 1997 The Walt Disney Company. **Page 31:** The Disney Wedding Pavilion on the Seven Seas Lagooon at Walt Disney World® Resort, Copyright 1998 The Walt Disney Compnay. **Page 44:** Disney's Wilderness Lodge, Copyright 1994 The Walt Disney Company. **Page 49:** The lobby of Disney's Wilderness Lodge, Copyright 1994 The Walt Disney Company. All Star Sports Resort room, Copyright 1994 The Walt Disney Company. **Page 64:** Camp Minnie-Mickey at Disney's Animal Kingdom® Theme Park, Copyright 1998 The Walt Disney Company. **Page 69:** Main Street USA, Copyright 1994 The Walt Disney Company. **Page 72:** Frontierland – Splash Mountain, Copyright 1994 The Walt Disney Company. **Page 73:** The Barnstormer, Copyright 1997 The Walt Disney Company. **Page 76:** Tomorrowland, Copyright 1998 The Walt Disney Company. The Magical Moments Parade, Copyright 1998 The Walt Disney Company. **Page 77:** Monorail to Future World, Epcot®, Copyright 1994 The Walt Disney Company. Test Track in Future World, Copyright 1997 The Walt Disney Company. **Page 81:** Honey I Shrunk the Audience, Copyright 1996 The Walt Disney Company. **Page 84:** Video Game Chairs at the Hammacher Schlemmer exhibit, Copyright 1994 The Walt Disney Company. Innoventions – Alec Tronic, Copyright 1994 The Walt Disney Company. **Page 89:** Hollywood Boulevard, Copyright 1994 The Walt Disney Company. **Page 92:** The Twilight Zone Tower of Terror™, Copyright 1995 The Walt Disney Company. **Page 97:** Discovery River Boat trip, Copyright 1998 The Walt Disney Company. Some of the cast at Disney's Animal Kingdom® Theme Park, Copyright 1998 The Walt Disney Company. **Page 100:** Festival of the Lion King, Copyright 1998 The Walt Disney Company. **Page 101:** The Boneyard, Copyright 1998 The Walt Disney Company. Kilimanjaro Safari, Copyright 1998 The Walt Disney Company. **Page 152:** Chef Mark Dowling at the Disney Institute's Culinary Program, Copyright 1996 The Walt Disney Company. **Page 153:** Rock climbing at the Sports and Fitness Program at the Disney Institute, Copyright 1996 The Walt Disney Company. **Page 160:** Typhoon Lagoon, Copyright 1995 The Walt Disney Company. **Page 161:** Blizzard Beach, Copyright 1995 The Walt Disney Company. **Page 189:** Downtown Disney, Copyright 1997 The Walt Disney Company. **Page 204:** Delicious foods at End Zone Food Court at Disney's All Star Sports Resort, Copyright 1994 The Walt Disney Company. **Page 205:** End Zone Food Court at Disney's All Star Sports Resort, Copyright 1996 The Walt Disney Company.

The author wishes to acknowledge the help of the following in the production of this book:

First Choice Holidays, Virgin Holidays, The Walt Disney Company, The Peabody Orlando, The Delta Orlando Resort, Dollar Rent A Car, All Cellular Phone Rental, The Orlando Tourism Bureau in London, The Orlando/Orange County Convention & Visitors' Bureau, The Florida Tourism Corporation, The Kissimmee/St Cloud Convention & Visitors' Bureau in London and Kissimmee, Walt Disney Attractions Inc, Universal Studios Florida, The Greater Orlando Aviation Authority, Orlando/Sanford International Airport, The Busch Entertainment Corporation, The Orange County Sheriff's Office, Seminole County Convention & Visitors' Bureau, HM Customs and Excise Office, Gatwick Airport, Canaveral Port Authority, Airtours and Thomson Holidays.

Plus, Oonagh McCullagh (Orlando Tourism Bureau), Joyce Leaver, Jason Bevan, Margaret Melia (Walt Disney), Jayne Telesca Behrle (Orlando CVB), Sarah Handy, Larry White (Kissimmee CVB), Rhonda Murphy (Universal), Carolyn Fennell (Orlando Aviation Authority), Det. Ray Wood (Orange County Sheriff's Office), Kjerstin Dillon (SeaWorld), Honoria Nadeau (Busch Gardens), Bernadette Davis (for Seminole County), Lisa (Old Town), Chris Bell (Gatorland), Andy Charalambous (Airtours), Jay Bennett (Dollar Rent A Car), Don & Fran Williamson (Unicorn Inn), Melissa Tomasso (Kennedy Space Center), Debra Johnson (Fantasy of Flight), Howard Mackinnon (Orlando/Sanford Airport), Rod Caborn (Gilbert & Manjura), Andrea Kudlacz (Renaissance Entertainment Services), Michele Carpenter, Marcia Harris and many, many more. Thank you all.

**Got a red-hot Brit Tip to pass on? The latest info on Disney's Animal Kingdom™ theme park? Found the best new restaurant in town? We want to hear from YOU about how to keep improving the Brit's Guide.**

**Why not drop us a line to:
Brit's Guide Travel Series (Orlando),
Foulsham, The Publishing House,
Bennetts Close, Cippenham, Slough, Berkshire SL1 5AP.**